SHAKING
THE
PUMPKIN

Jerome Rothenberg

SHAKING
THE
PUMPKIN

Traditional Poetry of the
Indian North Americas

Revised Edition

ALFRED VAN DER MARCK EDITIONS • NEW YORK

Editorial director: Robert Walter

Managing editor
and copy editor: Leonard Neufeld

Designer: Diane Ward

Typographer: Smith, Inc.

Cover photo used with permission of National Museums of Canada.

Library of Congress Cataloging-in-Publication Data
Main entry under title:

Shaking the pumpkin.

    Includes bibliographical references.
    1. Indian poetry — North America — Translations into
English.   2.   American poetry — Translations from Indian
languages.   I. Rothenberg, Jerome, 1931–
PM197.E3S5   1985   897   85-40038
ISBN 0-912383-10-0

Alfred van der Marck Editions
1133 Broadway, Suite 1301
New York, New York 10010

First printing: January 1986

ACKNOWLEDGMENTS

Grateful acknowledgment is made to the following for permission to reprint material copyrighted or controlled by them:

Charles L. Boilès for "Tepehua Thought-Songs," as originally printed in *Shaking the Pumpkin* (1972), by Jerome Rothenberg. Reprinted by permission of the author.

Katherine S. Branstetter for "A Story of the Eaters" (Tzeltal) in collaboration with W. S. Merwin and Santiago Mendes Zapata.

Allan F. Burns and the University of Texas Press for "Wizards," "Conversations in Mayan," "How Just One Poor Man Lives," and "Things That Happen to You," from *An Epoch of Miracles: Oral Literature of the Yucatec Maya,* translated by Allan F. Burns. Copyright © 1983 by the University of Texas Press. Reprinted by permission of the publisher.

Carl Cary for "The Origin of the Skagit Indians According to Lucy Williams," "Two Divorce Songs" (Tsimshian), and "One for Coyote."

Munro S. Edmonson for excerpts from *The Book of Counsel: The Popol Vuh of the Quiché Maya of Guatemala,* translated by Munro S. Edmonson. Reprinted by permission of the author.

The Etnografiska Museet for excerpts from N. Holmer and H. Wassén, *The Complete Mu-Igala.* Reprinted by permission of the publisher.

Edward Field for "Magic Words," "Magic Words to Feel Better," "Magic Words for Hunting Caribou," "Magic Words for Hunting Seal," "Orpingalik's Song," "Heaven & Hell," and "Hunger." Reprinted by permission of the author.

Lance Henson for "Two Cheyenne Poems," from *In a Dark Mist,* by Lance Hensen. Reprinted by permission of the author.

Anselm Hollo for "Poems to Ease Birth," "The Eagle Above Us," "what happened to a young man in a place where he turned to water," and "poem to be recited every 8 years." Reprinted by permission of the author.

Dell Hymes for selection from *"In Vain I Tried to Tell You": Essays in Native American Ethnopoetics,* by Dell Hymes. Reprinted by permission of the author.

Allan Kaprow for excerpt from "Soap." Reprinted by permission of the author.

Edward Kissam for "The Deadly Dance" and "To The Mother of the Gods." Reprinted by permission of the author.

Alison Knowles for "Giveaway Construction (1963)," from *By Alison Knowles,* copyright © 1965 by Something Else Press, Inc., New York. All rights reserved. Reprinted by permission of the author.

James Koller for "Wolf Songs & Others of the Tlingit," copyright © 1971 by James Koller, and "Sioux Metamorphoses," copyright © 1967 by Coyote Books.

Tom Lowenstein for "A Dispute Between Women," from *Eskimo Poems,* by Tom Lowenstein. Reprinted by permission of the author.

David P. McAllester for seven Navajo animal songs, from *Enemy Way Music,* by David P. McAllester, and for "A Song from Red Ant Way," from *Texts of the Navajo Creation Chants.* Reprinted by permission of David P. McAllester.

W. S. Merwin for "Crow Versions" and for "A Story of the Eaters," from *Selected Translations 1968–1978,* by W. S. Merwin. Reprinted by permission of the author.

Henry Munn for excerpt from Alvaro Estrada, *María Sabina: Her Life and Chants,* translated by Henry Munn. This version reprinted by permission of Henry Munn.

New Directions Publishing Corp. for "The Artist," from Denise Levertov, *With Eyes at the Back of our Heads.* Copyright © 1959 by Denise Levertov Goodman. Reprinted by permission of New Directions Publishing Corporation.

The University of New Mexico Press for "Things That Were Truly Remarkable," from *The Way to Rainy Mountain,* by N. Scott Momaday. Copyright © 1979 by the University of New Mexico Press.

Howard Norman for "Born Tying Knots," "Tree Old Woman," "Saw the Cloud Lynx," and two Wishing Bone poems, from *The Wishing Bone Cycle,* by Howard A. Norman. Reprinted by permission of the author.

The University of Oklahoma Press for excerpt from *The Book of Chilam Balam of Chumayel,* by Ralph L. Roys, with an introduction by J. Eric S. Thompson. New edition copyright © 1967 by the University of Oklahoma Press.

The University of Oklahoma Press for excerpt from *Popol Vuh: The Sacred Book of the Ancient Quiché Maya,* from the translation of Adrian Recinos. Copyright © 1950 by the University of Oklahoma Press.

The Estate of Charles Olsen for "A Myth of the Human Universe" from *Human Universe and Other Essays,* by Charles Olsen, edited by Donald Allen. Copyright © 1951, 1959, 1965, 1967 by Charles Olsen. Reprinted by permission of the estate of Charles Olsen.

Mary Oppen and Linda Mourelatos for four lines from "Psalm" by George Oppen.

Simon J. Ortiz for "Telling About Coyote," from *A Good Journey,* by Simon J. Ortiz. Reprinted by permission of the author.

Hilda Neihardt Petri for "The Horse Dance," from *Black Elk Speaks,* by John G. Neihardt, copyright © 1932, 1959, John G. Neihardt; published in the United States by Simon and Schuster, Pocket Books, and University of Nebraska Press.

George Quasha for "Somapoetics 73: Essie Parrish in New York." Reprinted by permission of the author.

Jarold Ramsey for "How Her Teeth Were Pulled" and "A Kalapuya Prophecy," by Jarold Ramsey. Reprinted by permission of the author.

Jerome Rothenberg for material originally published & copyrighted in *Shaking the Pumpkin,* by Jerome Rothenberg, Doubleday & Company, 1972. Copyright © 1972, 1985 by Jerome Rothenberg.

Armand Schwerner for poems originally printed in *Shaking the Pumpkin* (1972), by Jerome Rothenberg. Reprinted by permission of Armand Schwerner.

The Shoe String Press for visual image from Weston La Barre, *The Peyote Cult,* published by The Shoe String Press, 1959. Reprinted by permission of the publisher.

Smithsonian Institution Press, for permission to reprint excerpt from *Bulletin of the Bureau of American Ethnology Number 161,* "Seminole Music," by Frances Densmore. Smithsonian Institution, Washington, D.C., 1956.

Southern Methodist University Press for excerpts from Jack F. and Anna G. Kilpatrick, *Run Toward the Nightland,* copyright © 1967, Southern Methodist University Press.

Sunstone Press for three songs from Herbert J. Spinden, *Songs of the Tewa,* published by Sunstone Press, Santa Fe, N.M.

Nathaniel Tarn for "Rabinal-Achi: Act IV," copyright © 1972 and 1985 by Nathaniel Tarn, and published in *Alcheringa: Ethnopoetics,* no. 2, old series, 1971. Reprinted by permission of the author.

Barbara Tedlock for "From Ceremony of Sending: A Simultaneity for Twenty Choruses" and "They Went to the Moon Mother." Reprinted by permission of Barbara Tedlock.

Dennis Tedlock for "Zuni Derivations" and for "The Boy and the Deer" from *Finding the Center,* by Dennis Tedlock. Reprinted by permission of the author.

The University of Utah Press for excerpt from *Florentine Codex,* Book 2. Courtesy of the School of American Research and the University of Utah Press.

Alan R. Velie for Kiowa "49" Songs, from *American Indian Literature,* by Alan R. Velie, University of Oklahoma Press, 1979.

Viking Penguin Inc. for "The Invention of White People," by Leslie Marmon Silko. Copyright © 1977 by Leslie Silko.

Ray A. Young Bear for "four poems" from *Winter of the Salamander,* by Ray A. Young Bear. Reprinted by permission of the author.

An exhaustive effort has been made to locate all rights holders and to clear reprint permissions. This process has been complicated, and if any required acknowledgments have been omitted or any rights overlooked, it is unintentional and forgiveness is requested.

FOR AVERY JIMERSON & RICHARD JOHNNY JOHN

*Dane'ho niyo nengen' hojagowen'nondaat onen
di' nai hononho'n' gaiwayen'dahgon ne' yaden'nota
ennyenongai'daat.*

So this is how many words there are.
Now once again it rests with the two singers
to go on down to the end.

CONTENTS

PRE-FACE (1985)

When the book first came out, America was going through a spell of Indianismo.

Not for the first time & likely not the last.

Something like that happens periodically & can even leave some good behind.

Most notable this time around was the emergence of a new sense of identity among young Native Americans; & for many others the recognition not only of the injustices done but of the grandeur & persistence of what was here to start with.

Shaking the Pumpkin appeared in the midst of all that, & the spirit-of-the-time probably led many to approach it as a part of what they took to be their own awakening.

For myself the propositions of the book are even clearer in the aftermath.

To begin with: that the first peoples of this continent created a poetry (a charged & ritualized language, or a range of such) as diverse as the peoples themselves. As classic for its times & places as Homer was for Europe or the Book of Songs for China. Rooted in oral tradition & the potentialities of human voice & presence.

Let me say it quickly, it is so difficult a point to get across. What that poetry transmits is not so much a sense of reverence or piety as of mystery & wonder.

The Great Spirit of some Indian translations is thus the Great Mystery of others: a world that opens up through language, not as a series of enduring answers but as a questioning of what that world may be.

"Can this be real," asks the Pawnee song, "can this be real, this life I am living?" And the Eskimo shaman, Aua, pointing out scenes of hunger & injustice in response to Knud Rasmussen's question about the meaning of life: "We explain nothing, we believe nothing, but in what I have just shown you lies our answer to all you ask."

The same phrase (Indian or not) turns up independently in the assertion by the surrealist master, André Breton, "that the mysteries which are not will give way someday to the *great Mystery*": a reconciliation, as in the Indian instance, of dream & chance with the reality of our immediate lives.

The approach is no more simple & no more complex "here" than "there."

Wherever it occurs, it enlivens the world, brings the human & other-than-human together in a shared reality: *natural* & super*natural* at once.

If such a vision of nature is ecologically meaningful, as many still believe, it isn't through some generalized good feeling about "nature" or "wilderness" but through a lived relation, rich in detail & enactment, to other beings & to the world at large.

Everything in such a world can be embodied & enacted.

The view here is "total" — as expansive as the mind can make it. As such it allows "contradictory" impulses & images to coexist, often with no apparent sense of contradiction.

Dream & fact.

Real & imagined.

Mental & physical.

Savage & human.

Sacred & sacrilegious.

At certain of its extremes (sexual, scatological, blasphemous, psychedelic), much of this was suppressed until recently in Euro-American culture. If its appearance in a gathering like this once seemed startling, it should be seen by now as what it really is: a part of a greater human world.

As such it may remind us that Western poets have also had to defend that image of a total world, & in the process we have come to value cultures (including aspects of our own) in which such a fullness was the norm.

The other side of Indian spirituality is its traditional & sanctioned irreverence: the sacred clowns & tricksters whose absurdity & black humors complement its sense of harmony & order.

This is a question of more than literary models. For what is at stake here — in traditional terms — is the survival of that sense-of-balance that many of the old shaman-poets saw as crucial to their acts of healing.

It is a stance shared by many peoples & threatened, maybe irreparably, by our own fears of otherness & contradiction.

Some part of this is buried in the past, but much of it (where the cultures remain most alive) carries into the present.

Within that present it defies whatever temptations we may feel to keep-it-old.

For a tradition in practice is a virtual collage of old & new ways, of many times & places. As in Barbara Tedlock's account, say, of a Zuni house prepared for Shalako:

> Cinderblock and plasterboard white walls are layered with striped serapes, Chimayó blankets, Navajo rugs, flowered fringed embroidered shawls, black silk from Mexico, and purple, red and blue rayon from Czechoslovakia. . . . Rearing buckskins above Arabian tapestries of Martin Luther King and the Kennedy brothers, The Last Supper, a herd of sheep with haloed herder, horses, peacocks.

I have tried to get something of that mix into the work presented here: some sense of the hybrid nature of all poetry — maybe all culture — & of its metamorphosis through time.

Mostly this turns up in small or subtle ways, at other times more obviously; but the reader, once tuned to it, will find it almost everywhere.

New events & places, new objects & textures, new languages & names — a mixture, always, of the old & new.

Toward much the same ends, I've tried — while recognizing the anonymity of authorship in many cultures — to direct attention to the individuals behind the poems, giving their names & some of their histories wherever possible.

Many have lived within this century or are still alive today — functioning as songmakers, storytellers, ritualists, healers, speculative thinkers; addressing traditional audiences or learning (as with María Sabina, Essie Parrish, even Black Elk) to address the outside world as well.

There & elsewhere I've looked for new themes & forms to set beside the old ones: the Mayan Conversations of Alonzo Gonzales Mó, the Wishing Bone Cycle of Jacob Nibenegenesabe, the native & English "49" songs of countless contemporary singers.

Beyond these I've included a small sampling of work by Indian poets like Simon Oritiz, N. Scott Momaday, & Leslie Silko, *writing* in English or in mixed languages, yet finding thereby a continuity of old traditions pursued by (sometimes) radically new means.

The time since *Shaking the Pumpkin* first appeared has also been one of continuing experiment with ways to translate the native poetries into English.

In that first edition there was already a stress by Dennis Tedlock & myself on "total translation" — each of us going at it from a very different direction. And since then key work ("total" or "partial") has come from Howard Norman, Dell Hymes, Allan F. Burns, Henry Munn, & Tom Lowenstein, among others.

Along with the efforts of the poet-translators & scholars cited in the earlier Pre-Face, these translations opened up whole worlds of vision & performance at a time when such openings are sorely needed.

When María Sabina says, "I cure with Language," she offers us a clue to what those needs may be.

For poetry at its source involves a metaphor of healing, & metaphor at its source implies an act of transformation.

The hidden message of these works is what Lévi-Strauss spoke of as Rimbaud's *intuition*: that "metaphor can change the world."

Jerome Rothenberg
Encinitas, California
August 16, 1985

PRE-FACE (1971)

"Come not thus with your gunnes & swords, to invade as foes. . . .

"What will it availe you to take that perforce you may quietly have with love, or to destroy them that provide your food? . . .

"Lie well, & sleepe quietly with my women & children, laugh, & I will be merrie with you. . . ."

— Powhatan, to Capt. John Smith

1.

The awkwardness of presenting translations from American Indian poetry today is that it has become fashionable to deny the possibility of crossing the boundaries that separate people of different races & cultures: to insist instead that black is the concern of black, red of red, & white of white. Yet the idea of translation has always been that such boundary crossing is not only possible but desirable. By its very nature, translation asserts or at least implies a concept of psychic & biological unity, weird as such assertion may seem in a time of growing dis-integration. Each poem, being made present & translated, flies in the face of divisive ideology. The question for the translator is not whether but how far we can translate one another. Like the poet who is his brother, he attempts to restore what has been torn apart. Any arrogance on his part would not only lead to paternalism or "colonialism" (LeRoi Jones's term for it from a few years back), it would deny the very order of translation. Only if he allows himself to be directed by the other will a common way emerge, true to both positions.

To submit through translation is to begin to accept the "truths" of an other's language. At the same time it's a way of growing wary of the lies in one's own, a point of vigilance that translators & poets should be particularly keyed to. I learned, for example, that the Senecas with whom I lived call the whites "younger brothers" & themselves *"real* people." To understand the Seneca experience (including where I stand with relation to them) I have to submit to terms like these & to get to a truth about them which includes the Seneca truth. As I do, it becomes clear to me that the very nature of "Indian" & "white" (words basic to the process I'm describing) is itself a question of language & translation.

If the term "younger brother" would later be neutralized or come to suggest contempt, what relationship did it originally express in a culture that didn't practice primogeniture & individual ownership of land — in which forests & clearings (the men were hunters, the women farmers) were a common ground for brothers as children of one mother & members of one clan? Whether by birth or adoption didn't matter either: descended from a single mother (ultimately the Earth), "older" & "younger" was for them a matter of precedence in time & place, their relative experience of the shared environment. Thus the Senecas as older brothers recognized the rights of both to start with, but the whites (children of the "old world" patriarchy) came to the land prepared for dispossession & fratricide. In the overthrow of the older — refusing adoption to the real-personhood of the Indian way, while asserting their own great-white-fatherhood — they triggered a disruption of the natural (ecological) order that's now making all of us its victims.

A "real" person in these terms is one who hasn't forgotten what & where things are in relation to the Earth. Earth-rooted, he is royal too, not by precedence of birth, but insofar as he has & shares a knowledge of the realm. He has only to maintain a true eye for his surroundings & a contact with the Earth, to recognize himself as the inheritor of reality, of a more real way of life. At any rate that seems to be the claim implicit in the language & confirmed by the events that have followed its denial.

The issue, writes David Antin, is reality. The *real* person (reality-person, in fact) lives, like the "primitive" philosopher described by Radin, "in a blaze of reality" through which he can experience "reality at white heat." This is a part of the tribal inheritance (not Indian only but worldwide) that we all lose at our peril — younger & older alike. Remember too how many elements are active in that situation, where we would concentrate on the words as being particularly the "poem" (many Indian poems in fact dispense entirely with words): elements, I mean, like music, non-verbal phonetic sounds, dance, gesture & event, game, dream, etc., along with all those unstated ideas & images the participants pick up from the poem's context. Each moment is charged: each is a point at which meaning is coming to surface, where nothing's incidental but everything matters terribly.

Now, put all of that together & you have the makings of a high poetry & art, which only a colonialist ideology could have blinded us into labeling "primitive" or "savage." You have also the great hidden accomplishment of our older brothers in America, made clear in the poetry & yet of concern not only to poets but to all (red, white & black) who want to carry the possibilities of reality & personhood into any new worlds to come. The yearning to rediscover the Red Man is part of this. It acknowledges not only the cruelty of what's happened in this place (a negative matter of genocide & guilt) but leads as well to the realization that "we" in a larger sense will never be whole without a recovery of the "red power" that's been here from the beginning. The true integration must begin & end with a recognition of all such powers. That means a process of translation & of mutual completion. Not a brotherhood of lies this time but an affiliation based on what the older had known from the start: that we're doomed without his tribal & matrilocal wisdom, which can be shared only among equals who have recognized a common lineage from the earth.

2.

The question, then, was how to deliver the poetry of the first discoverers of America & civilizers of themselves. I had previously been retranslating (I wasn't unique in this among American poets) & anthologizing Indian & other tribal &/or "primitive" poetries mostly from the abundant volumes of myths & texts gathered over the previous hundred or so years by scores of Boasian anthropologists & others. That work had resulted in a worldwide anthology called *Technicians of the Sacred* (subtitle: *A Range of Poetries from Africa, America, Asia, & Oceania*), which included, in addition to my own contributions, workings by such poets as Pound, Williams, Tzara, Waley, Merwin, Sanders, Kelly, & R. Owens, plus very solid translations by anthropologists, etc. like Densmore, Berndt, Quain, Matthews, Bleek & Lloyd, McAllester, Beier, & many others. Not to mention all the workers (some even better known than these) whose gatherings from around-the-world served as sources for the poems that emerged in English.

There are a couple of points from *Technicians* that I want to reiterate here. First it seemed clear to me that the range-&-depth of the materials previously collected was astonishing, & that the levels of the poetry were in no obvious relationship to the economic or industrial development of the cultures from which they derived (or if they were, that the powers of the poetry declined as those of technology & the political state increased) — clear, I mean, in spite of considerable mistranslation in even the "literal" & interlinear texts, & the fact that many of the translated poems were practically unreadable as first presented. Second, the range of the tribal poets was even more impressive if one avoided a closed, European definition of "poem" & worked empirically or by analogy to contemporary, limit-smashing experiments (as with concrete poetry, sound poetry, intermedia, happenings, etc.). Since tribal poetry was almost always part of a larger situation (i.e. was truly intermedia), there was no more reason to present the words alone as independent structures than the ritual-events, say, or the pictographs arising from the same source. Where possible, in fact, one might present or translate *all* elements connected with the total "poem" — a concern that continues into the present book.

From 1968 on, I followed a number of such concerns into a concentration on Indian tribal poetry, which seemed for obvious reasons most relevant to where-we-all-are in U.S.A. As poet I was able to experiment with more direct approaches to translation: (1) in collaboration with Seneca songmen, who acted at the very least as intermediary translators, & from whom I could get a clearer picture of how the poetry (songs, prayers, orations, visions, dreams, etc.) fitted into the life; & (2) through working with ethnomusicologist David McAllester on cooperative translation from Navajo of *The 17 Horse Songs of Frank Mitchell.* With McAllester & on my own, I became interested in the possibility of "total translation" — a term I use for translation (of oral poetry in particular) that takes into account any or all elements of the original beyond the words. All of which (plus a growing sense of the grandeur & significance of Indian poetry & thought whether partially or totally translated) led me to the idea of a book that would offer a new look at all that in the light of the possibilities of poetry opening to us in this very time & place.

Unlike *Technicians* this gathering is largely a poet's book, & that in itself is an important step toward the larger work of translation & recovery I'd been hoping to develop. Several included herein had already been working in this area: Bill Merwin for at least the previous decade but with more recent emphasis on Plains Indian texts out of Lowie; Edward Field going the length of a book of adaptations from Rasmussen's Eskimo collections; Carl Cary working from anthropological texts & from his earlier Skagit contacts; & James Koller naturalizing works from Tlingit & Sioux toward an immediate grasp of some of the levels of vision they represent. Some others responded directly to my request for help — Schwerner & Hollo with greatest energy; Tarn equally so, but bringing to it also a considerable personal acquaintance with the contemporary Mayans of Guatemala — working from earlier translations into French, Spanish & German, or from English versions that had failed to match the life of their sources. But new works by anthropologists were important too, especially where they disclosed actual structural possibilities or ways of showing those in translation: Dennis Tedlock's total translations of Zuni narratives, say, which forever did away with the idea that "prose" could be the medium of a spoken narrative, or Munro Edmonson's verse reconstruction of the *Popol Vuh.* To say nothing of McAllester's Navajo horse songs, which were the solid basis for whatever workings I was then able to perform.

In each case the translator's voice is very different — which is the way it should be. For the translator — if he's to match the interest of the original — must extend its meanings into his own language & by means of his own voice. (This assumes a poet's voice to begin with.) He needn't lose his personhood but may extend that too & make it real — in translation as well as in any of his other workings. This has always been the way of the great poet-translators — Catullus or Chaucer or Marpa or Pound — & its beginnings here may hopefully mark the real emergence of Indian poetry into the consciousness of the non-Indian world.

Hopefully too it may coincide with Indian efforts to hold, expand or (for many) to return to the sources of their own power — even to understand that power as not only particular to its immediate place-of-origin, but as part of an historically proven & worldwide manifestation of such poetic & trans-poetic powers.

3.

As an arrangement of "classical" American poetry (i.e. of poetry in the first languages of America & respresenting modes or models for tribes present & to come), this anthology isn't more than a beginning. It tries above all to show the range of such poetries in the Americas north of Panama, but shies away from a division by region & tribe or from representing the major tribes & nations in anything like just proportions. (The reader who wants to see how the book breaks down along such lines can check the tribal index on page 345). Even so, I hope the gathering is a true reflection of Indian poetry (at least of some of its faces) that would be of use to those alive & growing at this time.

With a sense too that the best minds in our own culture & assorted counter-cultures will be freely rearranging any such collection, I've deliberately avoided an organization into very tight compartments. Certain works (particularly those that involve new approaches to translation or act as mini-anthologies of specialized kinds) I've isolated under separate headings; otherwise the poetry appears in four miscellaneous sections or services ("service" in the sense of a religious ritual), with each one corresponding to an evening's public reading under those circumstances in which we commonly share poetry with one another. Any other organizing principles are either self-evident or dealt with in the "commentaries" section, in which I also try to establish contexts for the poems where possible or useful, & to carry forward discussions of Indian & tribal poetry, philosophy or history as lightly touched on in this introduction. Unlike the parallel section in *Technicians,* I've here chosen not to make much of the considerable analogies between the native American classics & the work of our contemporary poets. (I do, on the other hand, say more about the poetry's relation to our own social & environmental dilemmas.) This is partly because *Technicians* already exists as a guide to all that, but mostly from a sense that these levels of poetry are so fundamental & deep-seated in human consciousness that they need no justification by resemblance to anything else in this world. Not once the old definitions have been laid to rest.

After which, it only remains to acknowledge the help I've gotten along the way & to stress again the cooperative nature of most of what's going on here. The suggestion for a pan-Indian book came from Ann London, who had hoped to do it as the first issue of a poetry magazine she was starting in Buffalo, & many of the pieces I'm printing here were originally gathered for that effort. My own experiments with oral translation were helped by a grant-in-aid from the Wenner-Gren Foundation, which followed in turn from Stanley Diamond's suggestion that I try an in-the-field translation project. I'm grateful to him for that, but also for the conscience & intelligence he's brought to bear both on anthropology & poetry — & the same holds true for David McAllester, without whose generosity the most experimental of these pieces would never have happened. Then, too, I owe great thanks to Richard Johnny John & Avery Jimerson (both for what they gave & what they withheld), as I do to all the poets & translators who are included in these pages & to many (but particularly Gary Snyder, Simon Ortiz & Larry Little Bird) who aren't.* Lenny Neufeld & Kathy Acker read the script with me; Loren Shakely & Dan Dyer typed it; Matthew helped me sing the songs; & Diane shared her empathy & knowledge.

But the deepest gratitude I have is for those sacred poets, named & unnamed in this book, who first saw the visions & who spoke & sang the words.

Jerome Rothenberg
1969 / 1971

*Ortiz, of course, turns up in the present revised version (page 91). —J. R.

PRELUDES

what the informant said to Franz Boas in 1920

Keresan

long ago her mother
had to sing this song and so
she had to grind along with it
the corn people have a song too
it is very good
I refuse to tell it

— English version by Armand Schwerner

THANK YOU: A POEM IN SEVENTEEN PARTS

Seneca

1.

Now so many people that are in this place.
In our meeting place.
It starts when two people see each other.
They greet each other.
Now we greet each other.
Now he thought.
I will make the Earth where some people can walk around.
I have created them, now this has happened.
We are walking on it.
Now this time of day.
This is he way it should be in our minds.

2.

Now he thought.
There should be grass & weeds should be all over the Earth.
Now this has happened.
Now he thought.
From this.
There should be some that will be used for medicine.
Now it blocks the way of it.
We aren't here forever.
Now this time of day.
We give thanks for grass & weeds.
This is the way it should be in our minds.

3.

Now he thought.
I will make Springs.
Where water will be coming from.
On this Earth.
There will be Springs.
The Rivers & the Lakes.
He thought.
There will be no trouble finding them.
Wherever you are on this Earth.

Now this time of day.
We give thanks for the things we named.
This is the way it should be in our minds.

4.

Now he thought.
There should be bushes & also the Forest.
He thought.
The people can keep warm from it.
Now a certain tree is there.
He gave authority for it to be the Head One.
In the Forest.
People will call it Maple.
There is a certain time here.
When water will be coming from it.
He thought.
The people could make use of it.
Now this has happened.
The water was flowing when the warm weather came to Earth.
Now this time of day.
We give thanks for the bushes, Forest & Maple.
This is the way it should be in our minds.

5.

Now he thought.
I will do this.
He left it for us.
Something that should be for the people's happiness.
They will be strong in body from it.
He left us all this food.
He scattered this all over the Earth.
Now we will give *one* thanks.
That he has left us all this food to live on.
On this Earth.
This is the way it should be in our minds.

6.

Now where the grass grows.
The first berry that ripens will be called the short strawberry.
He thought.

They should give thanks among themselves & also give thanks to him.
For all persons that are left on this Earth.
Now this time of day.
We give thanks for the Strawberries.
This is the way it should be in our minds.

7.

Now on this Earth.
He found out.
The Earth was so barren.
He made the animals & for them to be running around.
This is for the people to enjoy.
Now this has happened.
We give thanks for the animals running around on this Earth.
This is the way it should be in our minds.

8.

Now another thing   In the Air-&-Wind
He made the fluttering of the birds there.
& the different sounds of the birds.
This is for the people to hear.
This is for them to enjoy who I made for it.
Now this time of day.
Now we give thanks for the Birds that are fluttering in the air.
This is the way it should be in our minds.

9.

Now he thought.
At a certain place.
From which the air is moving around everywhere.
They will breathe easily by it.
While walking around on this earth.
Now this is happening.
Just the way he thought it to be happening.
Now this time of day.
We give thanks for the Air.
For the place with the net on it.
Which is making the Air move everywhere on Earth.
This is the way it should be in our minds.

10.

Now he thought.
I will give authority to them to carry the dampness & the Rain with them.
They will take care of rivers also to dampen the gardens.
Now this has happened he has these servants now.
He also made it
so that we are relatives.
The people should call them Our Grandparents.
The Thunderers.
Now this time of day.
We give thanks to the Thunderers.
For they come from the West.
This is the way it should be in our minds.

11.

Now he thought.
There should be a sky over their heads.
So they can look up at it.
Now this has happened.
We look up to see the sky over our heads.
Now this time of day.
We give thanks for the Sky.
This is the way it should be in our minds.

12.

Now in the sky.
He created two things.
That they should be in the sky.
They are the ones to give light.
So the people could see where they are going.
The people I created.
Now this has happened.
At this time of day.
There is plenty of light.
He has given authority.
To the one who gives light for the days to have light.
Now this time of day.
We give thanks to our Brother the Sun.
This is the way it should be in our minds.

13.

Now when the Sun has rested.
Because there is a length of time that he passes over the Earth.
The shadow will pass over the earth.
Now he has authorized another.
She will be the one to give light
so that everything will go on all right if something should happen to the
    families by night.
Now he has given her more things to do.
He has authorized her to take care of the months.
She just changes from one end of the month to the other.
Also there are little ones being born.
The people count it by these months.
Now this time of day.
We give thanks to our Grandmother the Moon.
This is the way it should be in our minds.

14.

Now in the sky.
He thought.
I will create all around her.
The stars will be all over the sky.
In the past.
They all had names also directions so that nothing would go wrong
    wherever you were on this earth.
It is still the same way that he made it.
Now we will set our minds yes we will give thanks for all the Stars in
    the sky.
This is the way it should be in our minds.

15.

Now.
He found out.
On this Earth.
All kinds of evil had come to it.
From a small item even.
Even just thinking it you were creating this evilness.
Now he thought.
I will come in through this person.

He will be the one to tell them what I think of it.
He picked out Handsome Lake.
Yes he is to tell these people.
What they should follow.
Now this has happened.
Now we hear the Word of our Creator.
Now this time of day.
We give thanks to our Big Man.
Handsome Lake.
This is the way it should be in our minds.

16.

Now he thought yes I should have servants.
Yes four Beings should be enough.
To protect the ones I had created.
Now this is in their power.
They are doing the job that he handed them.
Now we give thanks to the Four Beings.
This is the way it should be in our minds.

17.

Now he thought.
At a certain place.
I will stay there.
All that I made will be finding its end in it.
Now this time of day.
We have given our word & our thanks for it.
For whatever he gave us.
Now this time of day.
We will give him our thanks for it.
At this time of day.
This is the way it should be in our minds.

— *Translation by Richard Johnny John & Jerome Rothenberg*

THE ARTIST

Aztec

The artist: disciple, abundant, multiple, restless.
The true artist: capable, practicing, skillful;
maintains dialogue with his heart, meets things with his mind.
The true artist: draws out all from his heart,
works with delight, makes things with calm, with sagacity,
works like a true Toltec, composes his objects, works dexterously, invents;
arranges materials, adorns them, makes them adjust.

The carrion artist: works at random, sneers at the people,
makes things opaque, brushes across the surface of the face of things,
works without care, defrauds people, is a thief.

— English version by Denise Levertov

THEREFORE I MUST TELL THE TRUTH
(by Torlino)

Navajo

I am ashamed before the earth:
I am ashamed before the heavens:
I am ashamed before the dawn:
I am ashamed before the evening twilight:
I am ashamed before the blue sky:
I am ashamed before the darkness:
I am ashamed before the sun.
I am ashamed before that standing within me which speaks with me.
Some of these things are always looking at me.
I am never out of sight.
Therefore I must tell the truth.
That is why I always tell the truth.
I hold my word tight to my breast.

— Translation by Washington Matthews

SONG OF THE BALD EAGLE

Crow

we want what is real
we want what is real
don't deceive us!

— Translation by Lewis Henry Morgan

SHAKING THE PUMPKIN

SONGS & OTHER CIRCUMSTANCES FROM THE SOCIETY OF THE MYSTIC ANIMALS

Seneca

ENGLISH VERSIONS BY
JEROME ROTHENBERG & RICHARD JOHNNY JOHN

. . . but if everything's all right
the one who says the prayer tells them:
I leave it up to you folks & if you want to have
a good time, have a good time!

12 SONGS TO WELCOME
THE SOCIETY OF THE MYSTIC ANIMALS

(1)

T
h
e

The animals are coming

n
i
m
a
l
s

H E H E H H E H

H E H E H H E H

H E H **U** **H** H E H

H E H E H H E H

H E H E H H E H

(2)

T
h
e
                  o
The doings were beginning
  o   e
  i
  n
  g
  s

```
H  E  H  E  H  H  E  H
H  E  H  E  H  H  E  H
H  E  H  U  H  H  E  H
H  E  H  E  H  H  E  H
H  E  H  E  H  H  E  H
```

(3)

T
h
e
           t
The doings were begun
  o   o
  i
  n
  g
  s

```
H  E  H  E  H  H  E  H
H  E  H  E  H  H  E  H
H  E  H  U  H  H  E  H
H  E  H  E  H  H  E  H
H  E  H  E  H  H  E  H
```

(4)

A

A she-loon too soon
  h
  e
  -
  l
  o
  o
  n

```
H  A  H  A  H  H  A  H
H  A  H  A  H  H  A  H
H  A  H  U  H  H  A  H
H  A  H  A  H  H  A  H
H  A  H  A  H  H  A  H
```

(5)

```
A                         H  A  H  A  H  H  A  H

A he-loon soon too        H  A  H  A  H  H  A  H
   e
   -                      H  A  H  U  H  H  A  H
   l
   o                      H  A  H  A  H  H  A  H
   o
   n                      H  A  H  A  H  H  A  H
```

(6)

```
T                         H  O  H  O  H  H  O  H
h
e                         H  O  H  O  H  H  O  H
              o
She drifts on the water   H  O  H  U  H  H  O  H
   r      e
   i                      H  O  H  O  H  H  O  H
   f
   t                      H  O  H  O  H  H  O  H
   s
```

(7)

```
T                         H  O  H  O  H  H  O  H
h
e                         H  O  H  O  H  H  O  H
              t
He drifts on her water    H  O  H  U  H  H  O  H
   r          o
   i                      H  O  H  O  H  H  O  H
   f
   t                      H  O  H  O  H  H  O  H
   s
```

(8)

```
T                          H  E  Y  E  Y  H  E  Y
h
e                          H  E  Y  E  Y  H  E  Y

Caw caw the crow comes at us  H  E  Y  U  Y  H  E  Y
   r         n             H  E  Y  E  Y  H  E  Y
   o         e
   w                       H  E  Y  E  Y  H  E  Y
```


(9)

```
T                          H  E  Y  E  Y  H  E  Y
h
e                          H  E  Y  E  Y  H  E  Y

Caw caw the crow who's there  H  E  Y  U  Y  H  E  Y
   r    w                  H  E  Y  E  Y  H  E  Y
   o    o
   w                       H  E  Y  E  Y  H  E  Y
```

(10)

```
S HE  WA S
C shesna R
A washnm U
M rrreie N
E rruwni N
I nniann I
N nngsgH N
H assraI G
I hecrsG A
G amersH S
H inHrhH S
H IGHreE H
E HEYucY E
Y HEYHEY Y
```

(11)

```
H E   WA S
C hewhnm R
A asrene U
M runwii N
E nnnann N
I ninsgH I
N gasraI N
H hecrsG G
I ameuhH A
G inHneH S
H IGHncE H
E HEYnaY E
Y HEYHEY Y
```

(12)

THE SONGS

```
I  t h e t r i  B
S  s o n h e r  E
T  g s b e P n  G
H  e g i s U a  I
E  n h e o M m  N
I  r e P n P e  H
R  U M P g K H  E
N  K I N s I I  R
A  S i s b N G  E
M  t h e e S H  P
E  i r n g i H  U
H  a m e i s E  M
I  H I G n t E  P
G  H H E h h e  K
H  E E Y e e y  I
H  E E Y e e y  N
```

. . . Now I'm dumping the whole bag of songs in the middle, & each of you can sing whichever ones you want . . .

A SONG OF MY SONG, IN THREE PARTS

It's off in the distance.

•

It came into the room.

•

It's here in the circle.

CAW CAW THE CROWS CAW CAW

(1)

the crows came in

(2)

the crows sat down

TWO MORE ABOUT A CROW, IN THE MANNER OF ZUKOFSKY

(1)

Yond cawcrow's way-out

(2)

Hog (yes!) swine you're mine

```
        h                    h
    i       o        o       i
  g           o   o          g
  h              o           h
 h                            h
   o                      o
   y                      y
  a                        a
 h                            h
o                              o
o                                o
o                                  o
 o                                o
  o                          o
   o                      o
    o                  o
     o              o
   h                        h
```

THE OWL (1)
whose home was in
the hemlock

THE OWL (2)
could cure
by poison

THE OWL (3)
& hollow tree
& whistling

HE ASKED THEM WHAT DID THEY KNOW &
THEY TOLD HIM

i know all
about these
different
villages is
all i know

highyohoweyyehheyhighyohoweyyehheyhighyohoweyyeh

i know
all about these
different
hills is
all i know

highyohoweyyehheyhighyohoweyyehheyhighyohoweyyeh

i know all
about
these different
rivers is
all i know

highyohoweyyehheyhighyohoweyyehheyhighyohoweyyeh

h iiiiiiiiiiiiiiiiiiiiiiiiiiiiiiiiiiiiiiiiiiiiiiiiiiiiiiiiiiii h
e   e
e   THREE WAYS TO SCREW UP   e
e   ON YOUR WAY TO THE DOINGS   e
e   THREE WAYS   e
e   e
h iiiiiiiiiiiiiiiiiiiiiiiiiiiiiiiiiiiiiiiiiiiiiiiiiiiiiiiiiiii h

(1)
I fell down

(2)
I got lost

(3)
I lost my bucket

```
h        g a n e e w a     g a n e e w a h a     i
e                                                f
r
                                                 s
s        g a n e e w a     g a n e e w a h a     h
h                                                e
o
e                                                s
s        g a n e e w a     g a n e e w a h a     h
                                                 o
                                                 u
c                                                l
o        g a n e e w a     g a n e e w a h a     d
u
l                                                m
d                                                o
         g a n e e w a     g a n e e w a h a     c
b                                                k
u
r                                                u
n        ( i   m e a n   t h i s   w o m a n )   s
```

OF THREE FRIENDLY WARNINGS THIS IS THE FIRST

26

A POEM ABOUT A WOLF MAYBE TWO WOLVES

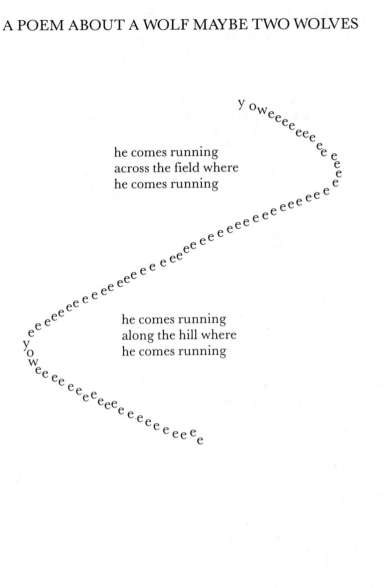

y o w e e e e e e e e e e e e e e e e e e e e e e e e e e e e e e e e e e e e e e e e e e e e e e e e e e e e e e e e

he comes running
across the field where
he comes running

he comes running
along the hill where
he comes running

y o w e e e e e e e e e e e e e e e e e e e e e e e e

WHERE THE SONG WENT WHERE SHE WENT
& WHAT HAPPENED WHEN THEY MET

the song went to the garden   (heh heh heh)
the song poked all around the garden   (heh heh heh)
she went to the garden   (heh heh heh)
she went to the garden   (heh heh heh)
she went like crazy in the garden   (heh heh heh)
that's where she went   (hah hah hah)

HEY WHEN I SING THIS SET OF 4 SONGS
LOOK WHAT HAPPENS!

hey when i sing
hey it can help her
yeah it can yeah it's so strong
hey when i sing
hey it can raise her
yeah it can yeah it's so strong
hey when i sing
hey her arm gets straighter
yeah it can yeah it's so strong
hey when i sing
hey her body gets straighter
yeah it can yeah it's so strong

A SONG ABOUT A DEAD PERSON — OR WAS IT A MOLE?

      YOHOHEYHEYEYHEYHAHYEYEYHAHHEH
I was going thru the big earth
      YOHOHEYHEYEYHEYHAHYEYEYHAHHEH
                          I went thru this big earth
      YOHOHEYHEYEYHEYHAHYEYEYHAHHEH
          I was going thru the big earth
      YOHOHEYHEYEYHEYHAHYEYEYHAHHEH
               I went thru this big earth
      YOHOHEYHEYEYHEYHAHYEYEYHAHHEH
                    I was going thru the big earth
      YOHOHEYHEYEYHEYHAHYEYEYHAHHEH
I went thru this big earth
      YOHOHEYHEYEYHEYHAHYEYEYHAHHEH
                              I was going
      YOHOHEYHEYEYHEYHAHYEYEYHAHHEH
th
      YOHOHEYHEYEYHEYHAHYEYEYHAHHEH

      YOHOHEYHEYEYHEYHAHYEYEYHAHHEH

      YOHOHEYHEYEYHEYHAHYEYEYHAHHEH

ANOTHER SONG ABOUT THAT SAME DEAD PERSON
OR MOLE — WHICHEVER IT WAS

YOHOHEYHEYEYHEYHAHYEYEYHAHHEH

I was going thru the big smoke

YOHOHEYHEYEYHEYHAHYEYEYHAHHEH

I went thru this big smoke

YOHOHEYHEYEYHEYHAHYEYEYHAHHEH

I was going thru the big smoke

YOHOHEYHEYEYHEYHAHYEYEYHAHHEH

I went thru this big smoke

YOHOHEYHEYEYHEYHAHYEYEYHAHHEH

I was going thru the big smoke

YOHOHEYHEYEYHEYHAHYEYEYHAHHEH

I went thru this big smoke

YOHOHEYHEYEYHEYHAHYEYEYHAHHEH

I was going

YOHOHEYHEYEYHEYHAHYEYEYHAHHEH

oke

YOHOHEYHEYEYHEYHAHYEYEYHAHHEH

YOHOHEYHEYEYHEYHAHYEYEYHAHHEH

YOHOHEYHEYEYHEYHAHYEYEYHAHHEH

OF THREE FRIENDLY WARNINGS THIS IS THE SECOND

h   ganeewa   ganeewaha   i
e   f
r

s   ganeewa   ganeewaha   h
h   e
o
e

s   ganeewa   ganeewaha   h
                                   o
c   u
o   ganeewa   ganeewaha   l
u   d
l
d   m
     ganeewa   ganeewaha   o
b   c
u   k
r   u
n   (i mean this woman)   s

YO OH HEYA YAH
YO OH HEYA YAH
YO HO HEYA YAH We made a mistake in this song
YO OH HEYA YAH
YO OH HEYA YAH

YO OH HEYA YAH
YO OH HEYA YAH
YO HO HEYA YAH We'll have to straighten it out
YO OH HEYA YAH
YO OH HEYA YAH

YO OH HEYA YAH
YO OH HEYA YAH
YO OH HEYA YAH This time we'll do it right
YO OH HEYA YAH
YO OH HEYA YAH

WE GOT EVERYTHING WE NEEDED HERE
AND AINT IT SOMETHING!

herezsometobaccozhere
herezsometobaccozhere
herezsometobaccozhere
herezsometobaccozhere
herez**sometobacco**zhere
herezsometobaccozhere
herezsometobaccozhere
herezsometobaccozhere
herezsometobaccozhere

herezsomepigmeatzhere
herezsomepigmeatzhere
herezsomepigmeatzhere
herezsomepigmeatzhere
herez**somepigmeat**zhere
herezsomepigmeatzhere
herezsomepigmeatzhere
herezsomepigmeatzhere
herezsomepigmeatzhere

herezsomekettlezhere
herezsomekettlezhere
herezsomekettlezhere
herezsome kettlezhere
herez**somekettle**zhere
herezsomekettlezhere
herezsomekettlezhere
herezsomekettlezhere
herezsomekettlezhere

herezsomemusssshzhere
herezsomemusssshzhere
herezsomemusssshzhere
herezsomemusssshzhere
herez**somemusssh**zhere
herezsomemusssshzhere
herezsomemusssshzhere
herezsomemusssshzhere
herezsomemusssshzhere

WHEN HE SAYS SO WE DANCE IN ALL DIRECTIONS—WOW!

                    YOHOWEYAH
                    YOHOWEYAH
                    YOWEYHEEE
                    YOWEYHEEE
              YOWEYHIGHEEEHEH
                    YOHOWEYAH
                    YOWEYHEEE
                    FROM   THE
                    SWAMPS   IS
                    WHERE ? I
                    COME   FROM
              YOWEYHIGHEEEHEH
                    YOHOWEYAH
                    YOHOWEYAH
                    YOWEYHEEE
                    YOWEYHEEE
              YOWEYHIGHEEEHEH
                    YOHOWEYAH
                    YOWEYHEEE
                    BEHIND   THE
                    EARTH   IS
                    WHERE ? I
                    COME   FROM
              YOWEYHIGHEEEHEH
                    YOHOWEYAH
                    YOHOWEYAH
                    YOWEYHEEE
                    YOWEYHEEE
              YOWEYHIGHEEEHEH
                    YOHOWEYAH
                    YOWEYHEEE
                    BEHIND   THE
                    HILLS   IS
                    WHERE ? I
                    COME   FROM
              YOWEYHIGHEEEHEH
                    YOHOWEYAH
                    YOHOWEYAH
                    YOWEYHEEE
                    YOWEYHEEE
              YOWEYHIGHEEEHEH
                    BEHIND   THE
                    EARTH   IS
                    WHERE ? I
                    COME   FROM
              YOWEEI'MDANCING
                    WOW

OF

THREE

FRIENDLY WARNINGS THIS IS THE THIRD

```
h   ganeewa   ganeewaha   i
e                         f
r
                          s
l   ganeewa   ganeewaha   h
e                         e
g
g                         s
i   ganeewa   ganeewaha   h
n                         o
g                         u
s                         l
                          d
c   ganeewa   ganeewaha
o
u                         m
l                         o
d   ganeewa   ganeewaha   c
                          k
b
u                         u
r   (i mean this woman)   s
n
```

35

```
P L E N T Y   O F   F L O W E R S
h                                 h
i                                 e
i                                 e
i           PLENTY OF FLOWERS     e
i           WHERE I'M WALKING     e
i                                 e
i                                 i
g                                 g
h                                 h
W H E R E   I ' M   W A L K I N G
```

```
C A T   T A I L S   A R E   G R O W I N G
h                                         h
i                                         e
i                                         e
i           CAT TAILS ARE GROWING         e
i           WHERE  I'M  WALKING           e
i                                         e
i                                         i
g                                         g
h                                         h
W H E R E   I ' M   W A L K I N G
```

I WAS SURPRISED TO FIND MYSELF OUT HERE
& ACTING LIKE A CROW

i didnt think i'd
shake the pumpkin
not just here & now
not exactly tonite
yahooondaaaaaheee
yohaaaaheeeeyooho
hohgaahaaaayeyhey
yohaaaaheeeeyoohoho

i didnt think i'd
rip some meat off
not just here & now
not exactly tonite
yahooondaaaaaheee
yohaaaaheeeeyooho
hohgaahaaaayeyhey
yohaaaaheeeeyoohoho

A FIRST SERVICE

Directions: Use the language of shamans.
Say "he turned my mind around" & mean
"he told me something."

Eskimo (Inuit)

MAGIC WORDS & MORE MORE MORE MAGIC WORDS

Eskimo (Inuit)

Magic Words (after Nalungiaq)

In the very earliest time,
when both people and animals lived on earth,
a person could become an animal if he wanted to
and an animal could become a human being.
Sometimes they were people
and sometimes animals
and there was no difference.
All spoke the same language.
That was the time when words were like magic.
The human mind had mysterious powers.
A word spoken by chance
might have strange consequences.
It would suddenly come alive
and what people wanted to happen could happen —
all you had to do was say it.
Nobody could explain this:
That's the way it was.

Magic Words to Feel Better (by Nakasuk)

SEA GULL
who flaps his wings
over my head
        in the blue air,

you GULL up there
dive down
        come here
take me with you
        in the air!

Wings flash by
my mind's eye
and I'm up there sailing
in the cool air,
        a-a-a-a-a-ah,
           in the air.

Magic Words for Hunting Caribou

You, you caribou
yes you
      long legs
yes you
      long ears
you with the long neck hair—
From far off you're little as a louse:
Be my great swan, fly to me,
big bull
      cari-bou-bou-bou.

Put your footprints on this land—
this land I'm standing on
is rich with the plant food you love.
See, I'm holding in my hand
the reindeer moss you're dreaming of—
so delicious, yum, yum, yum—
Come, caribou, come.

Come on, move them bones,
move your leg bones back and forth
and give yourself to me.
I'm here,
I'm waiting
      just
        for
          YOU

you, you, caribou
APPEAR!
COME HERE!

O sea goddess Nuliajuk,
when you were a little unwanted orphan girl
we let you drown.
You fell in the water
and when you hung onto the kayaks, crying,
we cut off your fingers.
So you sank into the sea
and your fingers turned into
the innumerable seals.

You sweet orphan Nuliajuk,
I beg you now
bring me a gift,
not anything from the land
but a gift from the sea,
something that will make a nice soup.
Dare I say it right out?
I want a seal!

You dear little orphan,
creep out of the water
panting on this beautiful shore,
puh, puh, like this, puh, puh,
O welcome gift
in the shape of a seal!

— *English versions by Edward Field, from Knud Rasmussen*

moon eclipse exorcism

Alsea

come out come out come out
the moon has been killed

who kills the moon? crow
who often kills the moon? eagle
who usually kills the moon? chicken hawk
who also kills the moon? owl
in their numbers they assemble
for moonkilling

come out, throw sticks at your houses
come out, turn your buckets over
spill out all the water don't let it turn
bloody yellow
from the wounding and death
of the moon

o what will become of the world, the moon
never dies without cause
only when a rich man is about to be killed
is the moon murdered

look all around the world, dance, throw your sticks, help out,
look at the moon,
                dark as it is now, even if it disappears
it will come back, think of nothing
I'm going back into the house
                        and the others went back

— English version by Armand Schwerner

poem to ease birth

Aztec

in the house with the tortoise chair
   she will give birth to the pearl
               to the beautiful feather

in the house of the goddess who sits on a tortoise
   she will give birth to the necklace of pearls
               to the beautiful feathers we are

there she sits on the tortoise
   swelling to give us birth

on your way on your way
   child be on your way to me here
           you whom I made new

come here child   come be pearl
              be beautiful feather

— English version by Anselm Hollo

CROW VERSIONS

1
I am making
    a wind come here

    it's coming

2
Child listen
    I am singing

    with my ear on the ground

    and we love you

                (by White-arm)

3
Your way
    is turning bad

    and nobody but you
    is there

4
If all of me is still there
    when spring comes
    I'll make a hundred poles

    and put something on top
    sun

for you
you

right there I'll make a small sweat lodge
      it's cold
      I'll sprinkle charcoal

   at the end of it
   my death

   sun
   it will all be for you

    I want to be still there
   that's why I'll do it

   thank you

    I want to be alive

    If my people multiply
   I'll make it for you

    I'm saying
   may no one be sick

   so I make it

   so

(by Plenty-hawk)

5

If there is someone above
who knows what happens

You

today I have trouble
give me something to make it
not so

if there is someone inside the earth
who knows what happens

I have trouble today
give me something
to make it not so

whatever makes these things
now just as I am
I have enough

give me just for me
my death

I have enough sadness

(by Double-face)

6
He was there
    Old Man Coyote

Water all over the earth
no animals

He looked around
    grabbed

    and there was a little bird

    a swallow
    they say

He told it Go down
    bring earth

    it brought none

Then a crow
    Go down
    get some mud

    it brought none

Wolf
    you bring it

    it brought none

Old Man said
    Nothing I can do

    grabbed a duck
    then duck gone

    it's gone

he said to himself it won't be back
    he brought earth

    made this world
    here

    then mud people
    mud man
    mud woman

at that time
    with only that much mud
    that was how

Afterward there was a baby
    a boy

then he had a baby
    a girl

so

        as they say again and again
        now there was
        being born

        more people
        came to be

        you get married
        you make others

(by Medicine-tail)

7

I am climbing
    everywhere is

    coming up

— English versions by W. S. Merwin, after Robert Lowie

From THE CHANTS
(by María Sabina)

Mazatec

Ah, Jesu Kri
I am a woman who shouts
I am a woman who whistles
I am a woman who lightnings, says
Ah, Jesu Kri
Ah, Jesusi
Ah, Jesusi
Cayetano García

> [SHE CALLS HIS NAME TO GET HIS ATTENTION.
> "YES," HE RESPONDS, "WORK, WORK."]

Ah, Jesusi
Woman saintess, says
Ah Jesusi

> [HERE SHE BEGINS HUMMING AND CLAPPING AND UTTERING THE
> MEANINGLESS SYLLABLES "SO" AND "SI." THROUGHOUT THE ENTIRE
> PASSAGE THAT FOLLOWS SHE GOES ON CLAPPING RHYTHMICALLY IN
> TIME TO HER WORDS.]

hmm hmm hmm
hmm hmm hmm
hmm hmm hmm
hmm hmm hmm
hmm hmm hmm
so so so si
hmm hmm hmm
hmm hmm hmm
Woman who resounds
Woman torn up out of the ground
Woman who resounds
Woman torn up out of the ground
Woman of the principal medicinal berries
Woman of the sacred medicinal berries

Ah Jesusi
Woman who searches, says
Woman who examines by touch, says
ha ha ha
hmm hmm hmm
hmm hmm hmm
She is of one word, of one face, of one spirit, of one light, of one day
hmm hmm hmm
Cayetano García

[HE ANSWERS, "YES. . . ." SHE SAYS: "ISN'T THAT HOW?" HE RESPONDS,
"YES, THAT'S IT." SHE SAYS: "ISN'T THAT IT? LIKE THIS. LISTEN."]

Woman who resounds
Woman torn up out of the ground
Ah Jesusi
Ah Jesusi

[IN THE BACKGROUND THE MAN LAUGHS WITH PLEASURE.]

Ah Jesusi
Ah Jesusi
Ah Jesusi
hmm hmm hmm
so so so
Justice woman
hmm hmm hmm   ["THANK YOU," SAYS THE MAN.]
Saint Peter woman
Saint Paul woman
Ah Jesusi
Book woman
Book woman
Morning Star woman
Cross Star woman
God Star woman
Ah Jesusi
Moon woman
Moon woman
Moon woman
hmm hmm hmm

hmm hmm hmm
Sap woman
Dew woman

[THE MAN URGES HER ON. "WORK, WORK," HE SAYS.]

She is a Book woman
Ah Jesusi
hmm hmm hmm
hmm hmm hmm
so so so
Lord clown woman
Clown woman beneath the sea
Clown woman

[THE OTHER WORD IS UNINTELLIGBLE.]

Ah Jesusi
hmm hmm hmm
hmm hmm hmm
so so so
Woman who resounds
Woman torn up out of the ground
hmm hmm hmm
Because she is a Christ woman
Because she is a Christ woman
ha ha ha
so so so
so so so
so so so
Whirling woman of colors
Whirling woman of colors
Woman of the networks of light
Woman of the networks of light
Lord eagle woman
Lord eagle woman
Clock woman
Clock woman
ha ha ha

so so so
so so so
so so so

["THAT'S IT. WORK, WORK," EXCLAIMS THE MAN.]

hmm hmm hmm
hmm hmm hmm
so so so
hmm hmm hmm
so so so
so so so
si si si
si si si
si si si
so sa sa
si si si
so sa sa sa
hmm hmm hmm
hmm hmm hmm
hmm hmm hmm
si so soooooooooiiiiii

THE END OF "SO" IS DRAWN OUT INTO A LONG TONE. SHE CALLS,
"CAYETANO GARCÍA." "WORK, WORK," HE REPLIES. SHE GOES ON
HUMMING, CLAPPING FASTER AND FASTER. "CAYETANO GARCÍA," SHE
CALLS AGAIN, IN BETWEEN HER HUMMING, ALMOST AS IF SHE WERE
BRINGING HIM TO LIFE WITH HER CLAPPING. "WORK, WORK," HE SAYS,
"DON'T WORRY." AND THE PASSAGE ENDS ON A LONG EXPIRING "SIIIIII."

— English version by Henry Munn

ARCHAIC SONG OF DR. TOM THE SHAMAN

Nootka

I know thee. My name is Tom.
I want to find thy sickness. I know thy sickness.
I will take thy sickness. My name is Tom. I am a strong doctor.
If I take thy sickness thou wilt see thy sickness.
My name is Tom. I don't lie. My name is Tom. I don't talk shit.
I am a doctor. Many days I haven't eaten.
Ten days maybe I haven't eaten. I don't have my tools with me.
I don't have my sack with me. My name is Tom.
I will take thy sickness now & thou wilt see it.

— English version by Jerome Rothenberg, after James Teit

MAGIC WORDS *from* RUN TOWARD THE NIGHTLAND

Cherokee

1.

Now! The Red Tobacco has come to strike your soul.

I have just come from the treetops: I have just come
    to step over you.

Ha! Do not think it too far: face your feet this way.

Ha! Without knowing it, you have just come to my
    door: let your soul be anxious.

Seven! You will be leaving your home, leading your
    soul toward me.

Now tonight — Seven! — you will be thinking of me:
    you will think that I am the only one living.

And I will let you go when the sun rises.

going to the bank at dawn he smokes the tobacco toward where the desired woman lives, after which he washes his face four times: he then smokes again at noon & at dusk: the smoking is done for four days

2.

I came from up there Above.
Now I have just come down from where You rest,
    You Ancient White One.

I have just come around a bend in the Pathway over
    there: I am not a lonely Crow.
I have just come around the bend: it is good on this
    side.
Let my soul be let down from Above: let you be the
    one who greets it.

Ha! You White Woman, you hunt your lonely soul,
    which will be moving about here and there.

Ha! In a friendly fashion the Sparrow Hawk has just
    flown in.

compelling his runaway wife to return

Ha! They will be offering you the body of a Crow.
  "Gha:!"
He corners me! *"Mi:ʔ!"*

They have just come to tell me that your soul is very
  lonely.
Now and then lonely Eyes will be living with you.

I am a man! I hunt your very lonely soul that lives
  about here and there.
I am a good one! My soul will not be appearing
  about, lonely.
My body is not lonely: you will find rest in my body.

3.

Your Pathways are Black: it was wood, not a human
  being!

Dog shit will cling nastily to you.

You will be living intermittently. *"Grr!"* you will be
  saying along toward the Nightland.

Your Black Guts will be lying all about. You will be
  lonely.

You will be like the Brown Dog in heat. You are
  changed: you have just become old. This is your clan.

In the very middle of the Prairie, changed, you will
  be carrying dog turds. *"Grr!"* you will be saying.

Your Pathway lies toward the Nightland!

for making
an enemy
insane: one
merely states
the name &
clan of the
victim, delivers
the incantation
four times, &
then blows
one's breath
toward him
after each
rendition

4.

Now! *Ha!* It was our Mother in front of You & me: a smooth tree leaf.

You and I have just come to cut the eyes and the souls of the people in the Seven Clan Districts.

A great wind has just thundered over our souls four times.

Thought has just descended in a column, face downward, and has just joined their souls that have just sunk into the sea.

for making them forget, to lessen argument, etc.

5.

The Black Men, those great Wizards who just arose in the Nightland, have just come to take away your soul. Seven!

a spell for remembering

They have just gone in through the Nightland, so that you will not know it.

They have just finished putting Seven Shadows over the Very Yellow Water.

They have just arrived, carrying your soul. Seven!

They are not to help you climb over. Seven!

The Black Men, those great Wizards, have just carried away your soul. Seven!

— *Translations by Jack Frederick Kilpatrick & Anna Gritts Kilpatrick*

THE KILLER
(after A'yunini)

Cherokee

Careful:	my knife drills your soul
	listen, whatever-your-name-is
	One of the wolf people
listen	I'll grind your saliva into the earth
listen	I'll cover your bones with black flint
listen	" " " " " " feathers
listen	" " " " " " rocks
Because	you're going where it's empty
	Black coffin out on the hill
listen	the black earth will hide you, will
	find you a black hut
	Out where it's dark, in that country
listen	I'm bringing a box for your bones
	A black box
	A grave with black pebbles
listen	your soul's spilling out
listen	it's blue

— English version by Jerome Rothenberg, after James Mooney

WIZARDS
(by Alonzo Gonzales Mó)

Maya

There is a Maker
that knows how to cure illness. He knows how to cure sickness too.
For if there is a person who makes you sick or who makes you ill with things,
who hates you like that,
who is going to make something happen, who is going to cast a spell on
 you like that,
that person goes to a Maker and talks like this:
"How much will it take to get you to make that woman sick?"
"Well, what particular sickness do you want me to make?
Do you want me to make her sick for the whole year?
Do you want me to make her shit worms or piss blood? Or do you want
 me to make her shit snakes?
Or do you want me to make her shit big cockroaches too? Or do you
 want me to make her give birth to a gopher?
Or do you want me to frighten her?
There are phantoms of cats, there are phantoms of dogs too.
There are phantoms of pigs too. There are phantoms of goats too."
When one of these phantoms is desired, the Maker can do it in her
 house like that.
You've gone to a Maker.
Well, you talk like this,
"I've just now arrived here in your presence, old man, so you can advise
 me with your saastun.
Is there anything wrong with me? I want to know what it is like that."
"Well, lady, let's see what sickness you have, what sickness brought you
 here.
I need a candle and a quart of liquor and a claw from a rooster too."
Well, he grabs the liquor and throws it in a glass.
Then he grabs the saastun, he puts it into the liquor too.
He puts the saastun into the liquor three times like that until it is done.
Then he grabs the candle, then he lights it like that.
Then he begins his work like this:
he begins to Talk in Secret. He says your name.
Then when he is done with the Talk in Secret like that, he pulls the
 saastun out for the last time.

Then he looks to see what will appear there in the saastun.
"Well, lady, here is what made you so sick: it is a sickness thrown on
 you too.
I'll have to cure it, I'll have to pull it out.
The thing that made you sick like that, it is a big cockroach in your stomach.
There is some medicine that will let you pass the big cockroach out.
 Wait here while I make up the medicine."
He grabs the claw and a red rose and breaks them apart in water. Then
 he puts all of it into a bottle like that.
It is to drink so that the big cockroach will pass.
Well, when he is done with that,
"I'm going to prescribe an herb bath too." Some of the herbs are "albajaca,"
 "siipche," "sinanche," "ruda."
He tears up the herbs like that on Friday and Tuesday.
That's how Makers work.
There are phantoms of bats too. There are phantoms of snakes like that.
They can be brought into a house like this:
he puts water into a trough, he puts a chhom flower in.
Then this is poured over a person's head.
Then when someone wakes up like that, when they lean over like that,
then their head will fall off like that.
Perhaps the husband is watching what happens,
when she is seen, when the wife is looked at,
when the head is seen like that, then the head falls off.
The eyes on the head just roll around like that.
You grab the head like that.
You put it into some lime powder. You put the head in like that.
When it comes out, when the wife comes out like that,
then she wants to grab the head but can't.
'Then tears begin to come out of the eyes like that.
"Oh my husband, give me my head.
Oh my husband, you don't love me. Give me my head right now."
He doesn't give her head back like that.
He grabs the body, he puts it in a house.
Then he grabs the head and puts it in a box like that.
After that the husband isn't left alone because of the head. When he
 looks at it it is looking cross-eyed like that.
The head is watching him like that. The head of the poor wife.
When the husband looks at it it is looking cross-eyed like that.

"Oh my husband, give me my head. You don't love me," it says, "poor
me." The husband is made to think all of this by the phantom.
Because he had been watched by his wife who is a phantom. Because
she is the return of the evil things like that.
She came to look for her husband so that she could take him too.
When sickness like this comes about, the husband begins to hop like
an armadillo,
until he is killed.
There it ends.

— Translation by Allan F. Burns

A SONG *from* RED ANT WAY

Navajo

The red young men under the ground
decorated with red wheels
& decorated with red feathers
 at the center of the cone-shaped house
 I gave them a beautiful red stone —
 when someone does the same for me
 I'll walk the earth
The black young women under the ground
decorated with black wheels
& decorated with black feathers
 at the center of the flat-topped house
 I gave them an abalone shell —
 when someone does the same for me
 I'll walk the earth
From deep under the earth they're starting off
the old men under the earth are starting off
they're decorated with red wheels & starting off
at the center of the cone-shaped house they're starting off
because I gave them a beautiful red stone they're starting off
when someone does the same for me I'll walk the earth like them &
 starting off
on the red road & on the road they're starting off
The black old women under the earth are starting off
they're decorated with black wheels & starting off
decorated with black feathers & starting off
at the center of the flat-topped house they're starting off
because I gave them an abalone shell they're starting off
when someone does the same for me I'll walk the earth like them &
 starting off
from deep under the earth they're starting off

— English version by Jerome Rothenberg, after Harry Hoijer

THE DEADLY DANCE

Aztec

That shaman, owl man,
               dressed himself in shining yellow feathers
once he had won.
             Then he planned that the people
should come together and dance.
                So the cryer went to the hill
and announced it,
             and called to all the people.
Everyone in the country around heard him
                and left quickly for
Texcalapa, that place in the rocky country.
                They all came,
both nobles and the people,
             young men and young women,
so many they could not be counted,
               there were so many.
And then he began his song.
             He beats his drum,
again and again.
             They begin to join in the dance.
They leap into the air,
             they join hands weaving themselves together,
whirling around, and there is great happiness.
The chant wavers
             up and breaks into the air,
returns as an echo from the distant hills
               and sustains itself.
He sang it, he thought of it,
             and they answered him.
As he planned, they took it from his lips.
It began at dusk
             and went on halfway to midnight.
And when the dance
             they all did together

reached its climax,

             numbers of them hurled themselves from the cliffs
into the gulleys.

          They all died and became stones.
Others, who were on the bridge over the canyon,

                           the shaman broke it
under them

       though it was stone.
They fell in the rapids

         and became stones.
The Toltecs

     never understood what happened there,
they were drunk with it,

        blind,
and afterwards gathered many times there to dance.
Each time,

     there were more dead,

           more had fallen from the heights
into the rubble,

      and the Toltecs destroyed themselves.

   — English version by Edward Kissam

A BOOK OF
NARRATIVES

A MYTH OF THE HUMAN UNIVERSE

Maya

. . . to be a man and a woman as sun was, the way he had to put up with Moon, from start to finish the way she was, the way she behaved, and he up against it because he did have the advantage of her, he moved more rapidly. In the beginning he was only young and full of himself, and she, well, she was a girl living with her grandfather doing what a girl was supposed to be doing, making cloth. Even then he had the advantage of her, he hunted, instead, and because he could hunt he could become a humming-bird, which he did, just to get closer to her, this loveliness he thought she was and wanted to taste. Only the trouble was, he had to act out his mask, and while he was coming closer, one tobacco flower to another toward the house, her grandfather brought him down with a clay shot from a blow gun. And sun fell, right into moon's arms, who took him to her room to mother him, for she was all ready to be a wife, a man's second mother as a wife is in these parts where birds are so often stoned and need to be brought back to consciousness and, if they have their wings intact, may fly away again. As sun was. Only he could also talk, and persuaded moon to elope with him in a canoe. But there you are: there is always danger. Grandfather gets rain to throw his fire at them and though sun converts to turtle and is tough enough to escape alive, moon, putting on a crab shell, is not sufficiently protected and is killed.

Which is only part of it, that part of it which is outside and seems to have all of the drama. But only seems. For dragonflies collect moon's flesh and moon's blood in thirteen hollow logs, the sort of log sun had scooped his helpless runaway boat out of, thinking he had made it, had moon finally for his own. Foolish sun. For now here he is back again, after thirteen days, digging out the thirteen logs, and finding that twelve of them contain nothing but all the insects and all the snakes which fly and crawl about the earth of man and pester people in a hot climate so that a lot die off before they are well begun and most are ready, at any instant, for a sickness or a swelling, and the best thing to do is to lie quiet, wait for the poison to pass. For there is log 13, and it reveals moon restored to life, only moon is missing that part which makes woman woman, and deer alone, only deer can give her what he does give her so that she and sun can do what man and woman have the pleasure to do as one respite from the constant hammering.

But you see, nothing lasts. Sun has an older brother, who comes to live with sun and moon, and sun has reason to suspect that something is going on between moon and the big star, for this brother is the third one of the sky, the devilish or waspish one who is so often with moon. By a trick, sun discovers them, and moon, dispirited, sitting off by herself on the river bank, is persuaded by the bird zopilote to go off with him to the house of the king of the vultures himself. And though a vulture is not, obviously, as handsome a thing as the sun, do not be fooled into thinking that this bird which can darken the sky as well as feed on dead things until they are only bones for the sun to whiten, has not his attractions, had not his attractions to moon, especially the king of them all. She took him, made him the third of her men, and was his wife.

But sun was not done with her, with his want of her, and he turned to that creature which empowered her, the deer, for aid. He borrowed a skin, and hiding under it — knowing as hot sun does the habits of vultures — he pretends to be a carcass. The first vulture comes in, landing awkwardly a distance off, hobbles his nervous way nearer until, as he is about to pick apart what he thinks is a small deer, sun leaps on his back and rides off to where moon is. He triumphantly seizes her, only to find that she is somewhat reluctant to return.

At which stage, for reasons of cause or not, sun and moon go up into the sky to assume forever their planetary duties. But sun finds there is one last thing he must do to the moon before human beings are satisfied with her. He must knock out one of her eyes, they complain she is so bright and that they cannot sleep, the night is so much the same as his day, and his day is too much anyhow, and a little of the sweetness of the night they must have. So he does, he puts out her eye, and lets human beings have what they want. But when he does more, when, occasionally, he eclipses her entirely, some say it is only a sign that the two of them continue to fight, presumably because sun cannot forget moon's promiscuity, though others say that moon is forever erratic, is very much of a liar, is always telling sun about the way people of the earth are as much misbehavers as she, get drunk, do the things she does, in fact, the old ones say, moon is as difficult to understand as any bitch is.

— *English version by Charles Olson*

From THE POPOL VUH: BEGINNINGS

Maya

This is the account of how all was in suspense, all calm, in silence; all motionless, still, and the expanse of the sky was empty.

This is the first account, the first narrative. There was neither man, nor animal, birds, fishes, crabs, trees, stones, caves, ravines, grasses, nor forests; there was only the sky.

The surface of the earth had not appeared. There was only the calm sea and the great expanse of the sky.

There was nothing brought together, nothing which could make a noise, nor anything which might move, or tremble, or could make noise in the sky.

There was nothing standing; only the calm water, the placid sea, alone and tranquil. Nothing existed.

There was only immobility and silence in the darkness, in the night. Only the Creator, the Maker, Tepeu, Gucumatz, the Forefathers, were in the water surrounded with light. They were hidden under green and blue feathers, and were therefore called Quetzal Serpent. By nature they were great sages and great thinkers. In this manner the sky existed and also the Heart of Heaven, which is the name of God and thus He is called.

● ● ●

So then came his word here.
  It reached
To Majesty
  And Quetzal Serpent
There in the obscurity,
  In the nighttime.
It spoke to Majesty
  And Quetzal Serpent, and they spoke.
Then they thought;
  Then they pondered.
Then they found themselves;
  They assembled
Their words,
  Their thoughts.
Then they gave birth —
  Then they heartened themselves.

Then they caused to be created
    And they bore men.
Then they thought about the birth,
    The creation
Of trees
    And shrubs,
And the birth of life
    And humanity
In the obscurity,
    In the nighttime
Through him who is the Heart of Heaven,
    1 Leg by name.
1 Leg Lightning is the first,
    And the second is Dwarf Lightning.
Third then is Green Lightning,
    So that the three of them are the Heart of Heaven.
Then they came to Majesty
    And Quetzal Serpent, and then was the invention
Of light
    And life.
"What if it were planted?
    Then something would brighten —
A supporter,
    A nourisher.
So be it.
    You must decide on it.
There is the water to get rid of,
    To be emptied out,
To create this,
    The earth
And have it surfaced
    And levelled
When it is planted,
    When it is brightened —
Heaven
    And earth."

— *Translations by Delia Goetz & Sylvanus G. Morley (prose)
and by Munro Edmonson (verse)*

From THE POPOL VUH: ALLIGATOR'S STRUGGLES WITH THE 400 SONS

Maya

. . . So these then are the deeds of Alligator in turn,
   The first son of 7 Parrot.
"I am the maker of mountains,"
   Said Alligator.
And so Alligator
   Was bathing at the edge of the water
When there passed by
   Four hundred sons,
Hauling a tree,
   A post for their house.
Four hundred of them were walking along,
   And they had cut
A great tree
   For the cross-beam of their house.
And there came Alligator
   And arrived where there were four hundred sons.
"What are you doing,
   You boys?"
"It's just a tree —
   We can't lift it."
"Shoulder it.
   I'll carry it.
Where does it go?
   What sort of use do you want from it?"
"It's just the cross-beam
   Of our house."
"All right,"
   He said then.
And when he had lifted it
   He put it on his shoulder and took it
To the door of the house
   Of the four hundred sons.
"Why don't you stay with us,
   Son?
Where are your mother

And your father?"
"I have none,"
   He said then.
"Let us perhaps press you then
   To get some more chopped tomorrow,
Another of our beams,
   A post for our house."
"Good,"
   He said again.
And then they took counsel,
   The four hundred sons.
"Here is this boy: what should we do with him?
   Let us kill him,
Because it is not good what he does:
   He lifts the beam all by himself.
Let us dig a big hole here,
   And then we'll make him go down there in the hole.
Go get it;
   Lift the dirt out of the hole, we'll tell him.
And when he is bending over down in the hole,
   Then we can throw a big beam down there
And thus he will die in the hole,"
   The four hundred sons said.
And so they dug a big hole that went very deep
   And then they called Alligator.
"We beg of you,
   Go and dig some more earth.
We can't do it," he was told.
   And he said, "All right,"
And then went down in the hole.
   "Call up
When the dirt is all dug up
   So that you have got really deep,"
He was told.
   "Yes," he said,
And began to dig the hole.
   Only the hole he dug was to save himself.
He knew he was to be killed,
   So he dug a branch in the hole to one side.
The second hole he dug

Was to save him.
"Well, how far along are you?"
The four hundred sons shouted down then.
"I'm digging it fast,
    So I'll call you just as soon
As the digging is finished up,"
    Said Alligator from down there in the hole.
But he was not digging the bottom of the hole
    Which was to be his grave,
But rather he was digging his own hole
    As a shelter for himself.
And so when Alligator finally called up,
    He was safe in the earth there in the hole when he called up.
"Come on then.
    Come.
Take the earth,
    The dirt from the hole.
It is all dug.
    I have made it really deep.
Can't you hear my call maybe?
    There it is now, your call,
Only down here
    It echoes
As though you were one remove
    Or two removes away,
It sounds like,"
    Alligator called up from the hole.
But he stayed hidden down there,
    Shouting up from down in the hole.
And so their big beam was dragged over by the boys
    And then they dropped the beam right down into the hole.
"He isn't there.
    He doesn't say anything.
Let's listen now while he groans
    Until he dies,"
They said to each other,
    But they whispered quietly,
And they just hid themselves, each one separately
    When they had dropped the beam down.
And so he spoke.

Then he groaned.
He called out just once more,
    The moment the beam was dropped.
"Ahah! It is done!
    Very good!
We've done it to him!
    He's dead!
What if further
    He had continued
What he was doing,
    What he was working at?
Why he would have become
    In fact the first,
And imposed himself with us
    And among us!
Even us,
    The four hundred sons!"
They said then,
    And again they rejoiced.
"It will be, for the making of our wine, three days,
    And three days having passed
Let us drink to our home,
    Our house,
Even we,
    The four hundred sons!" they said.
"So tomorrow we'll see,
    And the next day we'll see,
If the ants don't come
    From the ground.
When he is rotted,
    When he is decomposed,
Then it will console our hearts
    When we drink our wine," they said.
And Alligator, there in his hole, heard
    When the boys said "the next day."
And on the second day,
    Then the ants assembled.
They ran about.
    They swarmed around,
And then they got together

Under the beam.
Quickly they took in their mouths the hair
    And they took in their mouths the nails of Alligator,
And when they saw it,
    The boys said,
"Isn't that devil finished off?
    Just look at the ants!
They have already gathered there.
    They have swarmed there.
They have quickly seized his hair.
    Those are his nails that you can see!
We did it!"
    They said to each other then.
But Alligator was still alive.
    He had just cut the hair off his head.
He had just bitten off his nails
    In order to give them to the ants,
So that the fact that he had died
    Would be known to the four hundred sons.
And so they started on their wine on the third day
    And then all the boys drank heavily,
And all the four hundred sons got drunk
    Until they knew nothing further.
And then their house was pulled down
    On their heads by Alligator.
They were finished off
    And all of them destroyed.
There were not even one
    Or two of the four hundred sons who were saved.
They were killed by Alligator,
    The son of 7 Parrot.
And since they died,
    These four hundred sons,
They are said to have gone to be stars.
    "The Group" is the name for them,
Though that may only be a play on words.

— *English version by Munro Edmonson*

THE ORIGIN OF THE SKAGIT INDIANS ACCORDING TO LUCY WILLIAMS

Suelick is the greatest Indian power.
He is like your God.
When the world was flooded
he created four powers.
Schodelick.
Swadick.
Hode and Stoodke.
We call them the brothers of Suelick.
The oldest brother is something round.
Maybe canoe anchor.
Maybe something else.
Hode is fire.
Stoodke, knife.
I don't remember Swadick
but he's a big name around here.

One day Suelick tells his brothers
to create land and people.
So the boys leave home.
Schodelick comes to Skagit country.
Creates a man and woman
and some land.
He puts fish in the rivers and lakes.
Then he shows the man and woman
how to catch the fish
how to clean the fish
how to eat them.
Schodelick creates all living things.
Trees.
Animals.
Plants.
And Schodelick shows the man and woman how to use them.

When his work is done
Schodelick is at the waterfall above Marblemount.
He tells his brothers that his work is done.

He points to the big rock in the middle of the falls.
I'll be right here in the water near the big rock
he tells his brothers.
He dives into the water.
Sings and swims for a long time.
Nothing in his stomach.
Schodelick still lives there in the water
the greatest power of Skagit Indians.
If you walk by this place early in the morning
you hear the song of Schodelick.

Quaquach is the rock
he stands on before he goes into the water.

My people believed in the power search.
They lived by it.
They went for many days without eating
before they dived into water to receive words
from Schodelick.
Without power the Indian is no good.
No long lives.
No purpose.
All our young men and women went in search of this power.

Schodelick's brothers traveled into the Okanagan.
They created land and people.
They created trees, animals, plants.
Just like Schodelick did here.
They showed the poeple how to use everything.
Those Indians worship fire.
They play with hot rocks.
They become crazy men
and the only way they return to this world
is beating their heads in the fire.

This is all I know.
This is the true story of the beginning of my people.

— English transcription by Carl Cary

THE CREATION OF THE WORLD ACCORDING TO CHARLES SLATER

Cuna

God came from under the earth for himself. And then stood up from under the earth, and he started to thought himself how to make a woman. Because he could not stayed by himself; and whether he take palm of his hand to make a body of woman that he can compose the world. That time earth was without form and darkness. But god claimed that if he take him palm of his hand could not do because a hand will hurt a woman and if he take bottom of his feet would not do because the feet he will kick a woman. That time the earth was without form and firmament. And then God started to thought himself that if he take a heart that will do; because the heart is memory to the woman and then he take heart of string that which is gone down straight to blader, that which will make a woman way to come out of womb to form a child. And he take kineys blader, lungs, womb and liver. And then he take a soul to form of a white cloth. And then he spread out the white cloth on the table and then he put every things in it. And then he found a case to put every things in it and a key to lock every things in it. And then he carried into the four empty house and hide these and then God lay down on the bed and waiting for her to come to him. And then on 12 a clock in the night some one came crying and saying "Where is are you father? And on four days God heard a some one crying inside the case of the empty house. And then he took a key to opened the case. When he opened the case the child come from the womb and then she stood on the God key hole; and then she came upstairs and come crying and saying. "Where is my father"? God said: "here am I." And then she came and lay down with him on the bed. And then God to her My dear child my dear daughter and my dear wife and you is my heart and then I will name by the heart because you come forth of my heart and he called her name *Puna Olocueguintile.* And then God became two; and he started to thought himself to created the earth for the children to put therein. And then mother started to see white soul, yellow soul, black soul, dark soul, spotted soul, green soul and purple soul, blue soul, soft soul and red soul. And then God want it to form golden table out of his wife body. And he took bone part of just her below her neaple to form the golden table and then she start to see white soul and red soul. And then he form eight cups of it to find the soul how would became, then she spread out white soul on the golden table and then she wipe off to find the soul. And then he started to form a chair. And then mother started to see the soul again and then father called at her eight times and the last she saw the soul was round soul, and what he form chair of it and the mother never saw any more soul. And then he saw his wife bearing fruit. And then father saw it was so good to him. And he started to thought what he going to form first for his children and grand children. And then mother became sick on her day: and then God said am going to form first the earth. And then mother saw soul again and she first saw white soul and he form a different clays out of it. golden table and then she wipe off to find the soul. And then he could not bear it; but still she laugh; and God asked her how you feel!" and she said alright". And a grand children will be circumcise after me. And then mother saw soul again. When she saw soul a golden eel come auf of it. When the eel come down eel go crooked and twist: and then mother saw soul again and a gueb-gueb came out of it again. That time the earth was soft. And then God took a stomach out of the woman and also he took soul out of the mother to form a eight barrels of water. And then mother saw soul again and the father called to her again And then he start to thought by himself what am going to make for my children again. And their mother became sick again on her day; and then he form a water and put it in the barrels to make a river for us. And then God saw when a river flood that the earth could not stand from river flood; because the earth was to soft; and then God created stones and Ivory rock and sanctify rock and then God started to create a clays and he created sticky clay to defend the earth from river flood and he also created falls to defend the earth: trees to prevend the earth from falling. And then God created flint to make a looking glass with it. So he also putted in the river to prevent the earth from falling. And then mother started to see soul again: and she saw white soul and then father called to her. And then the girl child come forth for her mother's womb just come like a surenge; and then mother form a surenge out of it, and she put a surenge on top up of tanks; and the water start drop down on the tanks. And when a girl come forth from her mother's womb and the father said to her: "My dear child, my dear daughter and my dear wife". And then mother said to herself am going to created thunder. And then mother stand up on top up of tanks. And on the top of tanks and inside of the mother belly a great sound was heard and roared and from that mother form a thunder. And then mother begin swell her belly and then she stood up on top of eight tanks and then she drop every kind a soul, white soul, black soul, dark soul, blue soul and red soul, yellow soul to filled the eight tanks with it. And when the every kind soul drop upon the tanks; then the smoke rise up in the air to form a cloud and to come down to sinenage. And then mother going to let water run out of the barrels and then she lay down on top up of barrels lay wide opened and when she lay down and then mother start to see a soul again; and then the soul start to run out of the mother's belly to the mouth of the river. And the lord started to think to dress the mother body. And then God lay with his daughter and then he called on her and then she start to see her soul red soul and God says I will make red cloth of it, And then she start to see her soul again a yellow soul; and God says, I will make yellow cloth of it. And then she saw her soul again it was a red dish in the middle and the white soul was round of it and then God says whitish part it will make a cotton out it and the reddish part he make pink pouder out of it. And then she start to saw her soul again a white soul and God says, I will make white cloth out of it, and then daughter says it give me a pain; but she still feel good but she keep on going and then she start to see her soul again and it was spotted soul spotted dots and with crooked line and straight line that I will make apron out of it and then she start to see her soul again it was a blue soul and God says I will form blue drill out of it. And then she saw soul again come in form just like strings just beside the tubes thats to form a twine line out of it and just to make form a bridge. And then she start to see her soul again a round soul different kind of colours and that I will form eight different colours of a beads, yellow, red, white, green, blue, pink, yellowish an reddish beads out ot it. And then she start to see a soul again and came in a form yellowish looking piece out off her womb; that is to form a gold; goldnecklace; and gold-cross necklace and then she saw her soul again it came in a form reddish an yellowish colour under her neaples and God says that I will form earrings out of it. And then she saw her soul again it came in a form just like a net reddish and yellowish and dots and crooked lines and God says I will form a handkerchief out of that. And then she saw her soul again it came in a form same as a net and bluish and yellowish and dots and God says it will form a sarpo out of that. And then she start a see a soul again it came in a form a blood just like a netish thing a thing that which is on top of the heart and it came from her womb. And God says I will form bead necklace out of it. And then she see a soul again it came in a form whitish and shine just like a crystal and God says I will form a money out of it. And then God says I will take a bone part of it to form a looking glass out of it. And then she see her soul again came in a form just like a two hook and he form a scissors out of it. And then God got up and saw her dressed up and says Oh my I never saw a good looking woman in this world and I thought lay down her side again once more, and then God saw every things what he made it was a good to him. And then God says what am going to make for my children to eat for foods and for meats; and then he consider of her what he could do. And then he asked the mother what he will do. And then he put the mother on the top up of the golden table and he said to her my dear daughter, my child and my dear wife and then God stoop her down the golden table her down the golden table and he started to back scutle her and the very minute . . .

THE INVENTION OF WHITE PEOPLE
(by Leslie Marmon Silko)

Laguna Pueblo

The old man shook his head. "That is the trickery of the withcraft," he said.
"They want us to believe all evil resides with white people. Then we will
look no further to see what is really happening. They want us to separate
ourselves from white people, to be ignorant and helpless as we watch our
own destruction. But white people are only tools that the witchery manipu-
lates; and I tell you, we can deal with white people, with their machines and
their beliefs. We can because we invented white people; it was Indian
witchery that made white people in the first place.

Long time ago
in the beginning
there were no white people in this world
there was nothing European.
And this world might have gone on like that
except for one thing:
witchery.
This world was already complete
even without white people.
There was everything
including witchery.

Then it happened.
These witch people got together.
Some came from far far away
across oceans
across mountains.
Some had slanty eyes
others had black skin.
They all got together for a contest
the way people have baseball tournaments nowadays
except this was a contest
in dark things.

So anyway
they all got together
witch people from all directions

witches from all the Pueblos
and all the tribes.
They had Navajo witches there,
some from Hopi, and a few from Zuni.
They were having a witches' conference,
that's what it was
Way up in the lava rock hills.
north of Cañoncito
they got together
to fool around in caves
with their animal skins.
Fox, badger, bobcat, and wolf
they circled the fire
and on the fourth time
they jumped into that animal's skin.

But this time it wasn't enough
and one of them
maybe a Sioux or some Eskimos
started showing off.
"That wasn't anything,
watch this."

The contest started like that.
Then some of them lifted the lids
on their big cooking pots,
calling the rest of them over
to take a look:
dead babies simmering in blood
circles of skull cut away
all the brains sucked out.
Witch medicine
to dry and grind into powder
for new victims.

Others untied skin bundles of disgusting objects:
dark flints, cinders from burned hogans where the
dead lay
Whorls of skin
cut from fintgertips
sliced from the penis end and clitoris tip.

Finally there was only one
who hadn't shown off charms or powers.
The witch stood in the shadows beyond the fire
and no one ever knew where this witch came from
which tribe
or if it was a woman or a man.
But the important thing was
this witch didn't show off any dark thunder charcoals
or red ant-hill beads.
This one just told them to listen:
"What I have is a story."

At first they all laughed
but this witch said
Okay
go ahead
laugh if you want to
but as I tell the story
it will begin to happen.

Set in motion now
set in motion by our witchery
to work for us.

Caves across the ocean
in caves of dark hills
white skin people
like the belly of a fish
covered with hair.

Then they grow away from the earth
then they grow away from the sun
then they grow away from the plants and animals.
They see no life
When they look
they see only objects.
The world is a dead thing for them
the trees and rivers are not alive
the mountains and stones are not alive.
The deer and bear are objects
They see no life.

They fear
They fear the world.
They destroy what they fear.
They fear themselves.

The wind will blow them across the ocean
thousands of them in giant boats
swarming like larva
out of a crushed ant hill.

They will carry objects
which can shoot death
faster than the eye can see.

They will kill the things they fear
all the animals
the people will starve.

They will poison the water
they will spin the water away
and there will be drought
the people will starve.

They will fear what they find
They will fear the people
They kill what they fear.

Entire villages will be wiped out
They will slaughter whole tribes

Corpses for us
Blood for us
Killing killing killing killing.

And those they do not kill
will die anyway
at the destruction they see
at the loss
at the loss of the children
the loss will destroy the rest.

Stolen rivers and mountains
the stolen land will eat their hearts
and jerk their mouths from the Mother.
The people will starve.

They will bring terrible diseases
the people have never known.
Entire tribes will die out
covered with festered sores
shitting blood
vomiting blood.
Corpses for our work
Set in motion now
set in motion by our witchery
set in motion
to work for us.

They will take this world from ocean to ocean
they will turn on each other
they will destroy each other
Up here
in these hills
they will find the rocks,
rocks with veins of green and yellow and black.
They will lay the final pattern with these rocks
they will lay it across the world
and explode everything.

Set in motion now
set in motion
To destroy
To kill
Objects to work for us
objects to act for us
Performing the witchery
for suffering
for torment
for the still-born
the deformed
the sterile
the dead.

Whirling
whirling
whirling
whirling
set into motion now
set into motion.

So the other witches said
"Okay you win; you take the prize,
but what you said just now —
it isn't so funny
It doesn't sound so good.
We are doing okay without it
we can get along without that kind of thing.
Take it back.
Call that story back."

But the witch just shook its head
at the others in their stinking animal skins, fur
and feathers.
It's already turned loose.
It's already coming.
It can't be called back.

Coon cons Coyote, Coyote eats Coon, Coyote fights Shit-Men, gets immured in a rock-house, eats his eyes, eats his balls, gets out, cons Bird-Boy for eyes, loses them to the birds & gets them back

Nez Percé

his younger brother Coon said to Coyote Here's how I get this good fried fish. I use my skunk cabbages for a pillow, the morning sun shine turns them to fish. Coyote did that, he sat against the cabbages. At sunrise they were skunk cabbages

and Coon said Not that way! What I do, I put my prick into a nest of ants, they bite it, maybe hard, and there's a big fried fish, a little bite, I get a small fish. Well Coyote did it, he found the ants & put his prick in them, it really hurt when they bit; Coyote thought about his fish and pulled out his prick all red and sore. Home with no fish Coyote said to Coon They bit my thing and hurt it but I got no fish

and Coon said Not that way! What I do, I go to the trail and ask whoever's passing by. So Coyote went too and each got food. And Coyote stole from them and Coon told and ran with his own food. They beat up Coyote and took everything back and swelled up his eyes so he couldn't see. He went home feeling sick

Coyote said to Coon When you go crabbing watch out, black beings at the river shoot people. You can know them they say Spitspam Spitspam. Coyote charcoaled himself all up and went to the river and shot an arrow into Coon. Saying Spitspam Spitspam. Coon came home in pain. I told you said Coyote, let me take care of you. And Coyote bit his fatty places, he bit them out. O Coon screamed You hurt me. No Coyote said I cure you, and Coyote ate him. Coyote had a lot of food

then Coyote went here and there and couldn't decide and he said I wish I could have a fight with Shit-Man. Right away the Shit-Men hit him until he was unconscious. When he got up he smelled like shit all over and washed himself in the river

I wish I had a stone house, Coyote said, to protect me. And he had one. They couldn't get in or him out. After a long time there he got hungry and there was no food. So he pulled out his eyes and ate them, but he became thin and there was no food so he ripped out his balls and ate them

a person outside pecked and hammered; when Coyote cried out Sapsucker came. Coyote said Tell brown woodpecker, bluejay and redheaded woodpecker to break open this house and they did, and carried him out. He gave them the finest clothes and all those men went away happy

well Coyote was blind now. He heard Bird-Boy and called to him and he put flowers in his own eye-sockets. Coyote said Why don't you shoot that pheasant over there? your eyes are bad, let's trade. And each took the other's eyes. The boy ran here and there and he could see far but his eyes that were flowers wilted and dried and he was blind

Coyote would take one eye out and toss it up into the air saying Great it's mine. Birds passed by and noticed him they plucked his eyes from the air. Coyote said Great it's mine, he said it five times, but they had the eyes

Coyote reached an old one-eyed woman. O aren't they having a time with Coyote's eyes she said. She was grinding fern roots and he clubbed her to death and put on her clothes and ground fern roots. Then women came back and said to Coyote O aren't they having a time with Coyote's eyes!

the next day they took the old woman with them and she said to all the women Carry me on your back, a little lower down granddaughter. Then Coyote said That's just the right place down there. And the bearer said You're hurting me, you're sticking a thing into me. How, said Coyote, I have nothing to stick you with. But the youngest woman wouldn't put Coyote lower down and Coyote said It hurts granddaughter, a little lower down! But she threw Coyote down and they all went to the place of Coyote's eyes

they passed the eyes around and Coyote got them again and threw them into the air crying Great they're mine and Bluejay said to the others What's the old woman saying? and both eyes fell down and were his again. He took off the old woman clothes and ran away

— English version by Armand Schwerner, after Melville Jacobs

90

TELLING ABOUT COYOTE
(by Simon Ortiz)

Acoma Pueblo

Old Coyote...
"If he hadn't looked back
everything would have been okay
...like he wasn't supposed to,
                    but he did,
and as soon as he did, he lost all his power,
his strength."

"...you know, Coyote
is in the origin and all the way
through...he's the cause
of the trouble, the hard times
that things have..."

"Yet, he came so close
to having it easy.
                    But he said,
"Things are just too easy..."
Of course he was mainly bragging,
shooting his mouth.
The existential Man,
Dostoevsky Coyote.

"He was on his way to Zuni
to get married on that Saturday,
and on the way there
he ran across a gambling party.
A number of other animals were there.
                    He sat in
for a while, you know, pretty sure
of himself, you know like he is,
sure that he would win something.

                    But he lost
everything. Everything.
And that included his skin, his fur
which was the subject of envy
of all the other animals around.
Coyote had the prettiest,
the glossiest, the softest fur
that ever was. And he lost that.

            So some mice
finding him shivering in the cold
beside a rock felt sorry for him.
'This poor thing, beloved,'
they said, and they got together
just some old scraps of fur
and glued them on Coyote with pinon pitch.

And he's had that motley fur ever since.
You know, the one that looks like
scraps of an old coat, that one."

Coyote, old man, wanderer,
where you going, man?
Look up and see the sun.
Scorned, an old raggy blanket
at the back of the closet nobody wants.

"At this one conference
of all the animals there was a bird
with the purest white feathers.
His feathers were like, ah . . .
like the sun was shining on it
all the time but you could look at it
and you wouldn't be hurt by the glare.
It was easy and gentle to look at.
And he was Crow.
He was sitting at one side of the fire.
And the fire was being fed large pine logs,
and Crow was sitting downwind
from the fire, and the wind was blowing

that way . . .
        And Coyote was there.
He was envious of Crow because
all the other animals were saying,
'Wowee, look at that Crow, man,
just look at him,' admiring Crow.
Coyote began to scheme.
He kept on throwing pine logs into the fire,
ones with lots of pitch in them.
And the wind kept blowing.
all night long . . .
        Let's see,
the conference was about deciding
the seasons — when they should take place —
and it took a long time to decide that . . .
And when it was over, Crow was covered
entirely with soot. The blackest soot
from the pine logs.
And he's been like that since then."

"Oh yes, that was the conference
when Winter was decided
that it should take place
when Dog's hair got long.
        Dog said,
'I think Winter should take place
when my hair gets long.'
And it agreed that it would. I guess
no one else offered a better reason."

        Who?
        Coyote?
O,
O yes, last time . . .
when was it,
I saw him somewhere
between Muskogee and Tulsa,
heading for Tulsy Town I guess,
just trucking along.
He was heading into some oakbrush thicket,

just over the hill was a creek.
Probably get to Tulsa in a couple days,
drink a little wine,
tease with the Pawnee babes,
sleep beside the Arkansas River,
listen to the river move,
. . . hope it don't rain,
hope the river don't rise.
He'll be back. Don't worry.
He'll be back.

THE BOY AND THE DEER
(by Andrew Peynetsa)

Zuni

SON'AHCHI.

(*audience*) Ee —— so.

SONTI LO —— NG AGO.

(*audience*) Ee —— so.

THERE WERE VILLAGERS AT HE'SHOKTA

and

up on the Prairie-Dog Hills

the deer

had their home.

The daughter of a priest

was sitting in a room on the fourth story down weaving basket-plaques.

She was always sitting and working in there, and the Sun came up

every day when the Sun came up

the girl would sit working

at the place where he came in.

It seems the Sun made her pregnant.

When he made her pregnant

though she sat in there without knowing any man, her belly grew large.

She worked o —— n for a time

weaving basket-plaques, and

her belly grew large, very very large.

When her time was near

she had a pain in her belly.

Gathering all her clothes

she went out and

went down to Water's End.

On she went until

she came to the bank

Consult the Aids to Reading Aloud on page 116.

went on down to the river, and washed her clothes.

(Then)
having washed a few things, she had a pain in her belly.

She came out of the river. Having come out she sat down by a juniper
    tree and strained her muscles:
(the little baby came out).
She dug a hole, put juniper leaves in it
then laid the baby there.
She went back into the water
gathered all her clothes
and carefully washed the blood off herself.
She bundled
her clothes
put them on her back
(and returned to her home at He'shokta).

And the DEER
who lived on the Prairie-Dog Hills
were going down to DRINK, going down to drink at dusk.
(The Sun had almost set when they went down to drink and the little
    baby was crying.
"Where is the little baby crying?" they said.)
It was two fawns on their way down
with their mother
who heard him.
The crying was coming from the direction of a tree.
They were going into the water

(and there)
they came upon the crying.
Where a juniper tree stood, the child

(was crying).

The deer
the two fawns and their mother went to him.
"Well, why shouldn't we
save him?
Why don't you two hold my nipples
so
so he can nurse?" that's what the mother said to her fawns.

The two fawns helped the baby
suck their mother's nipple and get some milk.
(Now the little boy

was nursed, the little boy was nursed by the deer)
o —————— n until he was full.
Their mother lay down cuddling him the way deer sleep
with her two fawns
together
lying beside her
and they SLEPT WITH THEIR FUR AROUND HIM.
They would nurse him, and so they lived on, lived on.
As he grew
he was without clothing, NAKED.
His elder brother and sister had fur:
they had fur, but he was NAKED and this was not good.

The deer
(the little boy's mother)
spoke to her two fawns: "Tonight
when you sleep, you two will lie on both sides
and he will lie in the middle.
While you're sleeping

(I'll go to Kachina Village, for he is without clothing, naked, and
this is not good.")

That's what she said to her children, and
there
at the village of He'shokta

were young men
who went out hunting, and the young men who went out hunting looked
for deer.
When they went hunting they made their kills around the Prairie-Dog
Hills.
And their mother went to Kachina Village, she went o———n until
she reached Kachina Village.
It was filled with dancing kachinas.

"My fathers, my children, how have you been passing the days?"
"Happily, our child, so you've come, sit down," they said.
"Wait, stop your dancing, our child has come and must have
something to say," then the kachinas stopped.
The deer sat down, (the old lady deer sat down.
A kachina priest spoke to her):
"Now speak.
You must've come because you have something to say." "YES, in TRUTH
I have come because I have something to SAY.
(There in the village of He'shokta is a priest's daughter)
who abandoned her child.
We found him
we have been raising him.
But he is poor, without clothing, naked, and this
is not good.
So I've come to ask for clothes for him," that's what she said.
"Indeed." "Yes, that's why I've come, to ask clothes for him."
"Well, there is always a way," they said.
Kyaklo

laid out his shirt.
Long Horn put in his kilt and his moccasins.

And Huututu put in his buckskin leggings
he laid out his bandoleer.

And Pawtiwa laid out his macaw headdress.

Also they put in the BELLS he would wear on his legs.

Also they laid out

strands of turquoise beads
moccasins.
So they laid it all out, hanks of yarn for his wrists and ankles
they gathered all his clothing.
(When they had gathered it his mother put it on her back): "Well, I
    must GO
but when he has grown larger I will return to ask for clothing again."
That's what she said. "Very well indeed."
(Now the deer went her way.
When she got back to her children they were all sleeping.
When she got there they were sleeping and she
lay down beside them.
The little boy, waking up
began to nurse, his deer mother nursed him
and he went back to sleep.) So they spent the night and then
(with pleasure) the little boy was clothed by his mother.
His mother clothed him.

When he was clothed he was no longer cold.
He went around playing with his elder brother and sister, they would
    run after each other, playing.
They lived on this way until he was grown.
And THEN

they went back up to their old home on the Prairie-Dog Hills. Having
    gone up
they remained there and would come down only to drink, in the evening.
There they lived o——— n for a long time

until
from the village
(his uncle
went out hunting. Going out hunting
he came along
down around
Worm Spring, and from there he went on toward

the Prairie-Dog Hills and came up near the edge of a valley there.
When he came to the woods on the Prairie-Dog Hills he looked down and)
THERE IN THE VALLEY was the herd of deer. In the herd of deer
there was a little boy going around among them
dressed in white.
He had bells on his legs and he wore a macaw headdress.
(He wore a macaw headdress, he was handsome), surely it was a boy
(a male
a person among them.
While he was looking) the deer mothers spotted him.
(When they spotted the young man they ran off.
There the little boy outdistanced the others.)

"Haa——— , who could that be?"
That's what his uncle said. ("Who
could you be? Perhaps you are a daylight person.")
That's what his UNCLE thought and he didn't do ANYTHING to the deer.
(He returned to his house in the evening.)

It was evening
dinner was ready, (and when they sat down to eat
the young man spoke):

"Today, while I was out hunting
when I reached the top
(of the Prairie-Dog Hills, where the woods are, when I reached the
    top), THERE in the VALLEY was a HERD OF DEER.
There was a herd of deer

and with them was a LITTLE BOY:
whose child could it be?
When the deer spotted me they ran off and he outdistanced them.
(He wore bells on his legs, he wore a macaw headdress, he was dressed
    in white.")
That's what the young man was saying
telling his father.
It was one of the boy's OWN ELDERS
his OWN UNCLE had found him. (*audience*) Ee ——— so.
His uncle had found him.

Then
he said, "If
the herd is to be chased, then tell your Bow Priest."
That's what the young man said. "Whose child could this be?
PERHAPS WE'LL CATCH HIM."
That's what he was saying.
(A girl
a daughter of the priest said), "Well, I'll go ask the Bow Priest."
She got up and went to the Bow Priest's house.
(Arriving at the Bow Priest's house
she entered):
"My fathers, my mothers, how have you been passing the days?" "Happily,
    our child
so you've come, sit down," they said. "Yes.
Well, I'm
asking you to come.
Father asked that you come, that's what my father said," that's what she
    told the Bow Priest.

"Very well, I'll come," he said.
(The girl went out and went home), and after a while the Bow Priest
    came over.
He came to their house
while they were still eating.

"My children, how are you
this evening?" "Happy
sit down and eat," he was told.
He sat down and ate with them.
(When they were finished eating), "Thank you," he said. "Eat plenty,"
    he was told.
(He moved to another seat)

and after a while
the Bow Priest questioned them:
"NOW, for what reason have you
summoned ME?
Perhaps it is because of a WORD of some importance that you have
summoned me. You must make this known to me
so that I may think about it as I pass the days," that's what he said.
"YES, in truth
today, this very day
my child here
went out to hunt.
(Up on the Prairie-Dog Hills, there)
HE SAW A HERD OF DEER.
But a LITTLE BOY WAS AMONG THEM.
Perhaps he is a daylight person.
Who could it be?
He was dressed in white and he wore a macaw headdress.
When the deer ran off he OUTDISTANCED them:
he must be very fast.
That's why my child here said, 'Perhaps
they should be CHASED, the deer should be chased.'

He wants to see him caught, that's what he's thinking.
Because he said this
I summoned you," he said. "Indeed."
"Indeed, well

perhaps he's a daylight person, what else can he be?
It is said he was dressed in white, what else can he be?"
That's what they were saying.
"WHEN would you want to do this?" that's what he said.
The young man who had gone out hunting said, "Well, in four days
so we can prepare our weapons."
That's what he said.
"So you should tell your people that in FOUR DAYS there will be a
    deer chase."
That's what
he said. "Very well."

(*sharply*) Because of the little boy the word was given out for the deer chase.
The Bow Priest went out and shouted it.
When he shouted the VILLAGERS
heard him.
(*slowly*) "In four days there will be a deer chase.
A little boy is among the deer, who could it be? With luck
you might CATCH him.
We don't know who it will be.
You will find a child, then," that's what he SAID as he shouted.

Then they went to sleep and lived on with anticipation.
Now when it was the THIRD night, the eve of the chase

the deer
spoke to her son
when the deer had gathered:
("My son." "What is it?" he said.)
"Tomorrow we'll be chased, the one who found us is your uncle.

When he found us he saw you, and that's why

we'll be chased.
They'll come out after you:
your uncles.

(*excited*) The uncle who saw you will ride a spotted horse, and HE'LL
    BE THE ONE who
WON'T LET YOU GO, and
your elder brothers, your mothers
no
he won't think of killing them, it'll be you alone
he'll think of, he'll chase.
You won't be the one to get tired, but we'll get tired.
It'll be you alone
WHEN THEY HAVE KILLED US ALL
and you will go on alone.
Your first uncle
will ride a spotted horse and a second uncle will ride a white horse.
THESE TWO WILL FOLLOW YOU.
You must pretend you are tired but keep on going
and they will catch you.
But WE
MYSELF, your elder SISTER, your elder BROTHER
ALL OF US

will go with you.
Wherever they take you we will go along with you."
That's what his deer mother told him, (that's what she said).
THEN HIS DEER MOTHER TOLD HIM EVERYTHING: "AND
    NOW
I will tell you everything.

From here

from this place
where we're living now, we went down to drink. When we went down
    to drink
it was one of your ELDERS, one of your OWN ELDERS
your mother who sits in a room on the fourth story down making
    basket-plaques:
IT WAS SHE
whom the Sun had made pregnant.
When her time was near
she went down to Water's End to the bank
to wash clothes
and when you were about to come out
she had pains, got out of the water
went to a TREE and there she just DROPPED you.
THAT is your MOTHER.
She's in a room on the fourth story down making basket-plaques, that's
    what you'll tell them.

THAT'S WHAT SHE DID TO YOU, SHE JUST DROPPED YOU.
When we went down to drink
we found you, and because you have grown up
on my milk
and because of the thoughts of your Sun Father, you have grown fast.
Well, you
have looked at us
at your elder sister and your elder brother
and they have fur. 'Why don't I have fur like them?' you have asked.
But that is proper, for you are a daylight person.
That's why I went to Kachina Village to get clothes for you
the ones you were wearing.

You began wearing those when you were small
before you were GROWN.
Yesterday I went to get the clothes you're wearing now
the ones you will wear when they chase us. When you've been caught
you must tell these things to your elders.

When they bring you in
when they've caught you and bring you in
you
you will go inside. When you go inside
your grandfather
a priest
will be sitting by the fire. 'My grandfather, how have you been passing
    the days?'
'Happily. As old as I am, I could be a grandfather to anyone, for we
    have many children,' he will say.
'Yes, but truly you are my real grandfather,' you will say.
When you come to where your grandmother is sitting, 'Grandmother
    of mine, how have you been passing the days?' you will say.
'Happily, our child, surely I could be a grandmother to anyone, for we
    have the whole village as our children,' she will say.
Then, with the uncles who brought you in and
with your three aunts, you will shake hands.
'WHERE IS MY MOTHER?' you will say.
'Who is your mother?' they will say. 'She's in a room on the fourth story
    down making basket-plaques, tell her to come in,' you will say.

Your youngest aunt will go in to get her.
When she enters:
(*sharply*) 'There's a little boy who wants you, he says you are his mother.'
(*tight*) 'How could that be? I don't know any man, how could I have an
    offspring?'
'Yes, but he wants you,' she will say
and she will force her to come out.
THEN THE ONE WE TOLD YOU ABOUT WILL COME OUT:

you will shake hands with her, call her mother. 'Surely we could be
    mothers to anyone, for we have the whole village as our
    CHILDREN,' she will say to you.
'YES, BUT TRULY YOU ARE MY REAL MOTHER.
There, in a room on the fourth story down
you sit and work.
My Sun Father, where you sit in the light
my Sun Father
made you pregnant.
When you were about to deliver
it was to Water's End
that you went down to wash. You washed at the bank
and when I was about to come out
when it hurt you
you went to a tree and just dropped me there.
you gathered your clothes, put them on your back, and returned
to your house.
But my MOTHERS
HERE
found me. When they found me
because it was on their milk
that I grew, and because of the thoughts of my Sun Father
I grew fast.
I had no clothing
so my mother went to Kachina Village to ask for clothing.'
THAT'S WHAT YOU MUST SAY."

(That's what he was told), that's what his mother told him. "And
tonight
(*aside*) we'll go up on the Ruin Hills."
That's what the deer mother told her son. "We'll go to the Ruin Hills
we won't live here any more.
(*sharply*) We'll go over there where the land is rough
for TOMORROW they will CHASE us.
Your uncles won't think of US, surely they will think of YOU

ALONE. They have GOOD HORSES," that's what
his mother told him. It was on the night before
that the boy
was told by his deer mother.
(The boy became
so unhappy.)
They slept through the night
(and before dawn the deer
went to the Ruin Hills).

They went there and remained, and the VILLAGERS AWOKE.
It was the day of the chase, as had been announced, and the people
    were coming out.
They were coming out, some carrying bows, some on foot and
some on horseback, they kept on this way
o———n they went on
past Stone Chief, along the trees, until they got to the Prairie-Dog Hills
    and there were no deer.
Their tracks led straight and they followed them.
(Having found the trail they went on until
when they reached the Ruin Hills, there in the valley
beyond the thickets there
was the herd, and the
young man and two of his elder sisters were chasing each other)
by the edge of the valley, playing together. (Playing
they were spotted.)
The deer saw the people.
(They fled.)
Many were the people who came out after them
(now they chased the deer).
Now and again they dropped them, killed them.
Sure enough they boy outdistanced the others, while his mother and his
    elder sister and brother
still followed their child. As they followed him
he was far in the lead, but they followed on, they were on the run

and sure enough his uncles weren't thinking about killing deer, it was
   the boy they were after.
And ALL THE PEOPLE WHO HAD COME
      KILLED THE DEER
                   killed the deer
                            killed the deer.
Wherever they made their kills they gutted them, put them on their
   backs, and went home.
Two of the uncles

(then)
went ahead of the group, and a third uncle
(*voice breaking*) (dropped his elder sister
his elder brother
his mother.
He gutted them there) while the other two uncles went on. As they
   went ON
the boy pretended to be tired. The first uncle pleaded: "Tísshomahhá!
STOP," he said, "Let's stop this contest now."
That's what he was saying as
the little boy kept on running.
As he kept on his bells went telele.
O ———— n, he went on this way
on until
(the little boy stopped and his uncle, dismounting, caught him.
Having caught him):
(*gently*) "Now come with me, get up," he said.
His uncle
(helped his nephew get up, then his uncle got on the horse).
They went back. They went on
(until they came to where his mother and his elder sister and brother
      were lying
and the third uncle was there. The third uncle was there.)
"So you've come." "Yes."
(The little boy spoke): "This is my mother, this is my

elder sister, this is my elder brother.

They will accompany me to my house.

(They will accompany me," that's what the boy said.

"Very well."

His uncles put the deer on their horses' backs.)

On they went, while the people were coming in, (coming in, and still
the uncles didn't arrive, until at nightfall

the little boy was brought in, sitting up on the horse.

It was night and the people, a crowd of people, came out to see the boy
as he was brought in on the horse through the plaza

and his mother and his elder sister and brother

came along also

as he was brought in.

His grandfather came out. When he came out the little boy and his
uncle dismounted.

His grandfather took the lead with the little boy following, and they
went up.

When they reached the roof his grandfather

made a corn-meal road

and they entered.

His grandfather entered

with the little boy following

while his

uncles brought in the deer. When everyone was inside

the little boy's grandfather spoke: "Sit down," and the little boy spoke to
his grandfather as he came to where he was sitting):

"Grandfather of mine, how have you been passing the days?" (that's
what he said).

"Happily, (our child

surely I could be a grandfather to anyone, for we have the whole village
as our children." "Yes, but you are my real grandfather," he said.)

When he came to where his grandmother was sitting (he said the same thing.

"Yes, but surely I could be a grandmother to anyone, for we have many
children." "Yes, but you are my real grandmother," he said.)

He looked the way

his uncle had described him, he wore a macaw headdress and his clothes
    were white.

He had new moccasins, new buckskin leggings.

He wore a bandoleer and a macaw headdress.

He was a stranger.

He shook hands with his uncles and shook hands with his aunts.

"WHERE IS MY MOTHER?" he said.

"She's in a room on the fourth story down weaving basket-plaques," (he said.

"Tell her to come out."

Their younger sister went in.)

"Hurry and come now:

(some little boy has come and says you are his mother)."

(*tight*) "How could that be?

(I've never known any man, how could I have an offspring?" she said.)

"Yes, but come on, he wants you, he wants you to come out."

(Finally she was forced to come out.)

The moment she entered the little boy

(went up to his mother).

"Mother of mine, how have you been passing the days?"

"Happily, but surely I could be anyone's

mother, for we have many children," that's what his mother said.

(That's what she said.)

"YES INDEED

but you are certainly my REAL MOTHER.

YOU GAVE BIRTH TO ME," he said.

Then, just as his deer mother had told him to do

(he told his mother everything):

"You really are my mother.

In a room on the fourth story down

you sit and work.

As you sit and work
the light comes through your window.
My Sun Father
made you pregnant.
When he made you pregnant you
sat in there and your belly began to grow large.
Your belly grew large
you
you were about to deliver, you had pains in your belly, you were about
    to give birth to me, you had pains in your belly
you gathered your clothes
and you went down to the bank to wash.
When you got there you
washed your clothes in the river.
When I was about to COME OUT and caused you pain
you got out of the water
you went to a juniper tree.
There I made you strain your muscles
and there you just dropped me.
When you dropped me
you made a little hole and placed me there.
You gathered your clothes
bundled them together
washed all the blood off carefully, and came back here.
When you had gone
my elders here
came down to DRINK
and found me.
They found me

I cried
and they heard me.
Because of the milk

of my deer mother here
my elder sister and brother here
because of
their milk
I grew.
I had no clothing, I was poor.
My mother here went to Kachina Village to ask for my clothing.

That's where
she got my clothing.
That's why I'm clothed. Truly, that's why I was among them
that's why one of you
who went out hunting discovered me.
You talked about it and that's why these things happened today."
      (*audience*) Ee ——— so.
That's what the little boy said.

"THAT'S WHAT YOU DID AND YOU ARE MY REAL MOTHER,"
     that's what he told his mother. At that moment his mother
embraced him (embraced him).
His uncle got angry (his uncle got angry).
He beat
his kinswoman
(he beat his kinswoman).
That's how it happened.
The boy's deer elders were on the floor.
(His grandfather then)
spread some covers
(on the floor, laid them there, and put strands of turquoise beads on them.
After a while they skinned them.)
With this done and dinner ready they ate with their son.

They slept through the night, and the next day

the little boy spoke: "Grandfather." "What is it?"
"Where is your quiver?" he said. "Well, it must be hanging in the other
    room," he said.

He went out, having been given the quiver, and wandered around.
He wandered around, he wasn't thinking of killing deer, he just
    wandered around.
(In the evening he came home empty-handed.
They lived on

and slept through the night.
After the second night he was wandering around again.
The third one came)
and on the fourth night, just after sunset, his mother
spoke to him: "I need
the center blades of the yucca plant," she said.
"Which kind of yucca?"
"Well, the large yucca, the center blades," (that's what his mother said.
    "Indeed.)
Tomorrow I'll try to find it for you," he said.
(aside) She was finishing her basket-plaque and this was for the outer
    part. (audience) Ee ——— so.
That's what she said.
The next morning, when he had eaten
(he put the quiver on and went out).
He went up on Big Mountain and looked around until he found a large
    yucca
with very long blades.

("Well, this must be the kind you talked about," he said.) It was the
    center blades she wanted.
(He put down his bow and his quiver), got hold of the center blades,
    and began to pull.

(*with strain*) He pulled

it came loose suddenly
(and he pulled it straight into his heart.
There he died.)

He died (and they waited for him but he didn't come).

When the Sun went down
(and he still hadn't come, his uncles began to worry.
They looked for him.
They found his tracks, made torches, and followed him)
until they found him with the center blades of the yucca in his heart.

(Their
nephew
was found and they brought him home.
The next day

he was buried.)
Now he entered upon the roads
of his elders.
THIS WAS LIVED LONG AGO. LEE———SEMKONIKYA.

—Translation of performance by Dennis Tedlock

AIDS TO READING "THE BOY AND THE DEER" ALOUD

Line changes indicate brief silences (averaging a little less than one second) and double spaces between lines indicate longer ones (two to three seconds). In the printed version presented here, page breaks always indicate the shorter pause.

Loud words and passages are indicated by CAPITALS and soft ones (in parentheses).

Lengthened vowel sounds are indicated by ———, as in "She worked o——— n for some time," in which the o should be held for a full second or so.

When a line is set on different levels, each level indicates a single sustained pitch, almost as controlled as in singing. In the following example, the intervals are roughly fa, mi, do:

KILLED THE DEER
                killed the deer
                         killed the deer.

Special manipulations of voice quality (tone of voice) are indicated by italicized instructions in parentheses at the beginnings of affected lines. The same device (italics in parentheses) is also used to indicate interruptions by the audience.

In the Zuni words, the vowels should be given their continental values; double vowels are held a bit longer than single ones. The consonants should be pronounced as in English; ' indicates a glottal stop; double consonants are held a bit longer than single ones (ssh in "Tísshomahhá" is a double sh). Stress is on the first syllable except in "Tísshomahhá," which takes not only the initial stress but a final one as well.

A SECOND SERVICE

Directions: Thank someone for being that one. Then, while singing a song, walk with that one to the center of a room & back again. Burn something.

Seneca

WOLF SONGS & OTHERS OF THE TLINGIT

•

I keep dreaming I'm dead
keep feeling like I'm home

•

SHAMAN SONG

I don't have any place to come up through
think I'll go to Chillkat, come up there
I'll come up over there, & cry

•

Throw him into the river
let him float down
Crows can fish him out
downstream

•

HOW TO GET GRIZZLY SPIRIT

Come out of your body among us & we're all one
(we drop grease into the fire, before the grizzly's head
Whu Whu Whu is what we all say)

CRADLE SONGS

1.

I'm gonna marry my brother's wife
after he dies

2.

I like to crawl around the house after my brother's wife
I thought he might get up out of his grave & I was worried
I always follow her around town

3.

If I don't take anything to the party I'll feel bad
Little girls have to take something to a party or they'll feel bad
All you little girls better listen

4.

I'll shoot a little bird for little brother
I'll spear a little trout for little sister

•

FUNERAL SONG

You're like a drifting log with iron nails in it
I built my house from that log
I hope you float in like that log did
on a good sandy beach
The sun goes into the clouds
like you go into our great mother
That's why the world is so dark

•

That's a rich man coming
keep your feelings to yourself

- We've all been invited up to Killisnoo
all us high bred people are going to eat together

- How is it all gonna turn out
people on crow's river going up to wolf's town
I don't have any bad feelings about the crow people
never said anything at all about the wolf's children
if they'd come by I'd shake all their hands

- I wonder what eagle did to him
all those crows around him
it only took one crow to make the world

- I think about you & it's like having spirits come down on me
where is it that we were going to die together
don't you think you ought to do like you say

- I know how people get treated when they die
I'm gonna have a good time, a lot to drink

•

You surprise me, crow
whenever you see wolf people
you get way up on some branch

•

I'm gonna die & won't see you all any more
it doesn't matter that I'll lose lots of property
it's only what's gonna happen to me that I'm crying about

•

SONG ON THE WAY TO JAIL

They sound like howling wolves from here
everybody just beginning to get drunk
& I have to go away

•

SONG FOR THE RICHEST WOMAN IN WRANGELL

I used to make fun of you when you were a little girl & poor
where do you get all your whiskey & why aren't you ashamed

•

I don't know why you tell me I'm drunk
it's you been giving me all that whiskey

•

It's only whiskey that makes you pity me
what would it take to make you love me

•

My wife went away, left me
& like somebody who needs a good drink
I can't sleep

•

If you'd died I would've cut off my hair
I love you so much I would've blackened my face

•

Before he died
I saw his ghost

•

It would be very pleasant to die with a wolf woman
it would be very pleasant

•

He followed his own mind
got himself killed
can't blame anybody else

— English versions by James Koller, after John Swanton

ESKIMO SONGS ABOUT PEOPLE & ANIMALS

spring fjord

I was out in my kayak
I was out at sea in it
I was paddling
very gently in the fjord Ammassivik
there was ice in the water
and on the water a petrel
turned his head this way that way
didn't see me paddling
Suddenly nothing but his tail
then nothing
He plunged but not for me:
huge head upon the water
great hairy seal
giant head with giant eyes, moustache
all shining and dripping
and the seal came gently toward me
Why didn't I harpoon him?
was I sorry for him?
was it the day, the spring day, the seal
playing in the sun
like me?

the old man's song, about his wife

husband and wife we loved each other then
we do now
there was a time
each found the other
beautiful

but a few days ago maybe yesterday
she saw in the black lake water
a sickening face
a wracked old woman face
wrinkled full of spots

I saw it she says
that shape in the water
the spirit of the water
wrinkled and spotted

and who'd seen that face before
wrinkled full of spots?
wasn't it me
and isn't it me now
when I look at you?

dream

I dreamt about you last night
you were walking on the pebbles of the beach
with me
I dreamt about you
as if I had awakened
I followed you
beautiful
as a young seal
I wanted you like a hunter
lusting after a very young seal
who plunges in, feeling pursued.
That's how it was
for me

a man's song, about his daughter

That's
                your son? the brother
of your first-born boy?
That's what they say to me
well I've got some work to do again
a little better this time
if it's a boy I want
I need a sharp prick
well I'll sharpen it up and do the job again
and then if they say that I messed up
it'll be just the one time that's what

a woman's song, about men

first I lowered my head
and for a start I stared at the ground
for a second I couldn't say anything
but now that they're gone
I raise my head I look straight ahead I can answer
They say I stole a man
the husband of one of my aunts
they say I took him for a husband of my own
lies
fairy tales
slander
It was him, he
lay down next to me
But they're men
which is why they lie
that's the reason
and it's my hard luck.

— English versions by Armand Schwerner

KIOWA "49" SONGS

(1)
I don't care if you're married, I'll still get you,
I'll get you yet.

I don't care if you're married sixteen times,
I'll get you yet.

When the dance is over, sweetheart,
I will take you home in my one-eyed Ford.

(2)
If you really love me honey, hey-yah.
If you really love me honey, hey-yah.
Come back, come back if you really love me honey.

I'm from Oklahoma, far away from my home,
Down here looking for you.
If you'll be my honey, I will be your sugarpie.

I'm from Carnegie, so far away from my home,
Down here looking for you.
If you'll be my snag, I'll be your snag-a-roo.

(3)
You know that I love you, sweatheart, but every time I come around
You always say you got another one.
You know damn good and well that I love you.

To heck with your ole man.
Come up and see me sometime.

(4)
She said she don't love me anymore because I drink whiskey,
I don't care, I got a *better* one.

TWO DIVORCE SONGS

Tsimshian

1.

Now you love me;
Now you admire me,
but you threw me away
like something that tasted bad.
You treated me as if I were a rotten fish.
Now my old grandmother takes her dry
blackberries and puts them under her blanket.

2.

I thought you were good.
I thought you were like silver;
You are lead.

You see me high up on the mountain.
I walk through the sun;
I am sunlight myself.

—Translations by Carl Cary

Tsimshian mourning song

and now the words
      I'm grieving all by myself
      would rather be dead, what's the meaning
      of what I'm saying?
      I'll force the river to run upstream
      me sick at heart
      to do what I can't;
      little man at the corner of the sky
      boasting for nothing
      I'm way down like you
      why talk?
      this costly lament
      this song of moaning
      this one

— English version by Armand Schwerner, after Marius Barbeau

insult before gift-giving

Tsimshian

man you
             are
                a liar
what you say
                it's all
lies
                Now the words!
who's afraid of you snow-on-the-leaves,
melting away
I mean Where's your gun your money big mouth
                Now. Louder!
man what
you say it's all a crock of shit

— English version by Armand Schwerner, after Marius Barbeau

SPYGLASS CONVERSATIONS

Tule/Cuna

(A girl looking through a spyglass says)
You cannot see mountains and valleys in the clouds,
I see the clouds as big as trees,
when I look far away I see the clouds like cliffs of high, gray rocks.
I see a cloud that looks like a coconut tree.
The clouds come up and come up in different shapes.
There are clouds that look like breakers,
you don't see the colors and shapes of the clouds,
I see them like people moving and bending, they come up just like people.
There are clouds like many people walking.
I see them every time I look out to sea with the glass.
Sometimes a cloud comes up like a ghost, and sometimes like a ship.
I look far off through the glass and see everything.
I see a cloud that looks like a sea horse, a wild sea horse that lives in the
    water
I see a cloud like a deer with branching horns.

(The boy beside her says)
You don't see that at all.

(But the girl says)
From the time I was a child I didn't think I would see such things as
    these.
If I don't look through the glass I can't see them.
Now I find out the different things the clouds make.
Do you want to see them too?

(The boy says)
All right. I want to see them too. *(He looks through the glass.)*
Now *I* see funny things.

(The girl says)
Now you see all those funny things.

132

(Then the boy says to a younger girl)
You want to see them too?

(But she says)
I'm too young.

(The boy says to the older girl)
Look down into the water with the glass.

(The older girl says)
Now I see strange things under the water.
I see things moving around as though they were live animals.
I see things there that look like little bugs — many strange animals
    under the sea.

    — Translation by Frances Densmore

TWO CHEYENNE POEMS
(by Lance Henson)

HO DO VI I
for little fingernail

ho do vi i
        ma gi mi
                i yoda davo hi ah moo mii i

nivi payu gist ut
        vi hoo mi ni no

i yi mi zo zi yoo
hani
am mhoo ma zi soto zi
voo

ha ho
        ha ho

                        BUFFALO BLOOD
                        for little fingernail

                        buffalo blood
                                sumac berry
                                          blue sky

                        your pictures
                                look at them

                        they are walking
                        over the
                        mirror
                        of the morning star

                        thank you
                                thank you

NI HOI NIM MI NI HON   IDO MI MOO
for charles white antelope

ni hoi nim mi ni hon   ido mi moo
ni hoi nim mi ni hon   e inif
ni hoi das i woi nu
na wodstan ni hi vist
na dutz na ho utz

I AM SINGING THE COLD RAIN
for charles white antelope

i am singing the cold rain
i am singing the winter dawn
i am turning in the gray morning
of my life
toward home

CONVERSATIONS IN MAYAN
(by Alonzo Gonzales Mó)

Maya

CONVERSATIONS IN MAYAN

I'm going to bring you something,
I want to talk in Mayan like this.
When I'm done, I'll translate into Spanish
and English.
To do all of this, you have to write each line on the paper,
just as I'm telling you right now.
There are things I'm going to talk with you about that are large.
There are things I'm going to talk with you about that are small.
There are things strange;
there are things regular.
Maybe a small story can be put onto paper like this,
that's good.
Or if a small story can't be pulled out, then that's fine too.
That's how it will be.
Perhaps you'll have to write twenty pages for just one thing;
you'll have to do it.
Just the same, if you have to write one page about something,
that's what I'll bring you too.
I want to bring you a lot of things in Mayan.
I want to see how the words come out,
I want to learn how the words go.
I want to understand how they are sent around the world.

How Just One Poor Man Lives

How he found his life long ago,
how he finds his life today,
how he'll find his life tomorrow.
How a person is born,
how he grows among everything,
how a boy learns to work,
how a girl learns to work too.
How the boy finds a sweetheart,
how they "close their paths."
How they die too.
How a funeral is made for them,
for the dead.

Things That Happen to You

What Mérida looked like the first time you were there.
And all those things like that.
How things are made in a house;
how a kitchen is made to cook with too.
The house: how a house is built,
what a house is for too.
Corn: how it grows, what it is for.
The town: what it is for, what people do in it.
How it grows.
How a person goes hunting in the forest.
How a communal hunt is created to find deer in the woods.
How you catch gophers in the fields,
how you bake the meat.
How a "canteen" is made by people in the fields.
How things are made with honey and with bees.
How corn drinks are made; how a woman makes a meal.
Whatever you want to talk with me about.

— *Translations by Allan F. Burns*

NAVAJO ANIMAL SONGS

1.

Chipmunk can't drag it along
can't drag it along
Chipmunk holds back his ears

2.

Chipmunk was standing
jerking his feet
with stripes
he's a very short chipmunk

3.

Mole makes his pole redhot
Says: I'll shove it up your ass
Says: feel how it shakes your belly

4.

Wildcat was walking
He ran down here
He got his feet in the water
He farted
Wow, wow! says Wildcat

5.

A turkey is dancing near the rocks
shoves out his pelvis
woops-a-daisy we all go crazy

6.

Big Rabbit goes to see his baby
pisses
pissing all around him

7.

Pinionjay shits pebbles
now he's empty

— English versions by Jerome Rothenberg, after David McAllester

THREE CREE NAMINGS
(by Samuel Makidemewabe)

Swampy Cree

BORN TYING KNOTS

When he came out, into the world,
the umbilical cord
was around his toes.
This didn't trouble us,
that he was tying knots *that* early.
We untied it.

Later, he heard his birth
story.
It caused him to begin tying knots again.
He tied things up near his home,
TIGHT, as if everything might float away
in a river.

This river came from
a dream he had.

House things were tied up
at night. Shirts, other clothes too,
and a kettle. All those things
were tied to his feet
so they wouldn't float away
in the river he dreamed.
You could walk in
and see this.

Maybe the dream stopped
because it was no longer comfortable
to sleep with shirts tied to him.
Or a kettle.

After the dream stopped,
he quit tying things,
EXCEPT for the one night he tied up
a small fire.
Tied up a small-stick fire!
The fire got loose its own way.

TREE OLD WOMAN

She stood close to a tree and wrinkled
her face, TIGHT,
and this was her tree-bark face.
It felt like bark, too, when you ran fingers
over it.

Tree old woman,
even when she was young.

Then her face would smooth out
into a young girl again. Once, after doing
her tree-bark face, she said,
"I *was* a tree and I saw a woodpecker
who wanted my head! That's why
I smoothed out my face so quickly!"

We looked up in the trees for that woodpecker,
but it wasn't there. So, our eyes
turned back to her. She was gone too!
We found her in a lake. She was holding on
to some shore reeds
with her legs floating out behind.
She looked up at us WITH THE WRINKLED FACE
OF A FROG! We were certain of it!
Then she smoothed her face out,
saying, "The largest turtle in the world
was swimming for me, thinking I was a frog!
That's why I smoothed my face out
so quickly!"

We didn't even look
for that turtle.

This time we kept our eyes on her
as she went to sit
by an old man, the oldest
in the village.
She sat down next to him.

Their two faces were close together,
and hers began
to wrinkle up again.

Saw the Cloud Lynx

There was a boy in a village who made
wood stilts. Yes, he saw them made somewhere
and learned how. He spent a long time
knife whittling
and when he was finished
he walked on those stilts to the lake.
Walked around the shallows,
being tall.
Soon, others arrived to hunt fish
and he was UP IN THE AIR pointing out fish
to them.

He walked around with trees
for legs.

While he was up in the air he looked
far off in the distance
and saw a strange thing happen.
He saw a round cloud
grow an ear!
Then, it grew another ear!
He knew the wind did things such as this
to clouds, so he kept it to himself.
At first.

Then those ears
had a face between them.
It was
a lynx face!

The face was blowing toward THE LAKE
WHERE THEY WERE! He knew that giant lynx
would be coming toward them faster
as soon as it got the wind
to grow it legs.

That's when he told the others.

They ran, ha!
All the young ones!

Those wood stilts
stood STRAIGHT UP in mud
until he went back to get them.
After the sky cleared.

— *Translations by Howard Norman*

ORPINGALIK'S SONG: IN A TIME OF SICKNESS

Eskimo (Inuit)

My biggest worry is this:
that the whole winter long
I have been sick and helpless as a child.
  Ay me.

As long as I'm in this sorry condition
I really think it would be better
if my wife walked out on me
for I'm not much of a husband any more.
I should be taking care of her and getting food.
What good am I
now that I can't get up on my two feet?

Have you forgotten what a man you were? I ask myself.
Try to remember the beasts you hunted.
Remember and be strong again.

Yes, I remember once coming on a great white bear
who thought he alone was a fighter.
What a battle we had!
He came straight at me across the ice
rising high on his hind legs.
We grappled, and again and again
he threw me down,
but I didn't let go until he was dead.
When the bear came out of the water that day
and lay down calmly on the ice
he thought he was the only male around
but I came along and showed him!

I also remember a seal I once got
in a time when we were all weak with hunger.
Everyone was still asleep
when I went out on the ice that morning
and luckily found the breathing hole of a seal.

That blubbery beast was in there all right
about to come up for a breath of air
but he heard me, the sly one,
and waited to one side under the thick ice
where I could not spear him through the hole.
But just as I was ready to give up
he made a false move and I got my harpoon into him,
and we had his blubber and blood for breakfast that day!

Now with me sick
there is no blubber in the house
to fill the lamp with.
Spring has come
and the good days for hunting
are passing by, one by one.
When shall I get well?
My wife has to go begging skins for clothes and meat to eat
that I can't provide —
O when shall I be well again?

I can't understand it:
I was once a hunter
but now I've come to this.
I remember a fat caribou cow
swimming out in the open water,
and I went after her in my kayak
hardly believing I could ever catch up.
I chased hard
— I almost feel strong again remembering it —
and other kayaks were chasing too
thinking they would get the caribou first.
They were already shouting cries of victory
but I put everything I had into my paddle
— O I remember now how it feels to be a real man again —
and I won the race:
It was my caribou, all mine,
and the others got nothing at all!

— English version by Edward Field, after Knud Rasmussen

A BOOK OF
EVENTS (I)

DREAM EVENT I

Iroquois

After having a dream, let someone else guess what it was. Then have everyone act it out together.

DREAM EVENT II

Iroquois

Have participants run around the center of a village, acting out their dreams & demanding that others guess & satisfy them.

A MASKED EVENT FOR COMEDIAN & AUDIENCE

Lummi (Salish)

1. A comedian's mask is painted red on one side, black on the other; the mouth is twisted, the hair in disarray. For a costume he wears a blanket or a strip of fur which leaves his right hand free. He dances along with the other performers, often dances out-of-time to attract attention, & repeatedly annoys the dancers by quizzically scrutinizing their masks, poking at their eyes, looking at their noses, picking their teeth, etc. Sometimes the dancers whip the comedian vigorously with cedar boughs to drive him away, keeping time with the drums as they do so. When not annoying the dancers, the comedian goes around the room pretending to take lice from the singers' hair. He sometimes goes to a very old woman or a very pretty girl to do this, using it as a pretext to caress her.

2. The audience refrains from laughing.

BUTTERFLY SONG EVENT

Maricopa

A circular, roofless enclosure of willow poles is built, walled in with leafy branches. Across the top runs a series of parallel strings along which many yellow butterflies, cut out of mountain-sheep skin, are hanging. A singer sits at the center of the enclosure. As he sings he beats on an inverted basket with one hand, scraping a stick a foot long on it with the other. This makes the butterflies look as though they were fluttering, dancing in time to his tune.

AUTUMN EVENTS

Eskimo

A man & a woman both wear masks of seal skins, that of the woman being tattooed. The man's hair is arranged in a bunch protruding from the forehead, the woman's in a pigtail on each side & a large bunch at the back of the head. Their left legs are tied up by a thong running around the neck & the knee, compelling them to hobble as they walk.

1. *Threshold Event.* With their legs bound the man & woman must try to enter a hut while the occupants hold a long sealskin thong before them to keep them off. If they fall down in an attempt to cross the threshold, they are thoroughly beaten with a short whip or with sticks. After they succeed in entering a hut they blow out all the fires.

2. *Snow Event.* The organizers of the Autumn Events wake everybody up by climbing on their roofs & screaming & shouting. When all have assembled outside, the man & woman from the previous event sit down in the snow. The man holds a knife in his hand & sings:

> Oangaja jaja jajaja aja
> Pissiungmipadlo panginejernago
> Qodlungutaokpan panginejerlugping
> Pissiungmipadlo panginejernago.

To this song the woman keeps time by moving her body & her arms, at the same time flinging snow on the bystanders. Then everybody goes into a singing house & joins in dancing & singing. The men are first to leave & stand outside while the masked man & woman guard the entrance. With the men outside the women continue to sing, until the original couple leads them one by one to the waiting men. Each newly formed couple now re-enters the singing house & walks around the central lamp, all the men & women crying "hrr! hrr!" from both corners of their mouths. Each pair goes to the woman's hut & spends the night together.

TAMALE EVENT

Aztec

"For seven days all fasted. Only water tamales, soaked in water, were eaten, without chili, without salt, with neither saltpeter nor lime. And they were eaten only at midday. And he who fasted not at this time, if he were noted, he was punished. And much was this, the eating of water tamales, hallowed. And he who did not this, if he were not seen or noted, it was said — he was visited with the itch.

"And when the feast arrived, it was said: 'Ashes are put on faces,' & 'They are adorned with sea shells.' And it was when indeed all the gods danced. Thus it was named the dance of the gods.

"And all came forth as humming birds, butterflies, honeybees, flies, birds, giant horned beetles, black beetles — those forms men took; in these guises they came dancing. And still others were in the guise of sleep. Some had garlands of fruit tamales; birds' flesh tamales formed yet others' garlands. And before them was the maize bin, filled with fruit tamales.

"And soon also all these appeared — those who played the roles of the poor, those who sold vegetables, those who sold wood. Also appeared one in the guise of a leper. And still more took the forms of birds, large owls, screech owls. And even other birds they counterfeited."

MUD EVENTS

Navajo

1. The organizers of the event strip down & smear themselves & each other with mud & water from head to foot. They dip their headbands in mud before tying back their hair.

2. The participants run & dance about, then ask others to join them, lifting the newcomers high in the air, tossing them up & catching them again, or throwing them up & down in a blanket.

3. A small piece of sheepskin with a red blotch in the center (of fresh menstrual blood, excretion from the sore of a horse, etc.) is rubbed on the heads & backs of participants; some are made to sit on it.

4. Participants run into the audience & pull horsemen off their horses: then they oblige them to undress & join the mud event. The horsemen are smeared from foot to head, especially the back, face & hair. The original participants blow upon them, spit on them & put mud into their mouths. Horses are also caught & bathed with mud.

5. At the end of the event the organizers lie down flat on their stomachs one in line behind the other & so close that the head of each one touches the feet of the one in front of him. The last one gets up, walks along the trail of bodies & lies down; the next one does the same in leapfrog style until each participant has walked the length of the entire line. Some actually step on the prostrate bodies, while others place their feet on the ground close by the men. When this is over, all the participants stand up, form a snakeline & run over to a spring of water, where they sprinkle cornmeal on themselves & wash.

DAKOTA DANCE EVENTS

(1) *Hot Water Event*

Participants jump into a kettle of hot water & then run & dance where they please.

(2) *Fish event*

Four or five men lie down & imitate a fish out of water.

(3) *Half-Man Event*

They paint one-half their bodies with white clay & the other half black to represent a man split in two front & rear.

(4) *Moon Event*

A man & woman cut themselves & cry & dance for five days fasting. They cut through the skin of the breast & tie in a string. They tie the string to the top of the lodge, the man facing the woman.

(5) *Horse Event*

Putting boughs on the head. Men & women cut willows or boughs & trim their horses' heads & their own. They tie up the horses in one place & then the men dance around them.

GIFT EVENT

Kwakiutl

Start by giving away different colored glass bowls.
Have everyone give everyone else a glass bowl.
Give away handkerchiefs & soap & things like that.
Give away a sack of clams & a roll of toilet paper.
Give away teddybear candies, apples, suckers & oranges.
Give away pigs & geese & chickens, or pretend to do so.
Pretend to be different things.
Have the women pretend to be crows, have the men pretend to be
something else.
Talk Chinese or something.
Make a narrow place at the entrance of a house & put a line at the end
of it that you have to stoop under to get in.
Hang the line with all sorts of pots & pans to make a big noise.
Give away frying pans while saying things like "Here is this frying pan
worth $100 & this one worth $200."
Give everyone a new name.
Give a name to a grandchild or think of something & go & get everything.

LANGUAGE EVENT I

Eskimo

Use the language of shamans.

Say		*& mean*	
	the leash		the father
"	a road	"	the wind
"	someone with a something sticking out	"	a man
"	where things get soft	"	the guts
"	soup	"	a seal
"	Big Louse	"	a caribou
"	what makes me dive in headfirst	"	a dream
"	what cracks your ears	"	a gun
"	what looks like piss	"	your beads
"	a piece of frozen meat	"	a child
"	a piece of almost frozen meat	"	a grandchild
"	a jumping thing	"	a trout
"	what keeps me standing straight	"	your clothes
"	the person with a belly	"	the weather
"	the person with a belly getting up	"	it's morning
"	the person with a belly goes to bed	"	it's nightfall
"	little walker	"	a fox
"	walker with his head down	"	a dog
"	the bag it lies in	"	a mother
"	the bag it almost lies in	"	a stepmother
"	a person smoke surrounds	"	a live one
"	a floating one	"	an island
"	a neighbor	"	a wife
"	a flat one	"	a wolf
"	a shadow	"	a white man
"	another kind of shadow	"	a person
"	the dark one	"	the liver
"	making shadows	"	a seance
"	the shadow-maker	"	the shaman
"	he turned my mind around	"	he told me something

LANGUAGE EVENT II

Navajo

Hold a conversation in which everything refers to water.
If somebody comes in the room, say: "Someone's floating in."
If somebody sits down, say: "It looks like someone just stopped floating."

PICTURE EVENT, FOR DOCTOR & PATIENT
(to be performed after making a sandpainting of male & female dancing
figures with yellow legs from dancing knee-deep in pollen)

Navajo

1. Meal applied to divine figures.
2. Plumed wands erected.
3. Cup placed on the rainbow's hands.
4. Cold infusion made, sprinkler placed on cup.
5. Pollen applied to figures.
6. Doctor departs, unmasked.
7. Patient enters, song begins.
8. Patient sprinkles picture.
9. Patient sits, southeast, & disrobes.
10. Doctor, masked, returns as god.
11. Doctor sprinkles picture.
12. Assistant takes up meal from picture.
13. Doctor touches moistened sprinkler to figures.
14. Patient sits on picture.
15. Infusion offered to gods & given to patient.
16. Assistant moistens doctor's hands.
17. Sacred dust applied to patient.
18. Doctor yells into patient's ear.
19. Doctor departs, masked.
20. Patient leaves picture.
21. Patient fumigated.
22. Doctor returns, unmasked.
23. Plumed wands pulled out.
24. Picture despoiled.
25. Picture erased.
26. Material from picture taken out & discarded.

NAMING EVENTS

Papago

1. A shaman has a dream & names a child for what he dreams in it. Among such names are Circling Light, Rushing Light Beams, Daylight Comes, Wind Rainbow, Wind Leaves, Rainbow Shaman, Feather Leaves, A-Rainbow-as-a-Bow, Shining Beetle, Singing Dawn, Hawk-Flying-over-Water-Holes, Flowers Trembling, Chief-of-Jackrabbits, Water-Drops-on-Leaves, Short Wings, Leaf Blossoms, Foamy Water.

2. A person receives a name describing something odd about him, always on the bad side. Such names include: Grasshopper-Ate-His-Arrow, Gambler, Ass-Side-to-the-Fire, Pants-Fall-Down, Blisters, Fish-Smell-Mouth, Bed Wetter, Rat Ear, Yellow Legs.

3. A person receives a name describing something odd & sexual about the namer. Here the namer is a woman or a transvestite, who makes the name public by shouting it after the man named when others are present. The man invariably accepts it & is regularly called by it, even by his wife & family. Such names include: Down-Dangling-Pussy-Hairs, Big Cunt, Long Asshole.

4. A group of namers gathers around a dead enemy & shouts abusive names at the body. These names are then given to the shouters. They include: Long Bones, Full-of-Dirt, Back-of-a-Wildcat, Yellow Face, & Gold Breasts, the latter spoken of a girl.

5. A person buys a name or trades names with another person. For example, Devil-Old-Man exchanges names with Contrary, or Looking-for-Girls-at-a-Dance changes with Big Crazy, but has to give him four pints of whiskey in addition because of the desirability of the name.

PEBBLE EVENT

Omaha

Part One: The Painting. Those present at the pebble event sit along the sides of the room where the event is taking place. Four men leave their seats & go one by one to a place on the south side of the room, where a board with powdered charcoal has been set up for them. As each man reaches the board, he stoops & touches his hands to the earth, then passes them over his arms & body, down to his feet. Then he dips the fingers of his right hand into the charcoal & draws a black line from his mouth down the length of one arm, & a similar line down the other. After that he makes black lines on his body with his blackened fingertips. Taking some powder in the palm of his hand he goes back to the side of the room he came from, where he puts black lines down the arms of all those near him. When all four men have finished painting themselves & the others, they go to the rear of the room, where a pile of calico cloth has been placed, & stand there facing the east.

Part Two: The Shooting. The four men leading the pebble event bend over & make movements as though retching. After doing this for a while they begin to spit out pebbles. Then they circle the room, & as they do so, they "shoot" four other participants with their hands, shielding their shooting hands with an eagle wing held in the other: Each person "shot" immediately presses his hand on the "wound," assumes a tragic attitude, falls to the ground, & lays there rigid. The four leaders now circle the room again, with the other four joining them. Then these four "shoot" another four, who after circling the room shoot another four, and so on by fours until everybody has been "shot" & is circling the room. At that point a drum song begins & goes on for a while. Just before the event ends, each participant sings a song of his own choice — all these songs being sung simultaneously.

CRAZY DOG EVENTS

Crow

1. Act like a crazy dog. Wear sashes & other fine clothes, carry a rattle, & dance along the roads singing crazy dog songs after everybody else has gone to bed.

2. Talk crosswise: say the opposite of what you mean & make others say the opposite of what they mean in return.

3. Fight like a fool by rushing up to an enemy & offering to be killed. Dig a hole near an enemy, & when the enemy surrounds it, leap out at them & drive them back.

4. Paint yourself white, mount a white horse, cover its eyes & make it jump down a steep & rocky bank, until both of you are crushed.

ANIMAL SPIRIT EVENT

Lummi (Salish)

Imitate the spirit of the animal or thing inside you.

Let the one who imitates the wolf, dance squatting. Let him draw his arms up at the beginning of each measure bringing his bent wrists up below his chin with fingers pointing directly downwards. If he can, have him crack his knuckles & spurt blood.

Let the spirit of the sea, which appears half-bear & half-human & whose home is surrounded by hovering flies because there is so much food there, sing a song that goes: "O the flies in the home of the awful beast."

Let the spirit of the whistle imitate a whistle.

Let the spirit of the west wind sing: "Hey look out the west wind's going to blow."

Let the person who imitates a cedar be accompanied by five to ten other dancers. Have him warm up some cedar poles with mops of shredded cedar bark or twilled goat wool fastened at the ends, as he describes the approach of his spirit in a canoe. Let him sing the phrase, "Now the spirit is walking," then hand the poles to the other dancers who hold them vibrating from the waist. Then let him dance around the house with his own pole outstretched, the others joining him. Let him try to find food hidden in the house by prodding any bundles he sees with his pole, then toss what he finds into the center of the room, to be burnt as an offering to the dead or served to the assembled guests. Let the dance end with a great shout.

Let the spirit of the locomotive go through the locomotive's motions in his dance.

Let the man who imitates a fire swallow burning cedar bark.

VISION EVENT I

Eskimo

Go to a lonely place & rub a stone in a circle on a rock for hours & days on end.

VISION EVENT II

Eskimo

Let the person who wants a vision hang himself by his neck. When his face turns purple, take him down & have him describe what he's seen.

VISION EVENT III

Sioux

Go to a mountaintop & cry for a vision.

A BOOK OF EVENTS(II)

THEATER & RITUAL-THEATER

THE HORSE DANCE
(by Hehaka Sapa [Black Elk])

Oglala Sioux

[The Great Vision had come to him eight years before. Now at seventeen a terrible time began: fear & doubt, the voices of coyotes & crows repeating: "It is time! It is time! It is time!" The old holy man, Black Road, told him: "You must do what the bay horse in your vision wanted you to do. You must perform this vision for your people upon earth. You must have the horse dance first for the people to see. Then the fear will leave you." So they began to get ready for the horse dance.]

There was a man by the name of Bear Sings, and he was very old and wise. So Black Road asked him to help, and he did.

First they sent a crier around in the morning who told the people to camp in a circle at a certain place a little way up the Tongue from where the soldiers were. They did this, and in the middle of the circle Bear Sings and Black Road set up a sacred tepee of bison hide, and on it they painted pictures from my vision. On the west side they painted a bow and a cup of water; on the north, white geese and the herb; on the east, the daybreak star and the pipe; on the south, the flowering stick and the nation's hoop. Also, they painted horses, elk, and bison. Then over the door of the sacred tepee, they painted the flaming rainbow. It took them all day to do this, and it was beautiful.

They told me I must not eat anything until the horse dance was over, and I had to purify myself in a sweat lodge with sage spread on the floor of it, and afterwards I had to wipe myself dry with sage.

That evening Black Road and Bear Sings told me to come to the painted tepee. We were in there alone, and nobody dared come near us to listen. They asked me if I had heard any songs in my vision, and if I had I must teach the songs to them. So I sang to them all the songs that I had heard in my vision, and it took most of the night to teach these songs to them. While we were in there singing, we could hear low thunder rumbling all over the village outside, and we knew the thunder beings were glad and had come to help us.

My father and mother had been helping too by hunting up all that we should need in the dance. The next morning they had everything ready.

There were four black horses to represent the west; four white horses for the north; four sorrels for the east; four buckskins for the south. For all of these, young riders had been chosen. Also there was a bay horse for me to ride, as in my vision. Four of the most beautiful maidens in the village were ready to take their part, and there were six very old men for the Grandfathers.

Now it was time to paint and dress for the dance. The four maidens and the sixteen horses all faced the sacred tepee. Black Road and Bear Sings then sang a song, and all the others sang along with them, like this:

> "Father, paint the earth on me.
> Father, paint the earth on me.
> Father, paint the earth on me.
> A nation I will make over.
> A two-legged nation I will make holy.
> Father, paint the earth on me."

After that the painting was done.

The four black-horse riders were painted all black with blue lightning stripes down their legs and arms and white hail spots on their hips, and there were blue streaks of lightning on the horses' legs.

The white-horse riders were painted all white with red streaks of lightning on their arms and legs, and on the legs of the horses there were streaks of red lightning, and all the white riders wore plumes of white horse hair on their heads to look like geese.

The riders of the sorrels of the east were painted all red with straight black lines of lightning on their limbs and across their breasts, and there was straight black lightning on the limbs and breasts of the horses too.

The riders of the buckskins of the south were painted all yellow and streaked with black lightning. The horses were black from the knees down, and black lightning streaks were on their upper legs and breasts.

My bay horse had bright red streaks of lightning on his limbs, and on his back a spotted eagle, outstretching, was painted where I sat. I was painted red all over with black lightning on my limbs. I wore a black mask, and across my forehead a single eagle feather hung.

When the horses and the men were painted they looked beautiful; but they looked fearful too.

The men were naked, except for a breech-clout; but the four maidens wore buckskin dresses dyed scarlet, and their faces were scarlet too. Their hair was braided, and they had wreaths of the sweet and cleansing sage, the sacred sage, around their heads, and from the wreath of each in front a single eagle feather hung. They were very beautiful to see.

All this time I was in the sacred tepee with the Six Grandfathers, and the four sacred virgins were in there too. No one outside was to see me until the dance began.

Right in the middle of the tepee the Grandfathers made a circle in the ground with a little trench, and across this they painted two roads—the red one running north and south, the black one, east and west. On the west side of this they placed a cup of water with a little bow and arrow laid across it; and on the east they painted the daybreak star. Then to the maiden who would represent the north they gave the healing herb to carry and a white goose wing, the cleansing wind. To her of the east they gave the holy pipe. To her of the south they gave the flowering stick; and to her who would represent the west they gave the nation's hoop. Thus the four maidens, good and beautiful, held in their hands the life of the nation.

All I carried was a red stick to represent the sacred arrow, the power of the thunder beings of the west.

We were now ready to begin the dance. The Six Grandfathers began to sing, announcing the riders of the different quarters. First they sang of the black horse riders, like this:

> "They will appear—may you behold them!
> They will appear—may you behold them!
> A horse nation will appear.
> A thunder-being nation will appear.
> They will appear, behold!
> They will appear, behold!"

Then the black riders mounted their horses and stood four abreast facing the place where the sun goes down.

Next the Six Grandfathers sang:

> "They will appear, may you behold them!
> A horse nation will appear, behold!
> A geese nation will appear, may you behold!"

Then the four white horsemen mounted and stood four abreast, facing the place where the White Giant lives.

Next the Six Grandfathers sang:

> "Where the sun shines continually, they will appear!
> A buffalo nation, they will appear, behold!
> A horse nation, they will appear, may you behold!"

Then the red horsemen mounted and stood four abreast facing the east.

Next the Grandfathers sang:

"Where you are always facing, an elk nation will appear!
May you behold!
A horse nation will appear,
Behold!"

The four yellow riders mounted their buckskins and stood four abreast facing the south.

Now it was time for me to go forth from the sacred tepee, but before I went forth I sang this song to the drums of the Grandfathers:

"He will appear, may you behold him!
An eagle for the eagle nation will appear.
May you behold!"

While I was singing thus in the sacred tepee I could hear my horse snorting and prancing outside. The virgins went forth four abreast and I followed them, mounting my horse and standing behind them facing the west.

Next the Six Grandfathers came forth and stood abreast behind my bay, and they began to sing a rapid, lively song to the drums, like this:

"They are dancing.
They are coming to behold you.
The horse nation of the west is dancing.
They are coming to behold!"

Then they sang the same of the horses of the north and of the east and of the south. And as they sang of each troop in turn, it wheeled and came and took its place behind the Grandfathers — the blacks, the whites, the sorrels and the buckskins, standing four abreast and facing the west. They came prancing to the lively air of the Grandfathers' song, and they pranced as they stood in line. And all the while my bay was rearing too and prancing to the music of the sacred song.

Now when we were all in line, facing the west, I looked up into a dark cloud that was coming there and the people all became quiet and the horses quit prancing. And when there was silence but for low thunder yonder, I sent a voice to the spirits of the cloud, holding forth my right hand, thus, palm outward, as I cried four times:

"Hey-a-a-hey! hey-a-a-hey! hey-a-a-hey! hey-a-a-hey!"

Then the Grandfathers behind me sang another sacred song from my vision, the one that goes like this:

"At the center of the earth, behold a four-legged.
They have said this to me!"

168

And as they sang, a strange thing happened. My bay pricked up his ears and raised his tail and pawed the earth, neighing long and loud to where the sun goes down. And the four black horses raised their voices, neighing long and loud, and the whites and the sorrels and the buckskins did the same; and all the other horses in the village neighed, and even those out grazing in the valley and on the hill slopes raised their heads and neighed together. Then suddenly, as I sat there looking at the cloud, I saw my vision yonder once again — the tepee built of cloud and sewed with lightning, the flaming rainbow door and, underneath, the Six Grandfathers sitting, and all the horses thronging in their quarters; and also there was I myself upon my bay before the tepee. I looked about me and could see that what we then were doing was like a shadow cast upon the earth from yonder vision in the heavens, so bright it was and clear. I knew the real was yonder and the darkened dream of it was here.

And as I looked, the Six Grandfathers yonder in the cloud and all the riders of the horses, and even I myself upon the bay up there, all held their hands palms outward toward me, and when they did this, I had to pray, and so I cried:

> "Grandfathers, you behold me!
> Spirits of the World, you behold!
> What you have said to me, I am now performing!
> Hear me and help me!"

Then the vision went out, and the thunder cloud was coming on with lightning on its front and many voices in it, and the split-tail swallows swooped above us in a swarm.

The people of the village ran to fasten down their tepees, while the black horse riders sang to the drums that rolled like thunder, and this is what they sang:

> "I myself made them fear.
> Myself, I wore an eagle relic.
> I myself made them fear.
> Myself, a lightning power I wore.
> I myself made them fear,
> Made them fear.
> The power of the hail I wore,
> I myself made them fear,
> Made them fear!
> Behold me!"

And as they sang, the hail and rain were falling yonder just a little way from us, and we could see it, but the cloud stood there and flashed and thundered, and only a little sprinkle fell on us. The thunder beings were glad and had come in a great crowd to see the dance.

Now the four virgins held high the sacred relics that they carried, the herb and the white wing, the sacred pipe, the flowering stick, the nation's hoop, offering these to the spirits of the west. Then people who were sick or sad came to the virgins, making scarlet offerings to them, and after they had done this, they all felt better and some were cured of sickness and began to dance for joy.

Now the Grandfathers beat their drums again and the dance began. The four black horsemen, who had stood behind the Grandfathers, went ahead of the virgins, riding toward the west side of the circled village, and all the others followed in their order while the horses pranced and reared.

When the black horse troop had reached the western side, it wheeled around and fell to the rear behind the buckskins, and the white horse band came up and led until it reached the north side of the village. Then these fell back and took the rear behind the blacks, and the sorrels led until they reached the east. Then these fell back behind the whites, and the buckskins led until they reached the south. Then they fell back and took the rear, so that the blacks were leading as before toward the western quarter that was theirs. Each time the leading horse troop reached its quarter, the Six Grandfathers sang of the powers of that quarter, and there my bay faced, pricking up his ears and neighing loud, till all the other horses raised their voices neighing. When I thus faced the north, I sent a voice again and said: "Grandfather, behold me! What you gave me I have given to the people — the power of the healing herb and the cleansing wind. Thus my nation is made over. Hear and help me!"

And when we reached the east, and after the Grandfathers had sung, I sent a voice: "Grandfather, behold me! My people, with difficulty they walk. Give them wisdom and guide them. Hear and help me!"

Between each quarter, as we marched and danced, we all sang together:

> "A horse nation all over the universe,
> Neighing, they come!
> Prancing, they come!
> May you behold them."

When we had reached the south and the Grandfathers had sung of the power of growing, my horse faced yonder and neighed again, and all the horses raised their voices as before. And then I prayed with hand uplifted: "Grandfather, the flowering stick you gave me and the nation's sacred hoop I have given to the people. Hear me, you who have the power to make grow! Guide the people that they may be as blossoms on your holy tree, and make it flourish deep in Mother Earth and make it full of leaves and singing birds."

Then once more the blacks were leading, and as we marched and sang and danced toward the quarter of the west, the black hail cloud, still standing yonder watching, filled with voices crying: "Hey-hey! hey-hey!" They were cheering and rejoicing that my work was being done. And all the people now were happy and rejoicing, sending voices back, "hey-hey, hey-hey"; and all the horses neighed, rejoicing with the spirits and the people. Four times we marched and danced around the circle of the village, singing as we went, the leaders changing at the quarters, the Six Grandfathers singing to the power of each quarter, and to each I sent a voice. And at each quarter, as we stood, somebody who was sick or sad would come with offerings to the virgins — little scarlet bags of the chacun sha sha, the red willow bark. And when the offering was made, the giver would feel better and begin to dance with joy.

And on the second time around, many of the people who had horses joined the dance with them, milling round and round the Six Grandfathers and the virgins as we danced ahead. And more and more got on their horses, milling round us as we went, until there was a whirl of prancing horses all about us at the end, and all the others danced afoot behind us, and everybody sang what we sere singing.

When we reached the quarter of the west the fourth time, we stopped in new formation, facing inward toward the sacred tepee in the center of the village. First stood the virgins, next I stood upon the bay; then came the Six Grandfathers with eight riders on either side of them — the sorrels and the buckskins on their right hand, the blacks and whites upon their left. And when we stood so, the oldest of the Grandfathers, he who was the Spirit of the Sky, cried out: "Let all the people be ready. He shall send a voice four times, and at the last voice you shall go forth and coup the sacred tepee, and who shall coup it first shall have new power!"

All the riders were eager for the charge, and even the horses seemed to understand and were rearing and trying to get away. Then I raised my hand and cried hey-hey four times, and at the fourth the riders all yelled "hoka hey," and charged upon the tepee. My horse plunged inward along with all the others, but many were ahead of me and many couped the tepee before I did.

Then the horses were all rubbed down with sacred sage and led away, and we began going into the tepee to see what might have happened there while we were dancing. The Grandfathers had sprinkled fresh soil on the nation's hoop that they had made in there with the red and black roads across it, and all around this little circle of the nation's hoop we saw the prints of tiny pony hoofs as though the spirit horses had been dancing while we danced.

Now Black Road, who had helped me to perform the dance, took the sacred pipe from the virgin of the east. After filling it with chacun sha sha, the bark of the red willow, he lit and offered it to the Powers of the World, sending a voice thus:

"Grandfathers, you where the sun goes down, you of the sacred wind where the white giant lives, you where the day comes forth and the morning star, you where lives the power to grow, you of the sky and you of the earth, wings of the air and four-leggeds of the world, behold! I, myself, with my horse nation have done what I was to do on earth. To all of you I offer this pipe that my people may live!"

Then he smoked and passed the pipe. It went all over the village until every one had smoked at least a puff.

After the horse dance was over, it seemed that I was above the ground and did not touch it when I walked. I felt very happy, for I could see that my people were all happier. Many crowded around me and said that they or their relatives who had been feeling sick were well again, and these gave me many gifts. Even the horses seemed to be healthier and happier after the dance.

The fear that was on me so long was gone, and when thunder clouds appeared I was always glad to see them, for they came as relatives now to visit me. Everything seemed good and beautiful now, and kind.

Before this, the medicine men would not talk to me, but now they would come to me to talk about my vision.

From that time on, I always got up very early to see the rising of the daybreak star. People knew that I did this, and many would get up to see it with me, and when it came we said: "Behold the star of understanding!"

— Translation by John G. Neihardt

SIXTY-SIX POEMS FOR A BLACKFOOT BUNDLE
with scenario for an accompanying bundle-event

> *Give a bundle of turnip leaves & other things to a woman.*
>
> *Have the woman & her husband follow the actions of another man & wife who are experts in transferring a bundle.*
>
> *Call the transferrers "mother" & "father," & the receivers "son" & "daughter."*
>
> *Seat any men who are watching on the north side & any women on the south. Seat the transferrers & receivers at the rear.*
>
> *Begin the event by singing a smudge song.*

1

I was looking for the powerful spring grass, how powerful
I was finding it I was lifting it up, how powerful

2

Oldman was coming in telling us he would like to have a sweat
Oldman says I want a real fast fisher I want a real white buffalo robe

3

Oldwoman was coming in
 she was saying ditto ditto ditto

4

Morningstar was coming in saying he would like to have a sweat
Morningstar says I want a real fast fisher I want some fine tailfeathers

5

Man was coming in saying let's go have a sweat
Man was giving all of us a real sense of security

6

Oldman says I want some black & white buffalo robes
Let's go have a sweat

7

Oldwoman says I want some black & white wolfhides
Let's go have a sweat

8

Oldman was coming in says hurry & fix me up a sweathouse
He was coming in & happy: now he wants another sweathouse

Now begin to make a smudge.

9

Now she wants another sweathouse
Man came in   He'd like to have a sweat

10

Morningstar shows up with lots of things

*Begin to bring in robes & clothes & tail-
feathers & other things.*

11

Oldman says this man's got to want some tailfeathers

12

Oldman wants some tailfeathers

13

Oldman says I want a hundred tailfeathers

14

Oldwoman says I want all different kinds of tailfeathers

174

15

Oldman says you better hurry up with my tailfeathers
Oldwoman says be sure & get me some other kinds of tailfeathers

16

Oldman says better not forget my white buffalo robe

17

Oldwoman says better not forget my different kind of elkrobe

18

Somebody up there sees me, how powerful
Oldwoman sings, I was just looking at the ground, how powerful

> *Have one of the "transferrers" level out the smudge place with the toe of a new moccasin.*
>
> *Touch moccasin to smudge place, then smoothe the loose earth over.*

19

I have lifted up the buffalo, how very powerful

> *Have the "transferrer" pick up the tailfeathers.*

20

Oldman says better hurry up & smudge me
Oldwoman says you better smudge me in a different place
Morningstar says smudge me in an even different place
Oldman says better paint me now
Oldwoman says you better paint me with a different paint
Morningstar says paint me even different

> *Smudge & bodypaint are applied as per instructions.*
>
> *The order of the paint is first yellow, then black, then with sundog symbols.*

21

A Song for the Rawhide on Which the Rattles Are Beaten

Man says I'm standing powerfully upon these mountains, how powerful
I powerfully am coming down
I come down powerfully in summer
I'm standing powerfully upon the earth

22

A Song for the Rattles

I'm in a hurry

> *Spread out the rawhide in front of the men.*
>
> *Have the men pick up rattles.*

23

Raven says I'm on the ground looking for something to eat
Now I found it, how powerful

24

Raven says I'm looking for some buffalo
Now I've got them

25

Oldman says don't I look good with rattles?
Now I'm shaking them

> *Begin to beat the rattles.*

26

Oldman says I'm looking for some timber, now I fond it I've taken it

> *Have the "father" pick up the smudgestick &*
> *make a new smudge.*

27

The Sun Dance Shelter

Let's put my sunhouse up & no one knock it over

28

The Turnip Bundle

It's been a long time now, Man
You'd best get up

29

Oldman comes in & squats, says I'm looking for my bundle
Now I found it, how powerful

30

Oldwoman just comes in, says I'm looking for my bundle
Ditto ditto

31

Oldman says I'm picking up my bundle
Now I'm getting full of power

32

Oldwoman says I'm carrying my bundle on my back now I'm getting
    full of power
How powerful

33

I'm picking up my bundle
Now it's starting up now it's stopping
Now it wants to sit down someplace powerful

> *Have the "father" lay the bundle down. He
> exposes the inner wrapping of badger-skin.*

34

The Badger's Song

The earth's my home, how powerful
I'm looking for my home, how very powerful

35

Oldwoman says why can't I see my bundle which is so damn powerful?

36

Song for the Bundle-Event Women

Oldman says those women looking at me must be pretty smart

> *Take turnip leaves from the badger-skin wrapping.*
>
> *Hold them up & shake them.*

37

My bundle wants to do some shaking

38

Man says I want some fine tailfeathers
My bundle says I want to sit down someplace powerful
Oldwoman says why can't I see my bundle?

39

Blacktail deer was running all around, how powerful

> *Remove cloth wrappings from the turnip leaves.*

40

Another Skin Song

Weasel's my headdress he was running all around, how powerful

41

The Doll / The Dwarf*

Boys are running all around, how powerful

42

The Teal Duck Is the Water Ouzel

Duck says this water is my medicine, how very powerful

43

Man says I want a buffalo tail

44

Lizard says hey man I'm getting angry

45

Song for a Scalplock Necklace

I'm picking up my necklace, how powerful
Man says I want to have that string of scalphair

46

A Woman's Dress

Elk were running all around, how powerful

47

Song for an Elkrobe

I've given you my elkrobe

48

A Song for White Paint

The earth's my medicine, how powerful

*Names for doll-shaped tobacco-seed containers.

49

I'm looking for some timber, now I found it I've taken it
How powerful

Have an assistant bring in a small cottonwood tree.

The "transferrer" hands him an ax, & he stands holding tree & ax, while someone tells a war story.

Then he cuts a point onto the tree butt.

50

Timber's looking for someplace powerful to sit

Stick the tree in the ground on the south side of the performance area.

Let the "mother" take up the headdress, followed by the "daughter."

Have both women make dancing movements with their bodies, while hanging the headdress on the tree & singing.

51

I'm looking for some timber I can sit on

52

A Song Without Words

Wow! Wow! Wow! Wow! Wow!

During the song-without-words, the "mother" takes the headdress from the tree, puts it on her head, her body swaying with the rhythm of the singing, makes hooking motions at the tree, rubs her head up and down the limbs, & then places the headdress upon her daughter. She also makes the whistling sound of the elk.

53

Song for a Digging Stick

I was looking for my medicine I've taken it, how powerful

54

I landed some buffalo they're looking for someplace powerful to sit

> *Tie dewclaws to the end of the stick.*

55

I'm digging up this powerful turnip

> *Have someone imitate a crane's call.*
>
> *Have the "mother" hold the stick on her back, then make four passes toward the smudge place before pulling the stick into position on the "daughter's" back.*
>
> *Now prepare the "son" by taking off his robe & having the "transferrer" paint him while both sing.*

56

I'm taking off this young man's robe

> *Paint the "son's" entire body & face with charcoal.*

57

Oldman says to take some black paint
I'm powerfully going to paint him up, how powerful

58

I want to paint the sun & dogs on him

Have the "transferrer" mark a half moon on the "son's" breast with his fingertip.

Mark a circle on his back for the sun; a bar on each cheek, the chin and the forehead, for the sundogs.

59

A Painting Song Without Words

WOOOOooOOOOOW!

Draw a line across the "son's" face at the bridge of the nose, while singing #60.

60

Buffalo trail, how powerful
Hey I'm going for a trip on it

Have the "transferrer" draw a circle around each wrist & ankle, then hand the "son" his robe again, while both are singing.

61

Hey I'm giving you your robe, Man

62

This man says I want some feathers

Tie tailfeathers in the "son's" hair.

63

Man wants a string of scalphair

Put on his necklace.

64

I'm looking for my whistle now I found it
It's whistling how powerful it sounds

65

I want a bow

66

I want an arrow

Place four bunches of sage grass about two feet apart at the north end of the performance area. At this point the four participants are standing up.

The "father" takes hold of the "son's" right leg & makes four passes toward the first bunch of sage. The "mother" does likewise with the "daughter." Then the pair are made to step from one bunch to the other.

Now the "father" takes the lead, the "son" next, then the "daughter," then the "mother," & all file out in procession.

—Adaptation & scenario by Jerome Rothenberg, after Clark Wissler

A DISPUTE BETWEEN WOMEN
(Songs of derision from a contest between Paninguaq [Little Daughter]
and her cousin Sapangajagedleq [The Pearl])

Eskimo (Inuit)

                        Little Daughter dances and sings:

It seems high time
I challenged you to song-contest!
Yes, my anger wakes!

I was out fetching fire
(domesticated as ever)
when you, in foolish vanity
began to flaunt yourself
before my step-father.
Do I lie or speak the truth?
Come forward: test me,
while my anger grows!

                    The Pearl jumps forward, dances and sings:

Come over to this side,
those who will defend me!
Take the wick of the lamp,
dip it in oil, light it,
allow the light
to fall on Little Daughter's face!
Do you hear me, cousin?
Do I lie or speak the truth?
I took you by surprise one day
in bed with Asarpana!
Mock her with me,
those who take my side!
Take her, friends,
and throw her to the ground!
Cousin, you don't still think
that you're a match for me?
Let's close our fists and punch!
Come, we'll have a race:
the winner takes the loser's man!

At this point, The Pearl jumps forward again, with a song intended to make
the audience laugh:

Ija-ja-hrra
ajai-jai-hrra,
aj-ja-a-ha!
Oh let me be
a little naughty!
Ai-ja-a-ha!
Just a little bad!
If only there were
someone who would stroke,
or only touch my cunt:
I shouldn't then
be angry or resent
another woman
smiling at my man!
Ai-ja-a-ha!

Little Daughter:

Umaya — ima,
Ha-ja-ja!
I'm easy to make jealous,
quick to rage!
Here I stand,
forgetting my poor songs.
But listen, cousin:
you're too eager
to deride me in your song;
let's pay a visit
to the people by the sand.
There I'll make an answer
to your clumsy mockery!

The company rises, and goes down to the village by the sand. On the way,
The Pearl sings:

I'll have no mercy
for the people by the sand:
they won't be friends of yours for long.

I'll show them
what you girls are really like:
all smiles outside,
but unchaste underneath,
willing to fuck casually with men,
and then give birth
in secret in the hills.
Do I lie or speak the truth?
I often envy
folk who slept at night
in ignorance of what went on.
Chaste people don't see anything.
But there are those who say
that you, too, secretly gave birth.
Do I lie or speak the truth?

At this, Little Daughter bursts into tears. And now The Pearl has an idea:

Let's sing,
let's go and see the people by the sand!
We'll open Little Daughter's sewing-box,
mess it up, reveal
her secrets!
Catch hold of Little Daughter, friends!

They grab her, and hold on to her, while The Pearl continues singing:

The festival unites us,
draws us close!
Twist her loins,
rock her hips!

And they force Little Daughter to dance, while The Pearl goes on singing:

We'll ruthlessly reveal,
her hidden thoughts!
Together we'll expose her:
she who always coveted my man.
My anger, cousin, has arrived!

They reach the village. But here The Pearl's husband unexpectedly leaps
forward into the circle and sings:

Now *my* anger wakes!
Do you hear! Do you hear!
I'm feeling like a fight!
Do you hear! Do you hear!
Let's break into the house,
upset the piss-pot,
tear the membrane window out,
chuck the lamp on the shit-heap,
let the boiled meat follow suit!
Destroy, destroy the racks
of meat and skins!
I'm ready for a fight:
I'm hot with rage,
I'm hot for song, for song!

Look, here's this wretched girl
I had my fun with.
Like animals in heat we were,
when we went walking in the hills.
Oh, I remember how we hid
up on the Great Lichen mountain,
that sweet playground
for male animals!
Wagging our tails,
we looked out on
the sunny country of the south,
while we threw ourselves
down into the heather . . .

But what is happening?
Will no-one answer me?
Then shut your mouths!
We're going home,
and you can rest.
Daylight envelops the mountain.
Dawn has taken over from the night.

— Translation by Tom Lowenstein, after Knud Rasmussen

RABINAL-ACHI: ACT IV

Maya

Quiché-Achí, speaks for the Tenth time, coming before Hobtoh Rabinal-Rahaual, Chief Five-Rains:

Cala-Achí!   Ha! Aha! Yeha! Ahau! Wow! Achí!   I: Quiché-
Achí   Balam-Achí   Balam-Quiché   Rahaual-Quiché-Vinak
iiiiiiiiiiiiiiiiiiiiiiii kiiiiiiiiii kikikikikikikikikikikiki   Quiché-Vinak
                                            to you: Hobtoh   Rabinal-Rahaual
Great Chief Five-Rains.

Oyeu Achí!   Hail Valiant!   Hail Warlike!

O.K. I'm here   O.K. I've just arrived
                        to the great walls' entrance
                        to the great fortress
over which you throw
                                    your hands
over which you throw
                                    your shadow.
You've heard about my presence
                                in your teeth
                                in your face.

I'm valiant   I'm warlike   because your valiant   your war-
    like   Galel-Achí
eminent among the warlike   vanguard of valiants   valiant of
    Rabinal
came to throw his challenge
                        his war-cry
                                    to my teeth
                                    to my face.

"O.K. I've told my Man about you
    Hobtoh Rabinal-Rahaual   Great Chief Five-Rains
                in the great walls.
    And he said right back:

188

Bring in this motherfucking valiant   this vinak
                                to my teeth
                                to my face
and let me see
                                his teeth
                                his face
how valiant he is   how warlike he is.
But tell him from me   this valiant   this warrior
to keep his mouth shut
I don't want any trouble   I don't wan't any noise.
Let him touch his toes
let him bend down his face
when he gets to the doors
                of the great walls
                of the great fortress."

That's what your valiant said   your warrior
                                to my teeth
                                to my face
Goddamn it I am a valiant   a warrior
and if I've got to bend down
                                bend down my face
here's what I'll bend with
what'll bend my knee.
This is my arrow
this is my shield
with which I'll break your destiny
your day of birth
                        your lower mouth
                        your upper mouth
and you'll swallow it
Great Chief Five-Rains!

*Ixok-mun, a Servant-girl, speaks for the Second time, as Quiché-Achí menaces
Five-Rains with his truncheon:*

Valiant!   Warlike!   Rahaual Cavek Quiché Vinak!
Don't kill my Man   my Governor   my Chief   Great Chief
        Five Rains
                in the heart of his great fortress!

189

Quiché-Achí, speaks for the Eleventh time:

O.K. go get my bench then   go get my seat
the way it was in my mountains   the way it was in my valleys
with my destiny shining   my day of birth.
Some bench that was!   Some seat that was!
Are you going to freeze me in this place
freeze me with ice   freeze me with cold?
I'm speaking

> to the sky-face here
> to the earth-face here.
> May sky
> and earth
> be with you
> Chief five-Rains!

Hobtoh Rabinal-Rahaual, Chief Five-Rains, speaks for the Fourth time:

Valiant!   Warlike!   Cavek   Quiché   Vinak!   iiikiiiiiiiiikikikiki
Quiché Vinak!

> thanks to sky
> thanks to earth

you've just arrived

> at the great walls
> at the great fortress

over which I throw

> my hands

over which I throw

> my shadow.

I   the grandfather   Great Chief Five-Rains.

O.K.   Tell us   open your mouth   let's hear
why you make like coyote   weasel   fox

> through the great walls
> through the great fortress

to call   to attract
my white children
my white sons
to call   to attract

> to the great walls

                    to the great fortress
                    in the corn-city   Iximche
to ferret out
to get your fingers on
THE YELLOW HONEY
the green honey of bees
my food for me   the grandfather
Great Chief Five-Rains?
You were the one who got the nine   the ten white children
and it's a miracle they weren't dragged off
to the Quiché mountains
to the Quiché valleys
                    if my valiance   if my bravura
                    v'oyeualal   v'achihilal
                    Galel-Achí   Rabinal-Achí
hadn't been there on guard
you'd have cut the vine there   cut the trunk
cut the lineage
of the white children
of the white sons!
And damn near got me at the baths as well!
Damn near got hooked out there
by the son of your arrow
the son of your shield!
You shut me in there
inside the stones
inside the chalk
of the Quiché mountains
of the Quiché valleys
and you'd have cut my vine there   cut my trunk
cut my lineage
                    if my valiance   if my bravura
                    v'oyeualal   v'achihilal
                    Galel-Achí   Rabinal-Achí
hadn't freed me from there
hadn't dragged me from there
with the son of his arrow
with the son of his shield
and brought me back
                    to the great walls

                  to the great fortress
And you also destroyed
                two   three   great cities
                cities with moats
In Hidden-Buzzard   Balanvac
where feet stamp the ground with great noise
in Calcaraxah   Cunu   Gozibal-Tagah-Tulul
as the names go.

Well how long are you going to be hung up
by the lust of your heart   your valiance   your bravura?
how long are they going to block you
and keep you rampaging here?
This arrogance   this bravura
weren't they buried once and for all
in Qotom   in Tikiram   in Belehe Mokoh   in Belehe Chumay?
This arrogance this bravura
didn't we beat them out of you   we Governors   we Men
                Men of the walls
                Men of the fortress?

But you'll pay for this here
                          under the sky
                          on the earth.
You've said goodbye
                  to your mountains
                  to your valleys
because you're going to die in this place
to disappear in this place
                          under the sky
                          and on the earth.
                          May sky
                          and earth
                          be with you
                          Cavek Quiché Vinak!

Quiché-Achí, speaks for the Twelfth time:

Cala-Achí!   Ha! Aha! Yeha!Ahau! Wow!Achí!   I: Quiché-
Achí   Balam-Achí   Balam-Quiché   Rahaual-Quiché-Vinak

iiiiiiiiiiiiiiiiiiiiiiiiiii kiiiiiiiii kikikikikikikikikikikiki   Quiché-Vinak
                                   to you: Hobtoh Rabinal-Rahaual
Great Chief Five-Rains
                        Now hear this
                                to the sky-face here
                                to the earth-face here
Sure
        these are the words
        these are the opinions
        you've gone on and on about
                                to the sky-face here
                                to the earth-face.

Sure
        I've done wrong.
You also said:
        "Didnt you call   attract
        the white children
        the white sons
        to ferret out   to get your fingers on
        THE YELLOW HONEY
        the green honey of bees
        my food for me   the grandfather
        Great Chief Five-Rains
                    in the great walls
                    in the great fortress?"
Sure
        I've done wrong
        because of the hang-ups of my heart
        because I couldn't grab
        these beautiful mountains   these beautiful valleys
                                here   under sky
                                here on the earth
You also said:
        "and you destroyed
                    two   three   great cities
                    cities with moats
        in Hidden-Buzzard   Balanvac
        where feet stamp the ground with great noise
        in Calcaraxah   Cunu   Gozibal-Tagah-Tulul."

Sure
    I've done wrong
    because of the hang-ups of my heart
    because I cound't grab
    these beautiful mountains   these beautiful valleys
                        here   under sky
                        here on the earth
You also said:
    "Kiss your mountains goodbye
    and your valleys
    because you're going to die in this place
    to disappear in this place
    we'll cut your vine here   your trunk
    we'll cut your lineage here

                        here under sky
                        here on the earth."
Look:
    I don't give a damn for your words
    you go to hell with your orders

                        to the sky-face here
                        to the earth-face
    because of what I want in my heart.
And if I have to die here
if I really have to disappear in this place
then this is what I've got for you

                        in your teeth
                        in your face:
Since you're so rich here
since you don't know what to do with all you've got
                in the great walls
                in the great fortress
I'll borrow your food
I'll have a go at your drinks
those cool drinks called Ixtatzunin
those twelve drinks
those twelve stoning liquors
sweet   fresh   jubilant   lip-smacking
    you drink before sleep
                in the great walls
                in the great fortress

and also
the marvels of my Mother
the marvels of my Lady.
I'll try them out just once
as a sort of signal of my death
to mark my disappearance under sky   and on the earth.

                    May sky
                    and earth
                    be with you
                    Hobtoh Rabinal-Rahaual!

Hobtoh Rabinal-Rahaual, Chief Five-Rains, speaks for the Fifth time:

Valiant!   Warlike!   Cavek iiiiiiiiiiiii kiiiiiiiiiiii kikikikikikikikiki
    Quiché-Vinak:
This is what you came up with

                    to the sky-face
                    to the earth-face:

"Give me your food
your drinks
I'll try them out"   is what you said.
"As a sort of signal of my death
to mark my disappearance"   is what you said.

O.K. Fine.
Here they are take them
here they are I'm lending them.
Men   Girls   Get my food and drink!
Give them to this Valiant   this Achí   Cavek-Quiché-Vinak
as a supreme signal of his death
and of his disappearance

                    here   under sky
                    here on the earth.

A Servant: (bringing a low table with food and drinks)

Yessir! My Chief   My Governor!
I'm giving them to this Valiant   this Achí   Cavek-Quiché-Vinak.
Try a little of the food   of the drink
of my Chief   my Governor   grandfather   Chief Five-Rains

in the great walls
in the great fortress
in which he lives enclosed.

*Quiché-Achí eats and drinks disdainfully, then dances in the midst of the court, then
returns and speaks for the Thirteenth time:*

Ha!   Aha!   Yeha!   Ahau!   Wow!   Achí!   I: Quiché-
     Achí   to you
Hobtoh Rabinal-Rahaual
Great Chief Five-Rains:

Hey   call this food?
call this drink?
you crazy or something?
Comments?   Forget it!
                                        to my mouth
                                        to my face!

Look if you ever tried just once
                    in *my* mountains
                    in *my* valleys
what *I* call drink
sweet   fresh   jubilant   lip-smacking
drinks *I* drink
                    in my mountains
                    in my valleys
Man   you wouldn't ask
                                        the sky-face here
                                        the earth-face here!

Are *these* your groaning dishes
your overflow of drinks?
Hey but this skull right here
is my grandfather's skull!
this skull right here
is my father's skull!
Right?   Couldn't you do the same
with my head's bones?
with my skull's bones?
chisel my mouth?
engrave my face?

Then   when they quit my mountains
then   when they quit my valleys
to push five loads of cacao-coin
to push five loads of cacao-liquor
                      from my mountains
                      from my valleys

my sons
my children can say
Hey   this is grandpappy's skull!
Hey   this is our old man's skull!
and sing all day long!

And here's my arm-bone
for a silver gourd's handle
to sound and thunder
                      in the great walls
                      in the great fortress
And here's my leg-bone
hey   that's a great drumstick
for the big drum
for the little drum
the sky can throb to
the earth can throb to
                      in the great walls
                      in the great fortress!

And while I think of it:
how's this for a suggestion?
O.K.   Repeat after me:
     "I'll lend you the great cloth also
     smooth   brilliant   resplendent
     very well woven by God
     my Mother made   my Lady
     so you can wear it
                      in the great walls
                      in the great fortress
                      in the four corners
                      along the four walls
                      as a sort of signal of your death
                      to mark your disappearance

                              here   under sky
                              here on the earth."

Hobtoh Rabinal-Rahaual, Chief Five-Rains, speaks for the Sixth time:

Valiant!   Warrior!   Cavek iiiiiiiiiiii kiiiiiiiiiiii kikikikikikikiki
Quiché-Vinak:
What the hell are you coming up with?
O.K. nevertheless   here's what I'll do
I'll give you that
as a sort of signal of your death
to mark your disappearance

                              here   under sky
                              here on the earth.

Men   girls   go get that cloth
smooth   brilliant   resplendent
well woven here by God
                    in the great walls
                    in the great fortress
Give them to this Valiant   this Achí
as a supreme signal of his dying
and of his disappearance

                              here   under sky
                              here on the earth.

A Servant: (bringing a kind of shawl Quiché-Achí puts around his shoulders)

Yessir!   My Chief   My Governor!
I'll give this Valiant   this Achí
this cloth he's been begging for.
Man   here's the good-looking cloth
you've been panting for!
Take care not to spoil it now!

Quiché-Achí, speaks for the Fourteenth time:

Ha!   Aha!   Yeha!   Ahau!   Wow!   Achí!   I:
        Quiché-Achí   to you
Masters of the "tun" drum   Masters of the flute!

Hey   You   the flutes!
Hey   You   the drums!
Could you manage to make
like my flute
like my drum?
O.K. now
play the great melody
play the little melody
swing all those tunes!
Play my Toltec flute   play my Toltec drum
my flute from the Quiché   my drum from the Quiché!
the dance of my prisoner
the dance of my captive
                        among my mountains
                        among my valleys!
As if we were going to make the sky throb
as if we were going to make the earth throb
as our foreheads bend down
as our heads bend down
when we make great leaps and turns zapateando
when we dance and rock and beat the ground
with the men and the girls
                                    here   under sky
                                    here on the earth
That's what I have to say
                                    to the sky-face here
                                    to the earth-face.
                                    May sky
                                    and earth
                                    be with you
                                    O flutes   O drums!

*Quiché-Achí dances a round-dance in the midst of the Court and goes to each angle
in turn to shout his war-cry.*

Hey!   Chief Five-Rains!
                        Now hear this
                        to the sky-face
                        to the earth-face

This is what you lent me
This is what you let me have so far
I'm back to let you have it again
I'm taking it off here
    at the great walls
    in the great fortress.
Take good care of it put it back bury it
in the bundle in its box
    in these great walls
    in the great fortress.
You granted my desire
you granted my petition
        to the sky-face
        to the earth-face
I've made a big thing of it here
    in the great walls
    in the great fortress
    in the four corners
    along the four walls
    as a sort of signal of my death
    to mark my disappearance
        under sky here
        on the earth
But . . . if it's true you're so rich here
if you don't know what to do with all you've got
    in the great walls
    in the great fortress
then just for a minute let me have
    U Chuch Gug Mother of Feathers
    U Chuch Raxon Mother of Hummingbirds
    Yamanim Xtekoh the Brilliant Emerald
    come from Tzam-Gam-Carchag
    whose mouth hasn't ever been touched
    whose face hasn't ever been seen
so I can graze her mouth
so I can glimpse her face
so I can dance with her
so I can show her off
    in the great walls
    in the great fortress

in the four corners
along the four walls
as a supreme signal of my dying
and of my disappearance

                        under the sky here
                        and on the earth.
                        May sky
                        and earth
                        be with you
                        Great Chief Five-Rains!

Hobtoh Rabinal-Rahaual, Chief Five-Rains, speaks for the Seventh time:

Valiant! Warrior! Cavek iiiiiiiiiiii kiiiiiiiiiiii kikikikikikikiki
Quiché-Vinak:
Man   do you know what you're asking?
O.K.   O.K.
O.K. nevertheless   here's what I'll do
Because she's cloistered here

                        Our Feather-Mother
                        Mother of Hummingbirds
                        the Brilliant Emerald
                        come from Tzam-Gam-Carchag
                        whose mouth hasn't been touched
                        whose face hasn't been seen

I'll grant her to you
as a supreme signal of your dying
and of your disappearance

                        under the sky here
                        and on the earth.
Men   girls   bring us that Lady
                        Mother of Feathers
                        Mother of Hummingbirds
Give her to this Valiant   this Achí
since he asked for her
as a supreme signal of his dying
and his disappearance

                        under the sky here
                        and on the earth.

Ixok-mum, a Servant-girl, speaks for the Third time:

Very well my Chief   my Governor
I give her to this Valiant   to this Achí.

They bring the Mother of Feathers and present her to Quiché-Achí.

Here she is   Valiant   Achí   Cavek-Quiché-Vinak
I'm giving you what you wished for   what you asked for
                the Feather-Mother
                Mother of Hummingbirds
Don't offend her
don't wound her
But show her off
merely by dancing with her
                in the great walls
                in the great fortress.

Quiché-Achí salutes the young Lady who keeps her distance, dancing in front of him, turning away her face. He follows her in the same fashion, weaving before her, like a length of cloth — they dance round the Court to the sound of trumpets and then return before Chief Five Rains.

Quiché-Achí, speaks for the Fifteenth time:

Chief Five-Rains
Listen to me
                        to the sky-face
                        to the earth-face.
Here is the Lady
lent to me   conceded to me
as a companion.
I showed her off   I danced with her
                in the four corners
                along the four walls
                in the great fortress
Take her back now
and cloister her
                in the great walls
                in the great fortress.

Now I'm saying:
Remind yourself   remember   and lend me now
                    the Twelve Golden Eagles
                    the Twelve Golden Jaguars
                    Kablajuh u ganal Cot
                    Kablajuh u ganal Balam
I've met with night and day
arms in hand   spears in hand.
Lend them to me to go and shoot
with the son of my arrow   the son of my shield
                in the four corners
                along the four walls
                in the great walls
                in the great fortress
only . . .   only . . .
as a supreme signal of my dying
and of my disappearance

                                under the sky here
                                and on the earth.
                                May sky
                                and earth
                                be with you
                                Hobtoh Rabinal-Rahaual
                                Great Chief Five-Rains!

Hobtoh Rabinal-Rahaual, Chief Five-Rains, speaks for the Eighth time:

Valiant!   Warrior!   Cavek iiiiiiiiiiiiii kiiiiiiiiiiiii   kikikikikikiki
Quiché-Vinak:
You've said it now
                        to the sky-face
                        to the earth-face
that I should lend you
                the Twelve Golden Eagles
                the Twelve Golden Jaguars
O.K.
Here I lend you   here I concede to you
                the Twelve Golden Eagles
                the Twelve Golden Jaguars
that you beg of me   that you solicit

                              to my teeth
                              to my face.

Get going then

                O my Eagles
                O my Jaguars
and do what's needed
so that this Valiant   this Achí
parades with the son of his arrow
parades with the son of his shield
                    in the four corners
                    along the four walls!

Quiché-Achí, speaks for the Sixteenth time; Quiché-Achí going forward with the Eagles and the Jaguars and dancing a war-dance with them around the Court, then returning to the Gallery where Chief Five-Rains sits with his family:

Ha!   Aha!   Yeha!   Ahau!   Wow!   Achí!   I: Quiché-
    Achí   to you
Hobtoh Rabinal-Rahaual, Great Chief Five-Rains:

Listen to me   Approve of me
                          to the sky-face here
                          to the earth-face here.
You granted me
what I wished for   what I asked for
                    the Golden Eagles
                    the Golden Jaguars
I paraded with them
with the son of my arrow
with the son of my shield.
                COME ON NOW!
                Are *these* your Eagles then?
                Are *these* your Jaguars?
                HA!
You can't brag about these
                          to my teeth
                          to my face
                Some of them come on
                some of them don't come on
                they don't have any teeth

                    they don't have any talons
HA!   if you could spare a moment
                    in *my* mountains
                    in *my* valleys
                    how powerfully mine come on
                    how powerfully they gaze
                    they combat   they fight
                    with teeth
                    with talons!

Hobtoh Rabinal-Rahaual, Chief Five-Rains, speaks for the Ninth time:

Valiant!   Warrior!   Cavek iiiiiiiiiiiiiii kiiiiiiiiiiiii kikikikikikiki
Quiché-Vinak:
We've seen your Eagles' teeth
your Jaguars' teeth
in your mountains
in your valleys
          WELL
What's this sight
Where's this gaze
from your Eagles
from your Jaguars
in your mountains
in your valleys?

Quiché-Achí, speaks for the Seventeenth time:

Cala-Achí   Ha!   Aha!   Yeha!   Ahau!   Wow!   Achí!
I: Quiché-Achí   Balam-Achí   Balam-Quiché   Rahaual-Quiché-
Vinak   iiiiiiiiiiiiiiiiiiiiiiii   kiiiiiiiiiiiiiiiiiiiiiiiiiii   kikikikikikikikikikiki-
kikikikiki Quiché-Vinak

                          to you: Hobtoh Rabinal-Rahaual
Great Chief Five-Rains   OYEU ACHÍ!!!

Listen to me   Approve of me
                          to the sky-face
                          to the earth-face.
This is what I say
                          to your mouth

           to your face:
Allow me two hundred and sixty days
allow me two hundred and sixty nights
to go salute
         u vach nu huyabal
         u vach nu tagahal
         my mountains' faces
         my valleys' faces
where long   and long ago   I went alone
         to the four corners
         to the four walls
         to look for
         to encounter
         my needs   my food.

No one answers him. Then, dancing away, he disappears for a moment. Without returning to the Gallery where Five-Rains is seated, he approaches the Eagles and Jaguars posted in the middle of the Court around an altar.

              O Eagles!
              O Jaguars!
"He's gone" you said
a moment ago.
No   I hadn't gone
No   I hadn't disappeared
I went for a moment
to say goodbye
         to my mountains' faces
         to my valleys' faces
where long   and long ago   I went alone
         to find my food
         to find my meals
         in the four corners
         along the four walls.
            AAAAH   SKY!
            AAAAH   EARTH!
my valiance   my bravura
were no use.
I figured out my way
           below sky

                                    below earth

I opened my way
among grasses
among thorns.
My valiance   my bravura
were no use.
                                    AAAAH   SKY!
                                    AAAAH   EARTH!

Do I really have to die
to die in this place?
really disappear
disappear in this place?

                                O my gold!
                                O my silver!
                                O my arrow's sons!
                                O my shield's sons!
                                my Toltec war-club!
                                my Toltec axe!
                                my wreaths   my sandals!
                    go back to our mountains
                    go back to our valleys!
Take our news
to the teeth of our Man
to the face of our Governor
"It's a long time since
our valiance   our bravura
has looked for our food
has found our meals!"
says the word of our Man
the word of our Governor

He won't say so any more
now all I expect is my death
now all I expect is my disappearance
                                under sky here
                                and on the earth

                                AAAAH   SKY!
                                AAAAH   EARTH!

                                                            207

Since I can't do anything else but die
since I can't do anything else but disappear
                    under sky here
                    and on the earth
why can't I change fates with this squirrel with this bird dying on the branch
of the tree dying on the bud of the tree dying in their own little country
in which they've found their food   in which they've found their needs

                  chuvach cah
                  chuvach uleu?
                  under sky here
                  and on the earth?

            O Eagles!
            O Jaguars!

Come on then!
Let's get your work done
let's get your duty over with
           sink your teeth
           sink your talons
           get it over with
           in one moment

since I am a Valiant   an Achí
         from our own mountains
         from our own valleys
                May sky
                and earth
                be with you

            O Eagles!
            O Jaguars!

Eagles and Jaguars surround Quiché-Achí, Balam-Achí, Balam-Quiché, Rahaual-Quiché-Vinak — lay him on the sacrificial altar and open his breast. Then all present dance a general dance.

        — English version by Nathaniel Tarn

A THIRD SERVICE

Directions: Imitate the spirit of the animal or thing inside you.

Salish

the little random creatures

Fox

found a hole with a light in it, and saying
Whose?
        set a trap
with a bowcord for a noose.
A giant of light, something alive, dazzled the path
on its slow way up, blinding
the little random creatures
o something alive was dying in the bowcord and it said
        Allow me to choke to death
        And you'll have night forever
and they let the Sun go

— English version by Armand Schwerner, after William Jones

FIVE FLOWER WORLD VARIATIONS

Yaqui

[1]

   o flower fawn
          about to come out, playing
               in this flower water
  out there
          in the flower world
               the patio of flowers
 in the flower water
         playing
               flower fawn
  about to come out, playing
          in this flower water

[2]

  ah brother
         look at you
               a deer with flowers
 brother
         shake your antlers
             little brother
 shake your antlers
         deer with flowers
             why not let your belt
 your deer hoofs
         shake? why not vibrate
            cocoons
 strapped to your ankles
         brother
             shake them
 little brother
         shake & roll

[3]

  out in the mountain there
         these look like

doves

& in the flower water
            three of them
                        are grey & bobbing
three of them are walking
            grey & side by side
                        there in the flower world
the dawn
            out in the flower water
                        three of them
are grey & bobbing
            in the mountain there
                        these look like doves
out there
            & in the flower water
                        three are grey
& bobbing
            three of them are walkng
                        grey & side by side

[4]
    where are you standing
                in the wind
                            dead grasses
grey & shaking in the wind
                dead grasses
                        where are you standing
in the wind dead grasses
            grey & shaking in the wind
                        dead grasses
there in the wilderness
            the flower world
                        a pale blue cloud
will be grey water
            at its peak
                        the mist will reach
will rain down
            on the flower ground
                        & shining
reaching bottom

                    where you are
                              where you are only
          standing in the wind
                    dead grasses
                              grey & shaking in the wind
          dead grasses

[5]

SONG OF A DEAD MAN

          I do not want these flowers
                    moving
                              but the flowers
          want to move
                    I do not want these flowers
                              moving
          but the flowers
                    want to move
                              I do not want these flowers
          moving
                    but the flowers
                              want to move
          out in the flower world
                    the dawn
                              over a road of flowers
          I do not want these flowers
                    moving
                              but the flowers
          want to move
                    I do not want these flowers
                              moving
          but the flowers
                    the flowers
                              want to move

          — English versions by Jerome Rothenberg

214

the eagle above us

Cora

he lives in the sky
far above us
the eagle
looks good there
has a good grip on his world

his world wrapt in grey
but a living a humid
a beautiful grey

there he glides in the sky
very far
right above us

waits for what Tetewan
netherworld goddess
has to say

bright
his eye
on his world

bright
his eye
on the water of life
the sea
embracing
the earth

frightful his face
radiant his eye
the sun

his feet a deep red
there he is
right above us

spreading his wings
he remembers
who dwell down below

among whom the gods
let rain fall let dew fall
for life on their earth

there above us he speaks
we can hear him
his words make great sound

deep down they go
where mother Tetewan hears him and answers
we can hear her

here they meet
her words and the eagle's
we hear them together
together they make great sound

eagle words
fading
far above the water of life

mother words
from deep down
sighing away through the vaults of the sky

— English version by Anselm Hollo

A SONG OF THE RED & GREEN BUFFALO

Oto

. . . The fourth man to lead me was my nephew. He said, "In the early days there were many buffalos, but there was only one head among the buffalos. This buffalo was called One Rib. He had one red & one green horn. That is why old Indians paint their faces, one side red & the other side green." My nephew said, "I am going to sing a song for this buffalo & take this boy along the road to the end." The people said, "Hau! It is a great thing. It is going to be good."

THE SONG

All those buffalos have green horns.
Must go on with him towards the north
With the sole of your one green toe.

— *Translation by William Whitman*

From THE WISHING BONE CYCLE
(by Jacob Nibenegenesabe)

Swampy Cree

[1]

One time I wanted two moons
in the sky.
But I needed someone to look up and see
those two moons
because I wanted to hear him
try and convince the others in the village
of what he saw.
I knew it would be funny.
So, I did it.
I wished another moon up!
There it was, across the sky from the old moon.
Along came a man.
Of course I wished him down that open path.
He looked up in the sky.
He had to see that other moon!
One moon for each of his eyes!
He stood looking
up in the sky
a long time.
Then he suspected me, I think.
He looked into the trees
where he thought I might be.
But he could not see me
since I was disguised as the whole night itself!
Sometimes
I wish myself into looking like the whole day,
but this time
I was dressed like the whole night.
Then he said,
"There is something strange
in the sky tonight."
He said it out loud.
I heard it clearly.

Then he hurried home
and I followed him.
He told the others, "You will not believe this,
but there are ONLY two moons
in the sky tonight."
He had a funny look on his face.
Then, all the others began looking into the woods.
Looking for me, no doubt!
"Only two moons, ha! Who can believe you?
We won't fall for that!" they all said to him.
They were trying to send the trick back at me!
This was clear to me!
So, I quickly wished a third moon up there
in the sky.
They looked up and saw three moons.
They had to see them!
Then one man
said out loud, "Ah, there, look up!
up there!
There is only one moon!
Well, let's go sleep on this
and in the morning
we will try and figure it out."
They all agreed, and went in their houses
to sleep.
I was left standing there
with three moons shining on me.
There were three. . . I was sure of it.

[2]

One time
all the noises met.
All the noises in the world
met in one place
and I was there
because they met in my house.
My wife said, "Who sent them?"
I said, "Fox or Rabbit,
yes one of those two.

They're both out for tricking me back today.
Both of them
are mad at me.
Rabbit is mad because I pulled
his brother's ear
and held him up that way.
Then I ate him.
And Fox is mad because he wanted
to do those things first."

"Yes, then it had to be one of them,"
my wife said.

So, all the noises
were there.
These things happen.
Falling-tree noise was there.
Falling-rock noise was there.
Otter-mud-sliding noise was there.
All those noises, and more,
in my house.

"How long do you expect to stay?"
my wife asked them. "We need some sleep!"

They all answered at once!

That's why now my wife and I
sometimes can't hear well.
I should have wished them all away
first thing.

—*Translations by Howard Norman*

THE GREAT FARTER
(by Nakasuk)

Eskimo (Inuit)

The great farter, like they say
        because they couldn't get a
                meat-cache

open
        was called to fart at it.
                The great farter

answered:
        If I farted on it
                the meat no longer

would be good to eat!
        But when they kept on asking him to fart
                he let off a

tremendous fart
        & their blubber bags
                which they had

hammered
        with a stone
                but notwithstanding

no one could get loose
        I tell you
                now they burst

& being burst
        loose on the ground
                so could be used

for food
        but now they had
                a wicked smell

were simply
        thrown away.
                Not even the dogs
would eat them
        owing
            to the smell of fart.

— English version by Jerome Rothenberg, after Knud Rasmussen

ONE FOR COYOTE

Skagit

One day when Coyote
was walking through Snoqualmie Pass,
he met a young woman.

What do you have in your pack?
she said.
Fish eggs.
Can I have some?
If you close your eyes
and hold up your dress.

The woman did as she was told.

Higher.
Hold your dress over your head.

Then Coyote stepped out of his trousers
and walked up to the woman.

Stand still
so I can reach the place.

I can't.
There's something crawling between my legs.

Keep your dress up.
It's a bumble bee. I'll get it.

The woman dropped her dress.

You weren't fast enough.
It stung me.

— English version by Carl Cary

HOW HER TEETH WERE PULLED

Paiute

In the old time women's cunts had teeth in them.
It was hard to be a man then
Watching your squaw squat down to dinner
Hearing the little rabbit bones crackle.
Whenever fucking was invented it died with the inventor.
If your woman said she felt like biting you didn't take it lightly.
Maybe you just ran away to fight Numuzoho the Cannibal.

Coyote was the one who fixed things,
He fixed those toothy women!
One night he took Numuzoho's lava pestle
To bed with a mean woman
And hammer hammer crunch crunch ayi ayi
All night long:
"Husband, I am glad," she said
And all the rest is history.
To honor him we wear our necklaces of fangs.

— English version by Jarold Ramsey

THREE SONGS OF MAD COYOTE

Nez Percé

1.

Ravening Coyote comes,
red hands, red mouth,
necklace of eye-balls!

2.

Mad Coyote
madly sings,
then the west wind roars!

3.

Daybreak finds me,
eastern daybreak finds me
the meaning of that song:
with blood-stained mouth
comes mad Coyote!

—*Translation by Herbert J. Spinden*

Tzeltal

The eaters saddened every heart in Tenejapa.
The eaters couldn't be seen.
The eaters had powers that could murder the souls of people.
The eaters he eats the souls of grown people and children.
The eaters had great powers they could eat the souls of the dead.
The eaters went walking every night to houses because he is looking for
    someone who is open to sickness.
Those who pray and burn candles to God himself
So the eaters won't eat them.
Whoever does not burn candles to God himself
Many eaters come to his house with diseases.
The eaters takes souls and locks them up in the low city.
The eaters he gives people vomiting, diarrhoea and headache.
When the eaters locks up souls in the low city
Prayers set them free.
They make prayers for the souls that are locked up.
They pray they burn thirteen candles
Thirteen balls of incense
Five liters of cane alcohol
And one jug of cane wine
And a chicken
And a pack of cigarettes
And four gourds of our tobacco.
Every night the eaters want people. They go to dogs.
If a dog is crying at night like an orphan
The eaters are counting its hairs for it.
The eaters count the dog's hairs when they want people for eating.
It is not time for the dog's master to die
The dog tells the roosters
It's not time for his master to die.
The dog tells the roosters if the eaters come.
"Now you crow," the dog says, "because of my master."
The roosters are always ready
When the eater comes to the dog at night.

If the eater comes to the dog to count the dog's hairs
He stops half way for a rest counting the dog's hairs.
Then the dog cries like an orphan.
Then when the dog cries like an orphan all the roosters crow.
"Already the place is light.
Let's go now, the roosters are crowing,"
The eater says.
Thus no disease comes to the owners of the houses in Tenejapa.
In fact the dogs and the roosters protect it carefully from eaters.

— *Version by W. S. Merwin, from a literal translation by Katherine M. Branstetter*

THINGS THAT WERE TRULY REMARKABLE
(by N. Scott Momaday)

Kiowa

Mammedaty was the grandson of Guipahgo, and he was well-known on that account. Now and then Mammedaty drove a team and wagon out over the plain. Once, in the early morning, he was on the way to Rainy Mountain. It was summer and the grass was high and meadowlarks were calling all around. You know, the top of the plain is smooth and you can see a long way. There was nothing but the early morning and the land around. Then Mammedaty heard something. Someone whistled to him. He looked up and saw the head of a little boy nearby above the grass. He stopped the horses and got down from the wagon and went to see who was there. There was no one; there was nothing there. He looked for a long time, but there was nothing there.

There is a single photograph of Mammedaty. He is looking past the camera and a little to one side. In his face there is calm and good will, strength and intelligence. His hair is drawn close to the scalp, and his braids are long and wrapped with fur. He wears a kilt, fringed leggings, and beaded moccasins. In his right hand there is a peyote fan. A family characteristic: the veins stand out in his hands, and his hands are small and rather long.

Mammedaty saw four things that were truly remarkable. This head of the child was one, and the tracks of the water beast another. Once, when he walked near the pecan grove, he saw three small alligators on a log. No one had ever seen them before and no one ever saw them again. Finally, there was this: something had always bothered Mammedaty, a small aggravation that was never quite out of mind, like a name on the tip of the tongue. He had always wondered how it is that the mound of earth which a mole makes around the opening of its burrow is so fine. It is nearly as fine as powder, and it seems almost to have been sifted. One day Mammedaty was sitting quietly when a mole came out of the earth. Its cheeks were puffed out as if it had been a squirrel packing nuts. It looked all around for a moment, then blew the fine dark earth out of its mouth. And this it did again and again, until there was a ring of black, powdery earth on the ground. That was a strange and meaningful thing to see. It meant that Mammedaty had got possession of a powerful medicine.

things that were truly remarkable.

SWEAT-HOUSE RITUAL NO. 1

Omaha

listen   old man   listen
you rock   listen
old man   listen
listen   didn't i teach all their children
to follow me   listen
listen
listen   unmoving time-without-end   listen
you old man sitting there   listen
on the roads where all the winds come rushing
at the heart of the winds where you're sitting   listen
old man   listen
listen   there's short grasses growing all over you   listen
you're sitting there living inside them   listen
listen   i mean you're sitting there covered with birdshit   listen
head's rimmed with soft feathers of birds   listen
old man   listen
you standing there next in command   listen
listen   you water   listen
you water that keeps on flowing
from time out of mind   listen
listen   the children have fed off you
no one's come on our secret
the children go mad for your touch   listen
listen   you standing like somebody's house   listen
just like somewhere to live   listen
you great animals   listen
listen   you making a covering over us   listen
saying   let the thoughts of those children live with me & let them love
      me   listen
listen   you tent-frame   listen
you standing with back bent   you over us
stooping your shoulders   you bending over us
you really standing
you saying   thus shall my little ones speak of me
you brushing the hair back from your forehead   listen
the hair of your head

the grass growing over you
you with your hair turning white   listen
the hair growing over your head   listen
o you roads the children will be walking on   listen
all the ways they'll run to be safe   listen
they'll escape   their shoulders bending with age where they walk
walking where others have walked
their hands shading their brows
while they walk & are old   listen
because they're wanting to share in your strength   listen
the children want to be close by your side   listen
walking   listen
be very old & listen

— *English version by Jerome Rothenberg, from Alice Fletcher & Francis LaFlesche*

A POEM TO THE MOTHER OF THE GODS

Aztec

Oh, golden flower opened up
                         she is our mother
whose thighs are holy
                   whose face is a dark mask.
She came from Tamoanchan,
                       the first place
where all descended
                where all was born.
Oh, golden flower flowered
                   she is our mother
whose thighs are holy
                   whose face is a dark mask.
She came from Tamoanchan

Oh, white flower opened up
                   she is our mother
whose thighs are holy
                   whose face is a dark mask.
She came from Tamoanchan,
                   the first place
where all descended
                where all was born.
Oh, white flower flowered
                   she is our mother
whose thighs are holy
                   whose face is a dark mask.
She came from Tamoanchan.

· · · · · · · · · · · · · · · ·

She lights on the round cactus,
                   she is our mother
the dark obsidian butterfly.
                   Oh, we saw her as we wandered
across the Nine Plains,
                   she fed herself with deers' hearts.

She is our mother,
        the goddess earth.
                She is dressed
in plumes
      she is smeared with clay.
In all four directions of wind
            the arrows are broken.
They saw you as a deer
        in the barren land.
those two men, Xiuhnel and Mimich.

— English version by Edward Kissam

BEFORE THEY MADE THINGS BE ALIVE THEY SPOKE
(by Lucario Cuevish)

Luiseño

Earth woman lying flat her feet were to the north her head was to the south Sky brother sitting on her right hand side he said Yes sister you must tell me who you are She answered I am Tomaiyowit She asked him Who are you? He answered I am Tukmit. Then she said:

I stretch out flat to the Horizon.
I shake I make a noise like thunder.
I am Earthquake.
I am round & roll around.
I vanish & return.

Then Tukmit said:

I arch above you like a lid.
I deck you like a hat.
I go up high & higher.
I am death I gulp it in one bite.
I grab men from the east & scatter them.
My name is Death.

Then they made things be alive.

— English version by Jerome Rothenberg, after Constance G. DuBois

SIOUX METAMORPHOSES

(1st Set)

1.

He was an old wolf, no teeth, his tail all but bare. The war party thought he was one of them, singing with a young man's voice, until they saw him. He lay beside their fire, and they cut up their best buffalo meat for him, fed it to him. He taught them this song, and always since they carry their medicine in a wolfskin bag.

With powers you know nothing about
I made them come to life
with powers you cannot understand
I made them walk

Wolf people

With spirit powers
I made them walk
with spirit powers
I made them walk
with spirit powers
I made them walk
with spirit powers
I made them walk

2.

Everybody was there, but they heard somebody singing. One of them climbed the hill and looked over. A wolf was sitting there, looking far off and singing. The war party learned his song.

At daybreak
I go
I gallop
I go

At daybreak
I go

I trot
I go

At daybreak
I go
timidly
I go

At daybreak
I go
cautiously
I go

3.

I dreamed I came to a wolf den. Only the little wolves were there. They
were singing this song.

Father is away somewhere
will come home howling

Mother is away somewhere
will come home howling

Father is away somewhere
a buffalo calf in his belly

Mother is away somewhere
will come home howling

Now she returns
in a sacred manner she returns

4.

I thought I was a wolf
but the owls are hooting
& I'm afraid of the dark

I thought I was a wolf
but I'm so hungry
I'm tired from just standing

I am a wolf
I go to many places
I'm just tired of that one

(2nd Set)

I thought I saw buffalo
& called out
I thought I saw buffalo
& called out
let them be buffalo

They were blackbirds
I walked toward them
& they were blackbirds

I thought I saw buffalo
& called out
I thought I saw buffalo
& called out
let them be buffalo

They were swallows
I walked toward them
& they were swallows

(3rd Set)

1.

In wild flight
I sent the swallows

in wild flight
I made them go
in wild flight
before the clouds were gathered

In wild flight
I sent my horse
in wild flight
a swallow flying running
in wild flight
before the clouds were gathered

2.

My horse flies along
I wear blue earth & brown
I make myself fly along
I make my horse fly along
I make myself fly along
I have done it

3.

When I was courting
they told me
I had no horses
so I'm looking

Crow, Crow
watch your horses
they say I'm a horse thief

Keep your eyes open
I'm wandering around anyway
I might as well look for horses

Night is different
than day
may my horses be many

(4th Set)

1.

He comes from the north
he comes to fight
he comes from the north
see him there

I throw dust on me
it changes me
I am a bear
when I go to meet him

2.

Send word, bear father
send word, bear father
I'm having a hard time
send word, bear father
I'm having a bad time

3.

My paw is holy
herbs are everywhere
my paw
herbs are everywhere

My paw is holy
everything is holy
my paw
everything is holy

— English versions by James Koller, from Frances Densmore

A BOOK OF EXTENSIONS (1)

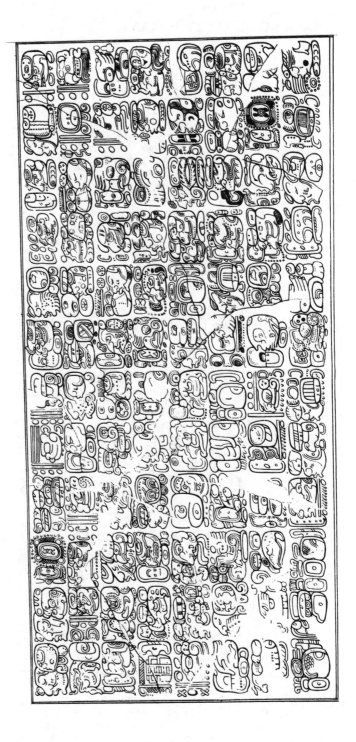

Maya

THE CALENDARS

Ojibwa

1. long moon, spirit moon 2. moon of the suckers 3. moon of the crust on the snow 4. moon of the breaking of snow-shoes 5. moon of the flowers & blooms 6. moon of strawberries 7. moon of raspberries 8. moon of whortle berries 9. moon of gathering of wild rice 10. moon of the falling of leaves 11. moon of freezing 12. little moon of the spirit

Mandan

1. moon of the seven cold days 2. pairing moon 3. moon of the weak eyes 4. moon of the wild geese / moon of the breaking up of the ice 5. moon in which maize is sown / moon of flowers 6. moon of ripe service berries 7. moon of ripe cherries 8. moon of ripe wild plums 9. moon of ripe maize 10. moon of the fall of the leaves 11. moon of the freezing of the rivers 12. moon of the little cold

Netchilli

1. it is cold, the Eskimo is freezing 2. the sun is returning 3. the sun is ascending 4. the seal brings forth her young 5. the young seals are taking to the sea 6. the seals are shedding their coats 7. reindeer bring forth their young / birds are brooding 8. the young birds are hatched 9. the reindeer is migrating southward 10. amerairui 11. the Eskimo lay down food depots 12. the sun disappears

Dakota

1. hard moon 2. racoon moon 3. sore eyes moon 4. moon in which the geese lay eggs / moon in which the streams are again navigable 5. planting moon 6. moon in which the strawberries are red 7. moon in which the chokecherries are ripe & the geese shed their feathers 8. harvest moon 9. moon in which wild rice is laid up to dry 10. drying rice moon 11. deer rutting moon 12. moon when deer shed horns

Tlingit

1. goose month 2. black bear month 3. silver salmon month 4. month before everything hatches 5. month everything hatches 6. time of the long days 7. month when the geese can't fly 8. month when all kinds of animal prepare their dens 9. moon child 10. big moon / formation of ice 11. month when all creatures go into their dens / the sun disappears 12. ground hog mother's moon

Loucheux

1. moon when dog is cold 2. moon of ice 3. moon of eagles 4. moon in which dog barks 5. moon of the break up of ice / moon of the sea 6. moon of moulting 7. moon of the long day 8. moon of the rutting reindeer 9. moon of the chase 10. moon of warmth 11. moon of mountain goats 12. moon in which the sun is dead

Cree

1. month in which the old fellow spreads the brush / extreme cold moon 2. month in which the young birds begin to chirp / old man 3. eagle moon 4. grey goose moon 5. frog moon 6. moon in which birds begin to lay their eggs / the leaves come out 7. moon in which birds cast their feathers 8. moon in which the young birds begin to fly 9. moon in which the moose deer cast their horns / snow goose month 10. rutting moon / the birds fly south 11. hoar frost moon / the rivers begin to freeze 12. moon in which the young fellow spreads the brush / whirlwind moon

Modoc

1. thumb 2. index finger 3. middle finger 4. ring finger 5. little finger 6. thumb 7. index finger 8. thumb 9. index finger 10. middle finger 11. ring finger 12. little finger

Kwakiutl

1. spawning season / season of floods   2. elder brother / first olachen run
3. raspberry sprouting season / no sap in trees   4. raspberry season
5. huckleberry season / oil moon   6. salalberry season / sockeye month
7. southeast wind moon   8. empty boxes   9. wide face   10. right moon
11. sweeping houses / dog salmon month   12. fish in river moon /
cleaned of leaves   13. split both ways

Tewa

1. ice moon   2. lizard belly cut moon   3. month leaves break forth
4. leaves open   5. tender leaf month / corn planting   6. dark leaf
month   7. horse month / month of ripeness   8. wheat cutting month
9. month when the corn is taken in / syrup is made   10. harvest month /
month of falling leaves   11. month when all is gathered in   12. ashes fire

Eskimo

1. season for top spinning / little sun   2. time of much moon / the first seals
are born / starting out to hunt reindeer   3. time of taking of hares in nets
/ time of creeping on game   4. time of cutting off (from the appearance
of sharp lines where the white of the ptarmigans' bodies is contrasted with
the brown of the new summer neck feathers)   5. geese come / time for go-
ing in kaiaks   6. time of eggs / time of fawn hunting   7. time of braining
salmon / geese get new wing feathers   8. time for brooding geese to moult
9. swans moult / time for velvet shedding   10. time for seal nets   11. time
for bringing in winter stores   12. time for the drum

Carrier

1. moon of the wind   2. moon of the snow storm   3. moon of the golden
eagle   4. moon of the wild goose   5. moon of the black bear / moon of the
carp   6. moon when they take to the water   7. the buffalo ruts / moon of
the land locked salmon   8. moon of the red salmon   9. moon of the bull
trout   10. moon of the white fish   11. during its half they navigate / the
fat of animals disappears   12. what freezes is covered with bare ice

LEAN WOLF'S COMPLAINT

Hidatsa

Four years ago

the white man

friends

with us

A lie

Done, finished,
"that is all"

ZUNI DERIVATIONS

I.

LIQUID, WATER
water in a shallow container
   honey
collection of water
   in water, floating
water on the surface
   lake, puddle
water on the surface coming out
   spring
   woman
sour water
   beer
   vinegar
water removed from a deep container
   whip
become water
   melt
water with a hot taste
   whiskey
   bilious phlegm
get water with a hot taste
   sick with an upset stomach

II.

GRAINS
grainy pants
    bluejeans
grainy jacket
    bluejean jacket
salty grains
    salt
sweet grains
    sugar
collection of grainy water
    Zuni Salt Lake
toward the collection of grainy water
  · south

III.

MOON, MONTH
what belongs to moon
    moonlight
instrument for what belongs to moon
    moon

IV.

DAYLIGHT
instrument for daylight
    sun
    clock

V.

TWO
multiplied with two
   twice
two tens
   twenty
coin of two
   quarter-dollar
two hearts
   witch

VI.

ON TOP
cause to be on top
    put on top
    bewitch
    (placing victim's lock of hair
    piece of clothing
   on top of a tree or bluff)

VII.

ANGULAR PROJECTIONS
(like the corners of a gunnysack)
like a witch
(a witch's hair projects
in two angular bunches
on each side of the head)
good angular projections
something perfectly square

VIII.

HOLLOW TUBE

hollow tube making rattling sounds
  empty-headed person
become a hollow tube
  faint, forget

IX.

DANCE

cause to dance
  sponsor in a dance
  bounce a child on the lap
  spin a top

X.

WICKERWORK

growing bunch of wickerwork
  pine needles
static wickerwork
  paper
make static wickerwork
  attend school
wickerwork together on the ground
  in single file

XI.

STAND

cause to stand
  stop
cause oneself not to stand
  run
stand together on the ground
  be a village

XII.

OLD
old ones
    parents
terrestrial old one
    dwelling-place of a deity
indeterminate old one
    calm, passive, quiet, shy
    inconspicuous
old person
    man, man of the house, husband

XIII.

BECOME BLUE, BECOME GREEN
one who is black and blue with bruises
one who is blue from the cold
valuable blue, valuable green
    turquoise
    blue corn

XIV.

BECOME LIGHT, BECOME WHITE
terrestrial light
    daylight
    life
cause to be light
    see
    make visible
valuable light
    white corn
    white shell necklace

— Selected & arranged by Dennis Tedlock

NAVAJO CORRESPONDENCES

(First Set)
1. red willow
Sun
yellow

2. arrow
Wind
Cicada
arrow-crossing
life

3. aspen
white
summer
pink

4. Bat
Darkness
wing feather
Big Fly

5. Big Fly
feather
Wind
skin at tip of tongue
speech

(Second Set)
1. black
Darkness
Black Wind
yellow squash

2. Black God
Black Star
Darkness

3. bull-roarer
lightning
snakes
pokers
danger line
hoops

4. ambush woods
emetic frames
pokers

5. cane
digging stick
arrow
water

(Third Set)

1. cotton
   motion
   clouds

2. Earth
   Yellow Wind
   Pink Thunder
   Reared-in-the-earth
   Pink Snake
   rainbow
   redshell
   sunglow
   Holy Girl

3. feather cloak
   yellow lightning

4. Frog
   hail
   potatoes
   dumplings

5. Old Age
   ax
   Frog

(Fourth Set)

1. cloud water
   fog
   moss

2. smoke
   cloud
   rain
   acceptance
   breathing in

3. spiderweb
   nerves & veins
   marrow
   conveyances

4. red willow
   water
   blue

5. yellow
   Yellow-evening-light
   Yellow Wind
   black squash

MUU'S WAY *or* PICTURES FROM THE UTERINE WORLD

Cuna

sunrise...& toward the sunrise stands the village of the Bow People...
  bowmen move around it

& place a net over the housetop bowmen are coming down from

a bowman sits & aims...bent over...crouching...with bow & arrow...
  arrow point goes whizzing

makes the earth rise in a cloud...it darkens the whole place...covers Muu's
  way

bird bowmen going down now

other bowmen too

& other bowmen

but doesn't leave Muu's roads...not a single alleyway of hers he sits defending the sick woman. . .sits protecting her

he calls "O Mountain dweller   dweller on the tops of mountains"

shaman calls the Lords of Animals. . .one like a jaguar. . .tied with iron
chains. . .the iron chains are rattling

the entrails make a noise. . .the entrails roar. . .an animal comes some-
where. . .now the animal comes up. . .it lifts its neck & comes with
flashing eyes & lifts its iron throat with terrifying eyes

with rattling iron chains. . .noise of its large links under the hammock of
the sick woman. . .three animals one like a jaguar tied with iron chains

while the iron chains are rattling. . .entrails screaming. . .while the entrails
make a noise & throw Muu's way into a panic. . .they defend the sick
woman. . .& protect her

"o mountain dweller o dweller on top of the mountain". . .the Shaman is
calling the lords of the Gold Water

257

the Little Gold Water answers. . .he's coming with lots of gold water

over her hammock he's pouring the strongest gold water

the strongest gold water is streaming. . .gold water is dripping. . .the strong gold waters are gathering. . .making a puddle of gold. . .on the ground

& he's turning them off. . .he's blotting them out on the road in front of the sick woman

"o dweller on mountains dweller on top of the mountain". . .the Shaman is calling the lord of the Silver Water

the Little Silver Water answers. . .he's coming with lots of silver water

Shaman calls "dweller on mountain o dweller on tops of the mountains". . . he's calling the lords of the Gold Net

& they come. . .down they come. . .with a gold net like a kerchief they cover her

they come with a gold net. . .to hang it over the treetops. . .to fasten a gold net. . .to make a gold net secure

a gold net starts looking like gold

a gold net is lowered. . .a gold net swells out. . .a gold net hangs down. . .a gold net forms meshes

shamans study a gold net to make sure it's straight. . .they sit down with a gold net. . .they kneel with it

shamans are swinging a gold net

shamans are swinging a gold net

shamans are swinging a gold net

shamans are putting on stockings

shamans are putting on shoes

shamans are polishing shoes

shamans are transforming shoes

shamans are giving each other endless advice

258

"with a fine piece of cloth you must wipe the child for me"

this medicine man has encouraged them . . . he has given all of them bones
. . . has adorned them with *tele*-flutes . . . brought them safely over the
Underground road . . . & all underground roads . . . he has put them
under the ground "to see if any man will take my castle"

& has put the gold net in front of the sick woman

with iron nails . . . or fastened with iron nails & giving light . . . they put the
gold net

& facing the opposite way. ∴ fastened with iron nails . . . held down with
nails of iron . . . they put the silver net

when the time is silent . . . when the time is midnight . . . my lady's essence
may try to escape . . . then take a care with it

under the ground . . . beneath its surface & below the earth . . . fastened with
iron nails . . . held down with nails of iron & giving light . . . they put the
gold net

"o dweller on the mountain o dweller on top of the mountain" the shaman
calls to his shaman

his shaman is calling the lords of the animals . . . Drinking Dog is an animal
. . . Sucking Dog is an animal . . . tied with an iron chain . . . the iron chain
rattles . . . the entrails are roaring . . . the entrails are making a noise

the animal . . . the animal is coming up . . . & comes with flashing eyes . . . lifts
its iron throat & comes . . . with terrifying eyes the iron chains . . . come

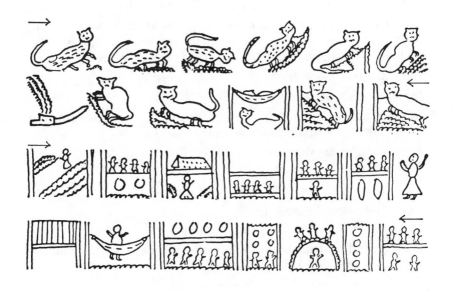

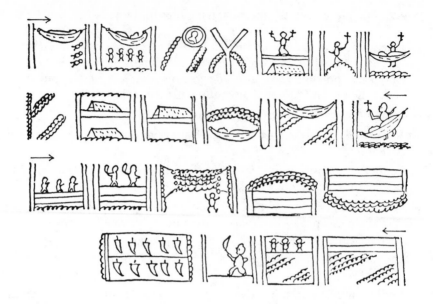

rattling. . .entrails roar beneath. . .the hammock of the sick woman

Drinking Dog is an animal. . .Sucking Dog is an animal. . .tied with an iron chain. . .the iron chain rattles. . .the entrails are screaming

& put Muu's way into a panic. . .while they defend her. . .they protect the sick woman

looking toward the sea. . .the South. . .the shamans are guarding the place . . .the shamans are listening. . .exactly four days

& facing the opposite way not leaving one of Muu's roads I put all these shamans here. . .dolls. . .to defend the sick woman. . .being invisible dolls. . .changing to shamans. . .you do things by seeing

the shamans are watching

the shamans are guarding the place

the shamans are listening. . .exactly four days. . .are defending the sick woman. . .the shamans are waiting around

& are facing. . .are watching. . .guarding the place. . .& they listen exactly four days

all over everywhere shamans are watching

shamans are guarding the place

shamans are listening. . .exactly four days

underground. . .shamans under the earth. . .are watching. . .guarding the place. . .they listen exactly four days

when the woman gets well. . .some people have gone where the plants grow
. . .but be careful!

beneath. . .the sick woman's hammock are shamans. . .carved. . .under
her hammock the shamans are rising

not stepping foot from her house the lords of the Silver Branch rise

the lords of the Silver Branch talk. . .the lords rise up. . .at the door of the
sick woman's house

the lords of the Silver Cross talk to the Silver Cross. . .to the fetus

entangling the road in front of the sick woman

they come to entangle the road in front of the sick woman

come to twist the road in front of the sick woman

pulling the gold net over her hammock. . .when the hour is silent the hour
is midnight

if Muu saw that the road through the woman was open. . .the shamans
would rise

& strike with their sticks. . .the shamans. . .are holding their sticks in a line

the shamans are swinging a gold net they put a gold net over the housefront

they drag a gold net as far as the sky

if Muu saw any road through the sky lying open. . .the shamans would rise

& would strike with their sticks

& hold their sticks in a line

— English version by Jerome Rothenberg, after Nils Holmer & Henry Wassén

261

A MOON PEYOTE ALTAR
(by Enoch Hoag)

Caddo

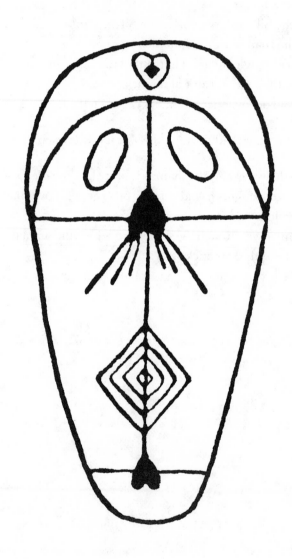

THE PICTURE WITH THE WATER FRINGE MOUTHS

Navajo

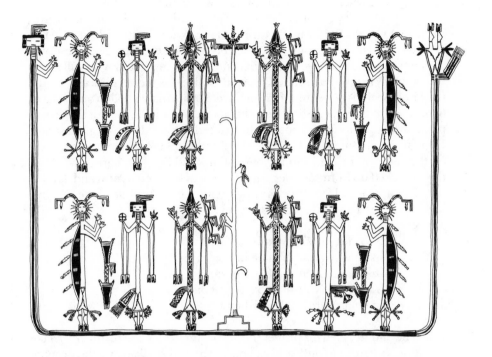

The Visionary and the gods were traveling. After passing the ridges of rock they came to a lake closely surrounded by high cliffs. The river flowed into the lake on one side and out at the other by two streams. The log floated to the middle of the lake and then circled around sunwise, in constantly widening circles until it touched the shore near the rocky wall, on the south side, where the Fringe Mouths of the Water lived, and here it stopped with its butt to the south. The gods pushed aside the waters and helped the Indian to get out of the log. At the same time the door of the house of the Fringe Mouths was thrown open. He entered and found many holy ones inside who awaited his coming.

The chief of the Fringe Mouths said to him, "We have heard that Bitahatini was coming to us; we have heard why he comes, and he comes not in vain. We shall give him what he seeks and then he will be a perfect chanter of the Night Chant." The Prophet did not speak. The Fringe Mouths led him four times around the lodge and placed him sitting in the south. Then they closed the door and bade him look down at the ground until they told him to lift his eyes. While he was looking down, they took from a shelf a sheet of cloud and spread it on the ground. When they bade him look up, he beheld the sheet of cloud covered with a picture in many colors and he saw four footprints and a trail drawn in white corn-meal extending from where he sat to the picture where there was a bowl of water.

The Visionary was told to arise and to examine the picture more carefully, that it was called The Picture with the Water Fringe Mouths. After he had looked at it for a long time, the holy ones asked: "Have you observed the picture well? Have you got it fixed in your mind so that you will never forget it?" When he had replied "Yes," he walked as the yei directed, on the tracks of meal to the center of the picture. He sprinkled pollen on the faces of the gods in the way we do it now; he sprinkled it up the stem of each corn-plant and down its three roots, as he uttered the words "Hozógo nasádo." He placed corn-meal on the feet, chest and mouth of each divine figure, on the bases of the ears and the base of the tassel of each cornstalk. After this he picked up from each deposit a portion of the sacred meal and handed it to Talking God. He stepped into the water in the middle of the picture, bowed his head and uttered this prayer:

> In beauty, I shall walk.
> In beauty, you shall be my picture.
> In beauty, you shall be my song.
> In beauty, you shall be my medicine,
> In beauty, my holy medicine.

When he had finished his prayer the yei began to beat the drum and shake the rattle. A Fringe Mouth and a goddess entered masked and the Prophet fell upon the ground in a fit.

— *Translation by Washington Matthews*

THE STORY OF GLOOSCAP, OR BLACK CAT: How He
Said Goodbye to Sable, How Sable Was Trapped in Snake's
Tent & Was Told to Bring a Straight Stick for His Own Gutting,
How Sable & Black Cat Planned Snake's Blinding with a
Crooked Stick, & How Black Cat Killed Snake Beside a Fallen
Hemlock Tree & Cut Him into Small Pieces

Passamaquoddy

OJIBWA LOVE POEM

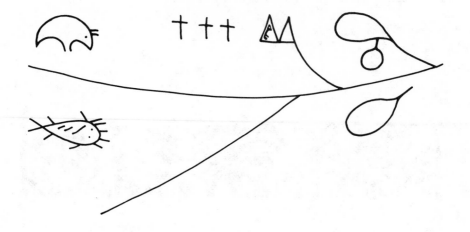

STRING GAMES

Bella Bella

1.

GETTING BERRIES

Where you going?
(Getting berries. Think I'll try a little farther.)
Why not go with this canoe?
(Don't guess we can use it. Not enough room for So-&-So's mother.)
Can't see how. Canoe's got room enough down in the baling hole.
(So-&-So's mother would use it for baling.)
Well I wish you'd go & capsize in the mouth of that river.
(Then they went & capsized in the mouth of that river.)

2.

GHOST & SHAMAN

Hey let's fight that shaman, let's fight that ghost first & then that shaman.
(See them running away. There goes that ghost & that old shaman.)
Well, take along his working box.
(Well, take along his crabapple box.)
Well, take along his viburnum box.
(Well, take along his dry-salmon box.)

3.

GETTING FIREWOOD

Where you going?
(Going to get firewood.)
Where's the firewood?
(Down to my house.)
Then you better come & get it.
(Why's your mouth all greasy?)
Been eating some old-woman grease.
(What you using for a grease dish?)
This old-woman clamshell.
(Well what's gonna be your mat then?)
This old-woman mat.
(How about your you-know-what?)

Some old-woman fishmeat.
(And what'll be your backboard?)
Old-woman backboard.
(How about your post?)
That's this old-woman digging stick.
(Then I guess you're the one to go & bring us some soaked salmon.)

4.

PIECES OF SNOT
Snot goes down.
(Snot goes back up.)
I said snot goes down.
(Now I guess it's dribbling out.)

5.

LYING DOWN
Don't lie down again.
(When you do lie down maybe hammer a stone.)
Raven & lover on their backs & facing.
(Somebody's asshole.)
Crane's ass is bloody. A lump on his neck.
(Runs out of the house with a mouth of soaked salmon.)

POEMS FOR THE GAME OF SILENCE

Chippewa

it is hanging
in the edge of sunshine
it is a pig   I see
with its double hoofs
it is a very fat pig
the people who live in a hollow tree
are fighting
they are fighting bloodily
he is rich
he will carry a pack toward the great water

Mandan

that
that
whose
track is it like?
grandfather
two-teeth
(he means the beaver!)
if it's like his track
if it is
follow it on
the man came to a wigwam
pounded the wigwam
with worn-out feet
with a wriggled bag
up high
lay a big fat
young buffalo calf
with a soft belly-button
walking
crumbling sticks
crab shells
have a dance
he
knocked his eye out

— *Translations by Frances Densmore*

SONGS & SONG PICTURES

Chippewa

SONG PICTURE NO. 17

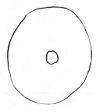

at the center of the earth
is where I'm from

SONG PICTURE NO. 27

when the water's calm
& the frog's just drifting in —
that's when I show up now & then

SONG PICTURE NO. 29

water's flowing
the sound
comes toward my home

SONG PICTURE NO. 30

when I show up
all those seething waters
cast their men up from below

SONG PICTURE NO. 34

sure thing
I'm a spirit!
see me becoming visible?
must be a male beaver

SONG PICTURE NO. 54

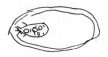

in the middle of the sea
long room of the sea
in which I'm sitting

SONG PICTURE NO. 56

I keep running around
shoot at a man & he falls down stoned
try feeling with my hand
see if he's still alive

SONG PICTURE NO. 58

I'm living in a cave
old Grandfather
got arms
with feathers
I must be a cave-man

SONG PICTURE NO. 64

know what I'll promise you?
skies be bright & clear for you
that's what I'll promise you

SONG PICTURE NO. 66

hunting song (i)

there's my war club
booming through the sky—
you animals better come when I
  call you

SONG PICTURE NO. 68

hunting song (ii)

this time I'll show up
everywhere on earth
I'll be dressed in skin of a marten

SONG PICTURE NO. 69

hunting song (iii)

shining like a star—
the animal that looks up's
dazzled by my light

273

SONG PICTURE NO. 71

the love charm

what's that you're telling me?
I'm dressed up like the roses —
just as beautiful as they are

SONG PICTURE NO. 82

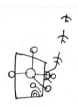

song of the man who succeeded

I'll test my power
on myself

SONG PICTURE NO. 83

song for a scalp dance

some people in the sky
must sure be jealous
me dancing around here
with this scalp

SONG PICTURE NO. 85

song of the crab medicine-bag

I can use it
good as any crab can

SONG PICTURE NO. 86

song of the fire-charm
flames are shooting
far up as my body

SONG PICTURE NO. 87

song of starvation
which of you
is going to take my body?
watch that old lady
making medicine

SONG PICTURE NO. 96

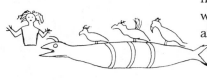

might have known it —
waterbirds come perching
all my body long

SONG PICTURE NO. 106

sound is fading out
it's more like five sounds
FREEDOM
sound is really fading out
it's more like five sounds

— *English versions by Jerome Rothenberg,
from Frances Densmore*

A BOOK OF
EXTENSIONS (II)

SOUNDINGS

SOUND-POEM NO. 1

Navajo

Óhohohó héhehe héya héya
Óhohohó héhehe héya héya
Éo ládo éo ládo éo ládo nasé
Hówani how owów owé
Éo ládo éo ládo éo ládo nasé
Hówani how owów owé
Hówani hówani how héyeyéye yéyeyáhi
Hówowów héya héya héya héya
Hówa héhehe héya héya héya
Óhohohó howé héya héya
Óhohohó héhehe héya héya
Hábi níye hábi níye
Há'huizánaha   síhiwánaha
Há'hayá éaheóo éaheóo
Síhiwánaha   há'huizánaha
Há'hayá éaheóo éaheóo éaheóo éaheóo éaheóo

SOUND-POEM NO. 2
(by Richard Johnny John)

Seneca

gah non   wey yo hey
             yahney heeyo
                     no heyah heyah
             yahney heeyo
                              ho wey yah heenay
yah ho ho yo
      o ho wey yo hey
             yahney heeyo
                     no heyah heyah
             yahney heeyo
             yahney heeyo
                         ho wey yah heenay

A POEM FROM THE SWEATBATH POEMS

Fox

A gi ya ni a gi yan ni i
A gi ya ni a gi yan ni i
A gi ya ni a gi yan ni i
A gi ya ni agi ya ni
Sky
A gi ya ni i a gi ya ni
A gi ya ni i a gi ya ni
A gi ya ni

From CEREMONY OF SENDING: A SIMULTANEITY FOR TWENTY CHORUSES

Osage

THE HIDDEN PEOPLE & THE STAR PEOPLE

THERE, TRULY THEY SAID IN THIS HOUSE
THERE, TRULY THEY SAID IN THIS HOUSE
The Hidden People sitting there said

said'nth'house   *The Water People of Seven Fireplaces*
said'nth'house   O! My Grandfather, they said to him
said'nth'house   *The Water People said*
said'nth'house   we have no suitable totem, My Grandfather
said'nth'house   *to The Star People sitting there*
said'nth'house   O! My Little Ones, he began
said'nth'house   *O! My Grandfather, they said to him*
said'nth'house   you say you have no suitable totem
said'nth'house   *we have no suitable totem, My Grandfather*
said'nth'house   I am a suitable totem
said'nth'house   *THERE, TRULY THEY SAID IN THIS HOUSE*
THERE, TRULY THEY SAID IN THIS HOUSE
You say you have no suitable totem

said'nth'house   He built a small house
said'nth'house   *I am a suitable totem*
said'nth'house   I have not built this house without purpose
said'nth'house   *the female cedar over there*
said'nth'house   I have built it as a place to break animal heads
said'nth'house   *truly I live in that body*
said'nth'house   I have not built this house without purpose
said'nth'house   *when the young take on my body*
said'nth'house   it is a symbol of the spider
said'nth'house   *they'll live to see old age as they walk*
said'nth'house   Indeed, I have built it as a trap
said'nth'house   *The male cedar right there*
said'nth'house   all small animals, whoever they may be
said'nth'house   *they'll walk with that totem*
said'nth'house   will ensnare themselves as they walk
said'nth'house   *the male cedar*
said'nth'house   and when the young use it, animals will appear
said'nth'house   *when they walk with that totem*

said'nth'house	Even before dawn
said'nth'house	*they'll live to see old age as they walk*
said'nth'house	animals will appear for them as they walk
said'nth'house	*THERE, TRULY THEY SAID IN THIS HOUSE*
	and also at dusk
said'nth'house	*And these waters*
said'nth'house	animals will appear for them as they walk
said'nth'house	*we'll unite with the two cedars as we walk*
said'nth'house	This bull buffalo right here
said'nth'house	*and these waters*
said'nth'house	this one
said'nth'house	*when they use them for old age*
said'nth'house	will make animals appear for them as they walk
said'nth'house	*they'll live to see old age as they walk*
said'nth'house	and this animal's blood
said'nth'house	*These grasses right here that never die*
said'nth'house	Even before dawn
said'nth'house	*when they use them also for old age*
said'nth'house	they'll drink his blood
said'nth'house	*they'll live to see old age as they walk*
said'nth'house	also at dusk
said'nth'house	*I stand here approaching old age*
said'nth'house	they'll drink this animal's blood
said'nth'house	*between these stooping shoulders*
said'nth'house	THERE, TRULY THEY SAID IN THIS HOUSE
	I stand here approaching old age
said'nth'house	These shall stand as suitable totems:
said'nth'house	*among these topmost white blossoms*
said'nth'house	The short-snake
said'nth'house	*I stand here approaching old age*
said'nth'house	the young will use as they walk
said'nth'house	*as the young stalks grow*
said'nth'house	there amongst the grass clumps
said'nth'house	*they'll live to see white hair as they walk*
said'nth'house	he suddenly lifted his head

said'nth'house

said'nth'house

Even though the young become spirits

said'nth'house

they'll regain consciousness as they walk

said'nth'house

When the young take on my body

said'nth'house

the four parts of their days

said'nth'house

they'll reach and enter as they walk

said'nth'house

And what totems shall they use?

said'nth'house

The long bull-snake

said'nth'house

the young will use as they walk

said'nth'house

there amongst the grasses

said'nth'house

he suddenly lifted his head

said'nth'house

the long bull-snake

said'nth'house

they'll use as they walk

said'nth'house

And even though the young become spirits

said'nth'house

they'll regain consciousness as they walk

said'nth'house

and the four parts of their days

said'nth'house

they'll reach and enter as they walk

said'nth'house

And what totems shall they use?

said'nth'house

The black-snake

said'nth'house

they'll use as they walk

said'nth'house

there amongst the grasses

said'nth'house

he suddenly lifted his head

said'nth'house

the black-snake

said'nth'house

Even though the young become spirits

said'nth'house

they'll regain consciousness as they walk

said'nth'house

and the four parts of their days

said'nth'house

they'll reach and enter as they walk

said'nth'house

And what totems will they use?

said'nth'house

The rattlesnake

said'nth'house

there amongst the grasses

said'nth'house

he lies buzzing nearby

said'nth'house

the rattler

said'nth'house

Even though the young become spirits

said'nth'house

they'll regain consciousness as they walk

said'nth'house

The rattlesnake

said'nth'house

hissing and hissing

said'nth'house

Beneath their feet

said'nth'house

he stands rattling and rattling

said'nth'house

Toward their necks

said'nth'house

he stands rattling and rattling

said'nth'house

Toward the east wind

said'nth'house

he stands rattling and rattling

said'nth'house

Toward the west wind

said'nth'house

he stands rattling and rattling

said'nth'house

    Toward the north wind

said'nth'house

    he stands rattling and rattling

said'nth'house

    Even though the young become spirits

said'nth'house

    they'll regain consciousness as they walk

said'nth'house

    When the young take on my body

said'nth'house

    the four parts of their days

said'nth'house

    they'll reach and enter as they walk

said'nth'house

    Those beautiful days

said'nth'house

    they'll reach and enter as they walk

said'nth'house

— Barbara Tedlock's version, after Francis La Flesche

TEPEHUA THOUGHT-SONGS

(1-3)

THOUGHT-SONG ONE

Knowing that the music knows

what those will give to Thought,
for whom it's needed

or where it will be entering & who
will ask for pardon

just as the music knows what will be played there.

Where it was going to be present
is where someone was going to a poor friend's home to visit

because he wants them to be looking out for him
because he wants them giving what he needs for living

that's what they did when giving us this light
when they were giving us commandments in this world

For way out there he'll use the thought they gave him
with which he'll enter in the place where he's arriving

& with it he will then begin his doings
& do it where he first went for a visit.

Thought-Song Two

Thought was

& though it had been
still remains

or it was hardly born when
boys & girls were.

Though they weren't Old Ones
they found their way with it —

so Thought was given them
so life was by their fathers.

When the music starts

it tells about the time Thought entered
it wants to speak about its happiness

to grasp the music way out there
knowing where it is

& knowing where to enter now
once it had gotten where its fathers were
it greeted them.

THOUGHT-SONG THREE

When they play like that where everyone is
everyone is

& everyone is seeing what is being done there
& what these ones are doing moving.

In that place some are coming in between
& moving things   asking favor for it.

This song is how the midwives & curers used to sing
this is how they did it

& the reason for their being there
& being asked for favor & forgiveness.

The asking of it from those there
is the same as what is played there

& what is spoken there
& done there

& the only reason that they play this music.

— *Translation by Charles Boilès, with working by Jerome Rothenberg*

From THE HAKO: A PAWNEE CEREMONY
(by Tahirussawichi)

THE MORNING STAR AND THE NEW-BORN DAWN

Explanation by the Ku'rahus

Now all have risen and have received the breath of the new life just born, all the powers above, all things below. Kawas has stood and spoken in the lodge; the Ku'rahus has heard and understood; the Son is awake and stands with the Ku'rahus awaiting the coming of dawn. The Ku'rahus has sent the server outside the lodge to watch for the morning star. We stand at the west and wait its coming. When it appears he sings the following song:

SONG
Words and Music

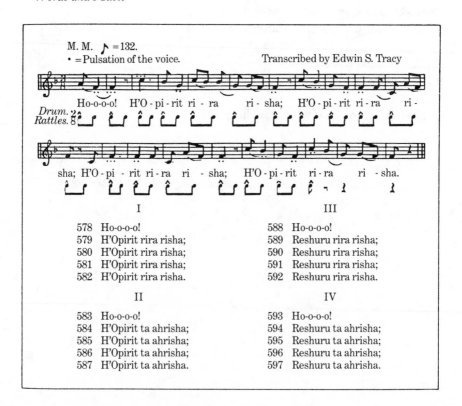

I		III	
578	Ho-o-o-o!	588	Ho-o-o-o!
579	H'Opirit rira risha;	589	Reshuru rira risha;
580	H'Opirit rira risha;	590	Reshuru rira risha;
581	H'Opirit rira risha;	591	Reshuru rira risha;
582	H'Opirit rira risha.	592	Reshuru rira risha.

II		IV	
583	Ho-o-o-o!	593	Ho-o-o-o!
584	H'Opirit ta ahrisha;	594	Reshuru ta ahrisha;
585	H'Opirit ta ahrisha;	595	Reshuru ta ahrisha;
586	H'Opirit ta ahrisha;	596	Reshuru ta ahrisha;
587	H'Opirit ta ahrisha.	597	Reshuru ta ahrisha.

578 Ho-o-o! An introductory exclamation.
579 H'Opirit rira risha.
    h', the symbol of breath, breathing forth life.
    Opirit, the Morning Star.
    rira, coming; approaching toward one.
    risha, something seen at a great distance; it seems to appear and then
        to be lost, to disappear. The word conveys the picture of a
        gradual advance, as from a great distance, where the object was
        scarcely discernable, to a nearer point of view, but still distant.
580, 581, 582 See line 579.

Explanation by the Ku'rahus

We sing this song slowly with reverent feeling, for we are singing of very sacred things.

The Morning Star is one of the lesser powers. Life and strength and fruitfulness are with the Morning Star. We are reverent toward it. Our fathers performed sacred ceremonies in its honor.

The Morning Star is like a man, he is painted red all over; that is the color of life. He is clad in leggings and a robe is wrapped about him. On his head is a soft downy eagle's feather, painted red. This feather represents the soft, light cloud that is high in the heavens, and the red is the touch of a ray of the coming sun. The soft, downy feather is the symbol of breath and life.

The star comes from a great distance, too far away for us to see the place where it starts. At first we can hardly see it; we lose sight of it, it is so far off; then we see it again, for it is coming steadily toward us all the time. We watch it approach; it comes nearer and nearer; its light grows brighter and brighter.

This is the meaning of this stanza, and the star comes as we sing it four times.

Translation of Second Stanza

583 H-o-o-o! An introductory exclamation.
584 H'Opirit ta ahrisha.
    h', the symbol of breath, life.
    Opirit, the Morning Star.
    ta, approaching.
    ahrisha, coming still nearer, but at the same time disappearing. The

word conveys the picture of the morning star by its increased brilliancy coming nearer, and then fading, disappearing in the light of day.

585, 586, 587 See line 584.

Explanation by the Ku'rahus

As we sing this stanza the Morning Star comes still nearer and now we see him standing there in the heavens, a strong man shining brighter and brighter. The soft plume in his hair moves with the breath of the new day, and the ray of the sun touches it with color. As he stands there so bright, he is bringing us strength and new life.

As we look upon him he grows less bright, he is receding, going back to his dwelling place whence he came. We watch him vanishing, passing out of our sight. He has left with us the gift of life which Tira'wa atius sent him to bestow.

We sing this stanza four times.

Translation of Third Stanza

588   Ho-o-o-o! An introductory exclamation.
589   Reshuru rira risha
      Reshuru, the Dawn.
      rira, coming toward one.
      risha, something scarcely to be seen because of its distance; it eludes,
          seems to appear and then to disappear.
590, 591, 592 See line 589.

Explanation by the Ku'rahus

As we sing this stanza we are still standing at the west of the lodge, looking through the long passageway toward the east. Now in the distance we see the Dawn approaching; it is coming, coming along the path of the Morning Star. It is a long path and as the Dawn advances along this path sometimes we catch sight of it and then again we lose it, but all the time it is coming nearer.

The Dawn is new born, its breath has sent new life everywhere, all things stir with the life Tira'wa atius has given this child, his child, whose mother is the Night.

We sing this stanza four times.

Translation of Fourth Stanza

593   Ho-o-o-o! An introductory exclamation.

594   Reshuru ta ahrisha.

      Reshuru, the Dawn.

      ta, approaching, coming,

      ahrisha, coming nearer but only to disappear. The Dawn comes nearer, nearer, grows brighter, but disappears in the brighter light of day.

595, 596, 597 See line 594.

Explanation by the Ku'rahus

As we stand, looking through the long passageway of the lodge, watching and singing, we see the Dawn come nearer and nearer, its brightness fills the sky, the shadowy forms on the earth are becoming visible. As we watch, the Dawn, like the Morning Star, recedes. It is following the star, going back to the place whence it came, to its birthplace.

The day is close behind, advancing along the path of the Morning Star and the Dawn, and, as we watch, the Dawn vanishes from our sight.

We sing this song four times.

    — Recorded and translated, 1898–1902, by Alice C. Fletcher,
      assisted by James R. Murie

THE 12TH HORSE SONG OF FRANK MITCHELL (BLUE)

Navajo

Key: wnn N nnnn N gahn   hawuNnawu   nngobaheegwing

Some are & are going to my howinouse baheegwing hawuNnawu N
   nngahn baheegwing
Some are & are going to my howinouse baheegwing hawuNnawu N
nngahn   baheegwing
Some are & some are gone to my howinouse nnaht bahyee nahtgwing
   buhtzzm bahyee noohwinnnGUUH

Because I was (N gahn) I was the boy raised Ng the dawn (n)(n) but some
   are & are gowing to my howinouse baheegwing
& by going from the house the bluestone hoganome but some are & are
   gone to my howinow baheegwing
& by going from the house the shahyNshining hoganome but some are &
   are gone to my howinow baheeGWING
& by going from the swollenouse my breath has blown but some are & are
   going to my howinouse baheegwing
& by going from the house the hohly honganome but some are & are gone
   to my howinow baheegwing ginng ginnng
& from the place of precious cloth we walk (p)pon (N gahn) but some are
   gone to my howinow baheegwing hawunawwing
with those prayersticks that are blu(u)(u) but some are & are (wnn N) gahn
   to my howinouse baheegwing
with my feathers that are b(lu)u but some are & are going to my howinouse
   baheegwing
with my spirit horses that are b(lu)u but some are & are going to my
   howinouse baheegwing
with my spirit horses that are blue & dawn but some are & are gone to my
   howinow baheegwing nngnnng
with those spirit (hawuN) horses that are bluestone (nawu) but some are
   & are gone to my howinow baheegwing
with those hoganorses that are bluestone but some are & are going to my
   howinouse baheegwing
with cloth of ever(ee)ee kind tgaahn & draw them on nahhtnnn but some
   are & are gone to my howinow baheegwing

with jewels of ever(ee)ee kind tgaahn & draw them on nahhtnnn but some are & are going to my howinouse baheegwing

with hoganorses of ever(ee)ee kind to go & draw them on nahhtnnn but some are & are going to my howinouse baheegwing

with sheep of evree(ee)(ee) kind tgaahn & draw them on nahhtnnn but some are & are going to my howinouse baheegwing

with cattle of every kind (N gahn) to go & draw them on nahhtnnnn but some are & are going to my howinouse baheegwing

with men of evree(ee)(ee) kind tgaahn & draw them on nahhtnnn but some are & are going to my howinouse baheegwing

now to my howinome of precious cloth in my backroom Ngahhnn where Nnnn but some are & are going to my howinouse baheegwing

in my house of precious cloth we walk (p)pon (N gahn) where Nnnn but some are & are going to my howinouse baheegwing

& everything that's gone before (mmmm) more we walk (p)pon but some are & are going to my howinouse baheegwing

& everything that's more & won't be (be!) be poor but some are & some are gone to my howinow baheegwing

& everything that's (nawuN) living to be old & blesst (bhawuN) some are & are going to my howinouse baheegwing

because I am the boy who goes & blesses/blisses to be old but some are & are going to my howinouse baheegwing hawuNnawu N nngahn baheegwinnng

Zzmmmm are & are gone to my howinow baheegwing hawuNnawu N nngahn baheegwing

Zzmmmm are & are going to my howinouse baheegwing hawuNnawu N nngahn baheegwing

Some are & some are gone to my house now naht bahyeee naht nwinnng buht nawuNNN baheegwinnng

THE 13TH HORSE SONG OF FRANK MITCHELL (WHITE)

Navajo

Key: nnnn N N gahn

Some 're lovely N nawu nnnn but some 're & are at my hawuz nawu wnn
   N wnn baheegwing
Some 're lovely N hawu nnnn but some 're & are at my howinow N wnn
   baheegwing
Some 're lovely N nawu nnnn but some are & are at my howzes nawu
   nahht bahyeenwing but bahyeesum nahtgwing

NNNOOOOW because I was (N gahn) I was the boy ingside the dawn but
   some 're at my house now wnn N wnn baheegwing
& by going from the house the wwwideshell howanome but some 're at my
   howinow N wnnn baheegwing
& by going from the house the darkned hoganome but some 're at my
   house N wnn bahhegwing
& by going from the swollen hoganouse my breath has blown but some 're
   at my house N wnn baheegwing
& by going from the house the hloly hoganome but some 're at my house
   N wnn N wnn baheegwingnnng
& from the plays of jewels we walk (naht gahn) (p)pon but some 're at my
   howinow N wnn baheegwing
with prayersticks that are white (nnuhgohn) but some 're at my house N
   wnn baheegwing
with my feathers that are white (mmm gahn) but some 're at my house N
   wnn baheegwing
with my spirit horses that are white (nuhgohn) but some 're at my house
   N wnn bahhegwing
with my spirit horses that are white & dawn (nuhgohn) but some 're at my
   house N wnnn baheegwing
with those spirit horses that are whiteshell nawuNgnnnn but some 're at
   my house N wnn baheegwing
with those howanorses that are whiteshell nawu but some 're at my
   howinouse wnnn baheegwingnnng
wiiiingth jewels of every kind d(go)nN draw them on nahtnnn but some 're
   at my howinow N wnn baheegwing

with cloth of every kind d(go)nN draw them on nahtnnn but some 're at
my howinow N wnn baheegwing
with sheep of every kind d(go)nN draw them on nahtnnn but some 're at
my house N wnn baheegwing
with horses of evree(ee)(ee) kind d(go)nN draw them on nahtnnn but
some 're at my howinow N wnn baheegwing
with cattle of every kind d(go)nN draw them on nahtnnn but some 're at
my howinow N wnn baheegwing
with men of every kind d(go)nN draw them on nahtnnn but some 're at
my house N wnn baheegwing
in my house of precious jewels in my back(acka)room (N gahn) where nnnn
but some 're at my howinow N wnn baheegwing
in this house of precious jewels we walk (p)pon (N gahn) where nnnn but
some 're at my house N wnn baheegwing
& everything that's g(h)one before mmmmore we walk (p)pon but some 're
at my howinow N wnn baheegwing
& everything that's more (   ) won't be (be!) be poor but some 're at my
house N wnn baheegwing
& everything that's now & living to be old & blesst nhawu but some 're at
my howinow N wnnn baheegwing
because I am the boy who blesses/blisses to be old but some 're at my house
N wnn baheegwing

Zzmmmm 're lovely N nawu nnnn but some 're & are at my howinouse
N wnn baheegwing
Zzmmmm 're lovely nawu N nnnn but some 're & are at my house N wnn
baheegwing
Zzmmmm 're lovely N nawu nnnn but some are & are at my howzes nahht
bahyeenahtnwing but nawu nohwun baheegwing

— Total translation by Jerome Rothenberg, with David P. McAllester

A FOURTH SERVICE

Directions: Go to a mountaintop & cry for a vision.

Sioux

THE NET OF MOON: A PAWNEE HAND GAME VISION

Full moonlit night   people
playing the Hand Game in a tent
everyone goes outside to dance
One man gets shakey
then starts crying   hands up
to the moon   (he says):   I felt it
something in my mind
when he went out   it seemed
I would be seeing something
it was coming
we went out   when we were dancing
I suddenly looked up
at the moon   Old Moon looks down
& sees me   & laughs at me
that's when I cried

— English version by Jerome Rothenberg

ESSIE PARRISH IN NEW YORK

Kashia Pomo

It is a test you have to pass.
Then you can learn to heal
with the finger, said Essie
pointing over our heads:
I went thru every test on the way,
that's how come I'm a shaman.
Be careful on the journey, they said,
the journey to heaven. They warned me.
And so I went.
Thru the rolling hills
I walked and walked,
mountains and valleys, and rolling hills,
I walked and walked and walked —
you hear many things there
in those rolling hills and valleys,
and I walked and walked and walked
and walked and walked until
I came to a footbridge,
and on the right side were a whole lot of people
and they were naked and crying out,
how'd you get over there,
we want to get over there too
but we're stuck here,
please come over here and help us cross,
the water's too deep for us —
I didn't pay no attention,
I just walked and walked and walked,
and then I heard an animal, sounded like a huge dog,
and there was a huge dog and next to him a huge lady
wearing blue clothes,
and I decided I had to walk right thru —
I did
and the dog only snarled at me.
Never go back.
I walked and walked and walked

and I came to one only tree
and I walked over to it and looked up at it
and read the message:
Go on, you're half way.
From there I felt better, a little better.
and I walked and walked and walked and walked
and I saw water, huge water —
how to get thru?
I fear it's deep. Very blue water.
But I have to go.
Put out the first foot, then the left,
never use the left hand,
and I passed thru.
Went on and on and on, and I had to enter a place
and there I had to look down:
it was hot and there were people there
and they looked tiny down there in that furnace
running around crying.
I had to enter.
You see, these tests are to teach my people
how to live.
Fire didn't burn me.
And I walked and walked and walked.
On the way you're going to suffer.
And I came to a four-way road
like a cross. Which is the right way?
I already knew.
East is the right way to go to heaven.
North, South, and West are dangerous.
And at this crossroad there was a place in the center.
North you could see beautiful things of the Earth,
hills and fields and flowers and everything beautiful
and I felt like grabbing it
but I turned away.
West was nothing but fog and damp
and I turned away.
South was dark, but there were sounds,
monsters and huge animals. And I turned away and
Eastward I walked and walked and walked
and there were flowers, on both sides of the road,

flowers and flowers and flowers
out of this world.
And there is white light, at the center,
while you are walking.
This is the complicated thing:
my mind changes.
We are the people on the Earth.
We know sorrow and knowledge and faith and talent
and everything.
Now as I was walking there
some places I feel like crying
and some places I feel like talking
and some places I feel like dancing
but I am leaving these behind for the next world.
Then when I entered into that place
I knew:
if you enter heaven
you might have to work.
This is what I saw in my vision.
I don't have to go nowhere to see.
Visions are everywhere.

— English transcription by George Quasha

FOR THE GOD OF PEYOTE

Huichol

FIRST PEYOTE SONG

Wirikota Wirikota
   Where the roses are born
   Where they flower
   Garlands of flowers & wind
    Wirikota
At the foot of Eternal Mountain
   Roses are breathing: breath of the gods
   The mother's moist love: the dew
   & from the peyote's heart fog emerges
   Blue Stag emerges
   Rain comes down
   Blue Stag comes down

   Maize takes root the rose lies open
   & the Rose sings: "I am the Stag"
   & the Stag: "I am the Rose"

And there on the Earth of the Gods they hear singing
   The gods are singing
   The mountains the hills are singing
   & the roses are singing
The song of life in Wirikota only heard in Wirikota
   Eternal song of Life
   Only there
   Only there & heard in Wirikota

SECOND PEYOTE SONG

Highway of roses
Peyote Highway

>   Stretches from here
>   to Wirikota
>   From here to Wirikota
They say you were just passing thru here

>   I'm coming to look for you
>   Coming to look for life
>   Coming to look for more life
& if I'm not your kind of pure

>   (meaning "sinless")
I'm passing thru here myself I'm coming for you

SONG OF AN INITIATE

climbed the blue staircase up to sky
climbed where the roses were opening
>   where roses were speaking

heard nothing   nothing to hear
>   heard silence

i climbed where the roses were singing
>   where the gods were waiting
>   blue staircase up in the sky

but heard nothing   nothing to hear
>   heard silence   silence

Third Peyote Song

Armara passed by. The Sea passed by.
Behind it the gods passed by.
Like flowers the gods trailed behind the Sea.
From where the gods came the placenta spewed forth.
      Gods were born here.
      From the placenta gods were flowing like clouds.
With the clouds the Sacred Place appeared.
      And the Stag appeared in it.
      Then the Stag became cloud.
      The Stag became maize.
Then the Sea spoke.
      Spoke to Southwater Lady.
      Spoke to Northwater Lady.
      Spoke to the Sunset.
      Spoke to the gods of Peyote Country.
And the Blue Stag rose from the Sea.
      And Mhari the Small Stag appeared.
      And the Arrow appeared in the Sea.
      The gods saw it & knew it.
And right next to the Arrow the face & horns of the Stag.
      He had changed into clouds & was raining.
And the Bed of the gods appeared called Ittari.
      And the gods brought the Arrow to Coamil
      & the face & horns of the Stag.
Later the gods stopped to see what was born.
      And Tall Grass was born
      & from it burst a yellow tassel.
The gods came near   loosening the yellow tassel.
      The gods became three yellow rays.
Anointed they would be looking like the maizeland
      this was the pollen of the maize.
The gods said: Tall Grass will be the Stag's cradle.
      And Marra Yuavi the Blue Stag appeared.
And in the five regions of the Earth Blue Stags were appearing.

HOW THE VIOLIN WAS BORN: A PEYOTE ACCOUNT

CEDAR CEDAR was born.
Born among stones & rocks.
                    BIG STAG made him.
                    BIG BRAIN worked him.
But CEDAR CEDAR didn't have a soul.
Heavy was his heart. His heart was silent.

Then Tahomatz the BIG BRAIN
                    sent Aimari the BIRD pure & fuckless
Aimari came singing: entered the tree
                    & became its pith.
                    And the tree's heart filled with music.
& CEDAR CEDAR sang. Quivered to caresses from the Wind.

— English versions by Jerome Rothenberg

THE FLOWERING WAR

Aztec

A Song of Chalco

In the sedge beyond Chalco
the god raised stones for his house

Green thrushes sang in the fire,
glowing, changing to roses
Over these ruins, these diamonds
the quetzal-bird
measured its voice into song

The river trembled with flowers, it
circled through flowers of jade,
deep perfumes

Lost among flowers
the tzinitzcan waited,
making their colors
its own

& the quetzal-bird
sang a new measure
The quetzal-bird ruled them

Being a poet
I sing: my song
grafts buds to these branches
Forests of flowers
rise, deep
fragrant perfumes

The flowers are dancing:
the deep perfume
moves to the beat of a drum

Dew globules
thicken with life
& run down the stems

The father stiffens
with pleasure
            A green sun
moves through the sky
In a jade urn
beautifully clothed
he sinks down

Throat bound by a
necklace of turquoise
While the flowers
rain shadows of color

Oh chieftains who sing
with me, chieftains
bringing him joy:
a new song to rise
from these flowers

The full flowers
tremble, the
flowers grow heavy
with Spring
bathed in sunlight

The sun's heart
throbs in the cup
His flesh
is the darkness of flowers

Who would not cry for
such flowers, oh
giver of life? who
would not rest in your hands
that hold death?
Opening buds & corollas
an endless thirst in the sun

I have gone from your house, I
sing in a dark heavy flower
My song fills rivers with petals

Oh day of libations, oh
flowers blown through the land
Oh deep perfumes

The god has opened his flowers:
flowers born in his house
are alive in this soil

A Song in Praise of the Chiefs

Here death is born among flowers:
the men of Tlapalla
our fathers
return to the earth

For this the song rises
with weeping
The dead take root in the sky
& the music
sticks in my throat, seeing
them lost in that city of shadows

As if a god spoke
the ordinance fell from the sky
You fulfilled it
dying, leaving
us orphaned & sad

Something inhuman
the way things fell out

The mind gets tired of asking:
who knows
if the life-giver
thinks of us now

Oh day of tears
& silence
when even the heart of our mother
is sad
Where have they taken the chiefs

Only a memory now:
the sadness breaks through my heart
when I think of Itzcoatl

No
I don't want to remember him
tired or weary
his face like a god's

Thinking
maybe he lives
in the life-giver's house
No one
braver than him
left
to grow old on this earth

Where can we go
Ah
the sadness breaks through my heart

They were carried away
hidden awhile in the earth
Warriors rulers & chiefs
vanished
leaving us orphaned

For this
the chieftains are sad

Where will my heart go

In search of Axayacatl
who left us here

Chanting the dirge
for Tezozomoctli

The chiefs who ruled here before us
handed this town
to the dogs

What sadness:
who knows if it ever will end
or grow less

Who knows if the grief
I squeeze through my lips
can be borne

A SONG FOR THE EAGLES & JAGUARS

I'd have these eagles & jaguars
embrace
till it sets their shields rattling

The rulers
plot at the banquet
They plan
to take prisoners

Scattering flowers
raining flowers of battle
over our heads
to placate the gods

This is the place of turmoil:
the place where we march
in disorder, place
of hot war, hunting
glory in back of our shields

This is the city of dangers
lost in the dust

The flowering war
will not end
We endure here, trapped
on the banks
of this river
The jaguars' flowers
show their corollas

This is the city of dangers:
dust from
the jaguars' garden
heavy with perfumes

Flowers drop on our heads
from the battlefield, raining
their fragrances on us

Oh soldiers
hunting glory & fame
Terrible flowers, oh
flowers alive in the heart

Flowers
torn from the battlefield
under the cries of war
& the chieftains
murdered for glory & fame

The eagles' shields
twist in the flags
of jaguars: armor
covered with feathers
Waves of plumed helmets
color of gold

The men of Chalcas
fell in the waves
They lie in mud
while the others
move in a line

through the turmoil
of war

The arrow snaps
with a cry
The obsidian point
turns to dust, staining
our shields
The water above us

THE EAGLE & THE JAGUAR

No one so strong, no one
so lovely
in all the things of this world

As the eagle
    ready for flight
& the jaguar
    whose heart
is a mountain

See how they carry
my shield now
These slaves

— *English versions by Jerome Rothenberg*

what happened to a young man
in a place where he turned to water

White Mountain Apache

1

no sleep for twelve days

then found himself in a circle of water girls

"come dance with us"

water people
they say
were dancing with him

ahead of the water they came
they were water
the water's soft feathers were theirs

closer they came
and to the very end of the water
closer and closer
their hands were electric

fog people
danced with him they say
where the fog was a wall
they came
they were fog
the fog's soft feathers
were theirs

closer they came
to the very end of the fog
closer and closer
their hands were electric

the moon before him they say
high as a woman's head
or no higher

the sun before him they say
no higher than a man's head
or as high

"come dance with us"

again no sleep for twelve days

2
he woke up and saw
only one had stayed
(remembered stumbling
over her foot in the dance)

they say those two
went away
to where the country is great with maize
there they sat down

they went
where the country grows beautiful pumpkins
there they lay down

great maize
         strong roots
                big stalks
big pumpkin
        long tendrils
               wide leaves

where the sun rises
as soon as it sets

yellow-top pumpkin
        big-bellied

strong maize
        with a bushy tassel

pollen
    and
       dew

3

he came back here
where people were living
his mother was angry but she forgave him
he went and hunted the deer with his brother

— English version by Anselm Hollo, after Pliny Earle Goddard

poem to be recited every 8 years
while eating unleavened tamales

Aztec

1

the flower
  my heart
        it opened
at midnight
  that lordly hour

she has arrived
        Tlaçolteotl
          our mother
            goddess desire

2

in the birth house
in the flower place
on the day called 'one flower'
  the maize god is born

in the vapor and rain place
  where we go angling for jewel-fish

  where we too make our young

3

soon day   red sky
quechol-birds in the flowers

4

down here on earth
  you rise in the market place and say

I am the lord Quetzalcoatl

let there be gladness among the flowering trees
   and the quechol-bird tribes
who are the souls of the brave

may they rejoice
   hear the word of our lord
the quechol-bird's word

'your brother whom we mourn
   will never be killed again
never again will the poison dart strike him'

5

maize flowers
   white and yellow
I have brought from the flower place

see there is the lord of the jewel land
   playing ball in his holy field

   there he is the old dog god
                  Xolotl

6

now go look if Piltzintecutli
   lord fertility himself
has yet lain down in the dark house
            in the house where it grows dark

o Piltzintli Piltzintli
   yellow feathers
you glue all over yourself

on the ball-playing field you lie down
   and in the dark house where it grows dark

7

here comes a merchant

a vassal of Xochiquetzal
    mistress of Cholula

(heart o heart
    I fear the maize god is still on his way)

a merchant a man from Chacalla
    sells turquoise spikes for your ears
and turquoise bands for your arms

8

the sleeper the sleeper he sleeps

with my hand I have rolled him to sleep

9

here
        the woman
here
        am I
here
                        asleep

— *English version by Anselm Hollo, from Eduard Seler*

HEAVEN AND HELL
(by Nalungiaq)

Eskimo (Inuit)

And when we die at last,
we really know very little about what happens then.
But people who dream
have often seen the dead appear to them
just as they were in life.
Therefore we believe life does not end here on earth.

We have heard of three places where men go after death:
There is the Land of the Sky, a good place
where there is no sorrow and fear.
There have been wise men who went there
and came back to tell us about it:
They saw people playing ball, happy people
who did nothing but laugh and amuse themselves.
What we see from down here in the form of stars
are the lighted windows of the villages of the dead
in the Land of the Sky.

Then there are other worlds of the dead underground:
Way down deep is a place just like here
except on earth you starve
and down there they live in plenty.
The caribou graze in great herds
and there are endless plains
with juicy berries that are nice to eat.
Down there too, everything
is happiness and fun for the dead.

But there is another place, the Land of the Miserable,
right under the surface of the earth we walk on.
There go all the lazy men who were poor hunters,
and all women who refused to be tattooed,
not caring to suffer a little to become beautiful.
They had no life in them when they lived

so now after death they must squat on their haunches
with hanging heads, bad-tempered and silent,
and live in hunger and idleness
because they wasted their lives.
Only when a butterfly comes flying by
do they lift their heads
(as young birds open pink mouths uselessly after a gnat)
and when they snap at it, a puff of dust
comes out of their dry throats.

— English version by Edward Field, after Knud Rasmussen

From THE BOOK OF CHILAM BALAM: A CHAPTER OF
QUESTIONS & ANSWERS

Maya

13 Etznab was the day when the land was established. 13 Cheneb was the day when they measured the cathedral off by paces: the dark house of instruction, the cathedral in heaven. It was also measured off by paces here on earth. . . .

Mani is the base of the land. Campeche is the tip of the wing of the land. Calkini is the base of the wing of the land. Itzmal is the middle of the wing of the land. Zaci is the tip of the wing of the land. Conkal is the head of the land.

In the middle of the town of Tihoo is the cathedral, the fiery house, the mountainous house, the dark house, for the benefit of God the Father, God the Son and God the Holy Spirit.

Who enters into the House of God? Father, it is the one named Ix-Kalem.

What day did the Virgin conceive? Father, 4 Oc was the day when she conceived.

What day did he come forth from her womb? On 3 Oc he came forth.

What day did he die? On 1 Cimi he died. Then he entered the tomb on 1 Cimi.

What entered his tomb? Father, a coffer of stone entered his tomb.

What entered into his thigh? Father, it was the red arrow-stone. It entered into the precious stone of the world, there in heaven.

And his arm? Father, the arrow-stone; and that it might be warmed in the sun, it entered the red living rock in the east. Then it came to the north and entered into the white living rock. After that it entered the black living rock in the west. Also it entered the yellow living rock in the south.

Son, how many deep hollows are there? These are the holes for playing the flute.

Son, where is the cenote? All are drenched with its water. There is no gravel on its bottom; a bow is inserted over its entrance. It is the church.

Son, where are the first marriages? The strength of the King and the strength of the other head-chiefs fail because of them, and my strength because of them also. It is bread.

Son, have you seen the green water-holes in the rock? There are two of them; a cross is raised between them. They are a man's eyes.

Son, where are the first baptized ones? One has no mother, but has a bead collar and little bells. It is the small yellow corn.

Son, where is the food which bursts forth, and the fold of the brain and the lower end of that which is bloated, and the dried fruit? It is the gizzard of a turkey.

Son, bring me that which hooks the sky and the hooked tooth. They are a deer and a gopher.

Son, where is the old woman with buttocks seven palms wide, the woman with a dark complexion? It is a certain kind of squash.

Son, show me the light complexioned woman with her skirt bound up who sells white flints. It is another kind of squash.

Son, bring me two yellow animals, one to be well boiled, and one shall have its throat cut. I shall drink its blood also. It is a yellow deer and a green calabash full of chocolate.

My sons, bring me here a score of those who bear flat stones and two married ones. They are a quail and a dove.

Son, bring me a cord of three strands, I wish to see it. It is an iguana.

Son, bring me that which stops the hole in the sky and the dew, the nine layers of the whole earth. It is a very large maize tortilla.

Son, have you seen the old man who is like an overturned tortilla pan? He has a large double chin which reaches the ground. It is a turkey-cock.

Son, bring me the old farmers, their beards come to their navels, also their wives. It is a muddy arrowroot.

Bring to me here with them the women who guard the fields, white complexioned women. I will remove their skirts and eat them. It is a root like a turnip.

Son, bring me the great gallants that I may view them. Perhaps they will not dance badly when I see them. It is a turkey-cock.

Son, where is the first collector? The answer is to undress, to take off one's shirt, cape, hat and shoes.

Son, where was it that you passed? Did you pass to the high rocky knoll which slopes down to the door of heaven, where there is a gate in the wall? Did you see men in front of you, coming side by side? A god called Ninth Heaven and the first town councillor are there. It is the pupils of the eyes and any pair of eyes.

Son, have you seen the rain of God? It passed beneath the mountains of God; it entered beneath the mountains of God, where there is a cross on the savannah. There will be a ring in the sky where the water of God has passed.

Son, where has the water of God passed when it comes forth from the living rock? Father, from a man's head and all a man's teeth, passes through the opening of his throat and comes forth beneath.

Son, whom did you see on the road just now?

. . . .

Son, what did you do with your companions who were coming close behind you? Here are my companions. I have not left them. I await the judgment of God when I shall come to die. This is a man's shadow.

Son, whom did you*see on the road? Did you see some old men accompanied by their boys? Father, here are the old men I saw on the road. They are with me; they do not leave me. This is his great toe with the little toes.

Son, where did you see the old women carrying their step-children and their other boys? Father, here they are. They are still with me so that I can eat. I can not leave them yet. It is my thumb and the other fingers.

Son, where did you pass by a water-gutter? Father, here is the water-gutter, it is right with me. This is my dorsal furrow.

Son, where did you see an old man astride a horse across a water-gutter? Father, here is the old man. He is still with me. My shoulders are the horse on which you say the old man sits astride.

Son this is the old man with you of which you spoke: it is manifest truth and justice.

Son, go get the heart of the stone and the liver of the earth. I have seen one of them lying on its back, and one lying on its face as though it were going into hell. They are a Mexican Agouti and a Spotted Agouti, also the first local chief and the first Town Councillor. As for the heart of the stone, it is the tips of the teeth; and that which covers the opening of hell is a sweet potato and another kind of root to eat.

Son, go and bring me here the girl with the watery teeth. Her hair is twisted into a tuft; she is very beautiful. Fragrant shall her odor be when I remove her skirt and her other garment. It will give me pleasure to see her. Fragrant is her odor and her hair is twisted into a tuft. It is an ear of green corn cooked in a pit.

Son, then you shall go and get an old man the herb that is by the sea. The old man is the rushes, and the herb is a crab.

Son, then you shall go and get the stones from the bottom of a forest pond. It is a *tzac*-fish.

Son, then you shall bring here the stones of the savannah. It is a quail.

Also bring the first sorcerers, there are four of them. They are the gopher, the Spotted Agouti, the Mexican Agouti and the peccary.

Son, then go and get the thigh of the earth. It is the cassava.

Son, go and bring here the green gallant and the green singer. It is a wild turkey hen and cock.

Son, you shall bring your daughter that I may see her in the sun tomorrow. First the smaller one shall be brought and behind her shall come the larger one. Her hair shall be bound with a feathered band; she shall wear a head-scarf. I will take off her head-scarf. Also the Town Councillor is behind her.

Son, then go and get a cluster of Plumeria flowers widely separated.

They should be there where the sun is tomorrow. What is meant is roasted corn and honey.

Here I have rolled something that you have which is flat and round. There are many rolls of it in the cave where you live. Then you shall roll it here that we may see it, when it is time to eat. It is a fried egg.

— Translation by Ralph L. Roys

her elegy

Papago

I'd run about
on the desert
me a young girl fierce to see
whatever I could. My heart
was not cool.
     When there was no Coyote
I saw Coyote
     then a spider
on the house-post, the central one,
stopped to look at me, just
ready to speak.
I made a song, about Coyote.
A shaman sang over me, to find out.
And when he spoke Father said — No
one shaman in the house is enough —
my body already sheltered
the divining crystals, growing in my body.
The shaman bent over me he sucked them one by one
out of my breast
     they were long
like the joint of my pinkie, white and moving like worms
o the shaman said See I've taken them out
before they got big
     He made a hole in a giant cactus
and put them away, inside

— English version by Armand Schwerner, after Ruth Underhill

THEY WENT TO THE MOON MOTHER

Zuni

ho-ho-ho he-he-he
ho-ho-ho he-he-he

"Rejoice holy bundles, sacred bundles!
By means of your wise thoughts
there in the east your Moon Mother spoke,
                     gave her word
when we went up there with the dragonfly,
                     entered upon her road.
Rejoice! You will be granted many blessings
                     flowing silt."
The Two Stars are saying this to all the sacred bundles
                     here now mmmmmm.
The Lying Star says this to all the sacred bundles
                     here now mmmmmm.

Maskers, rainmakers soaking the earth with rain
making lightning, thundering, coming, coming
stretching, stretching, stretching
                     hey-o hey-e neya, hey-o hey-e neya
                     awiyo-o heyena, awiyo-o heyeney
                     awiyo-o heye, awiyo-o
                     hahaha iihi hiya hiya
                     ha haha iihihi hiya hiya
                     hapiime, hapiime

By the Moon Mother's word
from the Middle Place all the way to Dawn lake
                     your paths will be complete.
                     You will reach old age.
I the masker say this to you the people
                     here now mmmmmm.

— *Translation by Barbara Tedlock*

four poems
(by Ray Young Bear)

Mesquaki (Sauk & Fox)

my reflection
seems upside-down

even when the daylight pushes
my shadow into
the ground

it is like that

*

this little house swallows
her prayer
through the green fire
and stone

i disappear
into the body of a mouse
sleeping over the warm
ashes

*

i am walking and i
notice that the road
seems bare

some of the stones
are missing

ahead is a toad
throwing stones
from his fingers

whatever thought
he is following
we are
following

*

through the cracks
along the walls of this
house

the sun reaches its peak

our dishes begin
to breathe

dance of the rain gods

Cora

now the thinkers our old ones remember
    the gods known as dancers

let's call the dancers
talking and thinking
                call them to come
            from their far away sky place
call for the rain gods
              explain the problem

the dancers receive the message
they put on their garments their crowns
their life-giving feathers
black as night
              white as cloud

veil their faces with beads
    talking
their faces are radiant

they take the great cross the great rattle
far away in their sky place
they concentrate
on the high east

then they rise high in the east
radiant as life in their feathers
they come down to talk to the earth

see the life-giving trees
    stand up
line their road

lovely fig trees and tuka trees
lovely anapa trees by their road

lovely the reed
　　rising
full of life the banana tree

life-giving reed
　　　　　　　there it stands

then the dancers appear
　　down east
stopping to wait for mother and elder brother

'dance you gods
　　　　　　bring the rain down
dance you dancers
　　　　　　　come down to your earth'
they wait for the fiddles
　　for the fiddlers to play
　　　　　　　　　now they hear them
the sound of their fiddles
　　sound known as 'words'

they listen to it
　　　　　　they start dancing

now it resounds on their earth
　　the dance of the 'dancers'
　　　　　　　who call themselves rain gods

and when it is over
they go
talking they go
　　west
to see Tsevimoa
the goddess
　　who sits on her rainstone
fade in the west
with all their thoughts

and the thinkers our old ones
leave them there
in their thought's power
turn back east to the altar
ending
     a good day's work

     — *English version by Anselm Hollo*

POSTLUDES

A KALAPUYA PROPHECY

In the old time, by the forks of the Santiam,
a Kalapuya man lay down in an alder-grove
and dreamed his farthest dream. When he woke in the night
he told the people, "This earth beneath us
was all black, all black in my dream!"
No man could say what it meant,
that dream of our greening earth.
We forgot. But then the white men came,
those iron farmers, and we saw them plow up the ground,
the camas meadow, the little prairies by the Santiam,
and we knew we would enter their dream
of the earth plowed black forever.

— *English version by Jarold Ramsey*

THE REMOVAL

Seminole

They are taking us beyond Miami
They are taking us beyond the Caloosa River
They are taking us to the end of our tribe
They are taking us to Palm Beach, coming back beside Okeechobee
    Lake
They are taking us to an old town in the west

— *Translation by Frances Densmore*

HUNGER
(by Samik)

Eskimo (Inuit)

You, stranger, who only see us happy and free of care,
If you knew the horrors we often have to live through
you would understand our love of eating and singing and dancing.
There is not one among us
who hasn't lived through a winter of bad hunting
when many people starved to death.
We are never surprised to hear
that someone has died of starvation — we are used to it.
And they are not to blame: Sickness comes,
or bad weather ruins hunting,
as when a blizzard of snow hides the breathing holes.

I once saw a wise old man hang himself
because he was starving to death
and preferred to die in his own way.
But before he died he filled his mouth with seal bones,
for that way he was sure to get plenty of meat
in the land of the dead.

Once during the winter famine
a woman gave birth to a child
while people lay round about her dying of hunger.
What could the baby want with life here on earth?
And how could it live when its mother herself
was dried up with starvation?
So she strangled it and let it freeze.
And later on ate it to keep alive —
Then a seal was caught and the famine was over,
so the mother survived.
But from that time on she was paralysed
because she had eaten part of herself.

This is what can happen to people.
We have gone through it ourselves

and know what one may come to, so we do not judge them.
And how would anyone who has eaten his fill and is well
be able to understand the madness of hunger?
We only know that we all want so much to live!

— English version by Edward Field, from Knud Rasmussen

THE CRIER
(by Philip Kahclamet)

Wishram Chinook

In the morning he steps out,
      he intones his words:
"This is Sunday morning,
      You people should know —
"I don't have to come round this morning
          to tell you —
          that you people should put on all your trappings;
          that you will come to church.
"You know
      that we were put here by the Great Spirit
      We have to worship him.
"I am getting to my old age.
      Some of you will have to take my place
         when I'm gone.
"When you hear the drum this morning,
      it's calling you
         to worship the Great Spirit.
"That's
      where all our ancestors went;
         if you go by the old religion,
            you will see them
               when you leave the earth.

"You know
    we are going to have to leave our flesh in the ground;
       only our souls go;
         and we'll be sure
            to meet our ancestors.
"You people know
    that we didn't come here ourselves.
      He who created us is above.
"He put us here.
    We have to be
      where we are today.
      "Me — I'm not telling you this myself
    I'm only giving you the revelations
      which I've learned from somebody else.
"When you hear these drums,
    go.
"We are Nadidánwit here,
    this is our country.
"These white people came;
    they brought Christianity.
"It's not for us.
    The Christianity was brought here for the white people only.
"The white people cheated us out of our country.
    So don't follow them,
      whatever they teach you.

"SHuSúgli was a Jew;
    he was not Nadidánwit,
      and he was not for the Nadidánwit.
"SHuSúgli i ju-i-kiXaX.
"Yaxdau i-pendikast,
        i-käthlik,
        'Presbyterian,'
        'Methodist,'
        kwadaw i-Sik,
    k'aya amXáwiXa,
      k'aya t'únwit amdúXa."

      — *Transcription from English & Wishram by Dell Hymes*

THREE GHOST DANCE SONGS

•

My children,
when at first I liked the whites,
I gave them fruits,
I gave them fruits.

•

I'yehe! my children —
my children,
we have rendered them desolate.
The whites are crazy — Ahe'yuhe'yu!

•

We shall live again.
We shall live again.

—*Translations by James Mooney*

COMMENTARIES

A BREAKDOWN BY LANGUAGE & TRIBE

THE COMMENTARIES

Page 3   WHAT THE INFORMANT SAID TO FRANZ BOAS IN 1920

SOURCE: F. Boas, *Keresan Texts,* Publications of the American Ethnological Society, Volume 8, 1928.

A FURTHER CAUTION. To the reader who imagines that a book like this can really hold the spirit-of-a-people, etc., the editor testifies that in instance after instance the best remains untold or its powers reserved for those who "have ears to hear," etc. But the rest of us have to begin somewhere.

Page 4   THANK YOU: A POEM IN SEVENTEEN PARTS

SOURCE: Written down at Allegany Reservation (Steamburg, New York), summer of 1968; first published in *El Corno Emplumado,* Number 30, Mexico, 1969, pages 125–131, "with a note on the process by Jerome Rothenberg."

J.R.'s note for the original publication reads: ". . . The poems themselves are translations of the traditional thanking formulas that the Seneca 'longhouse people' (followers of the Code of Handsome Lake [the late 18th-century Iroquois prophet]) use for opening of all group functions. The wording is R.J.J.'s, also by & large the pauses; I mostly followed his acute use of periods (he was writing it down as 'prose' alongside me), to mark out what appear as lines in this reading. I also asked questions in the process, but in general learned to leave well enough alone. No matter. Johnny John's a singer & songmaker in his own right, absolutely fluent in Seneca & with a poet's delight in getting the right combinations in whatever language. When he wasn't happy with what we were translating from the taped Seneca, he'd tell me: 'Play back just a little. I want to word it just the way it says there.' Which was how it became a poem in English."

Page 10   THE ARTIST

SOURCE: Denise Levertov, *O Taste & See,* New Directions, 1964. Based on Spanish translation from *Códice Matritense de la Real Academia de la Historia* (Nahuatl texts of the 16th-century informants of Bernardino de Sahagún).

Page 11   THEREFORE I MUST TELL THE TRUTH

SOURCE: Washington Matthews, *Navaho Legends,* American Folk-Lore Society Memoirs, Volume 5, 1897, pages 58–59.

"Old Torlino, a priest of *hozóni hatál* [= Blessing Way], sent a son to school at Carlisle, and when the young man returned he no doubt imparted to his father much that he had learned there. The writer sent for the old man to get from him the myth of *hozóni hatál.* Torlino began: 'I know the white men say the world is round, and that it floats in the air. My tale says the world is flat, and that there are five worlds, one above another. You will not believe my tale, then, and perhaps you do not want to hear it.' Being assured that the tale was earnestly desired, he proceeded. 'I shall tell you the truth, then. I shall tell you all that I heard from the old men who taught me, as well as I can now remember. Why should I lie to you?' And then he made the interesting asseveration which is here literally translated." (W.M., *ibid.*)

Page 11   SONG OF THE BALD EAGLE

SOURCE: Lewis Henry Morgan, *The Indian Journals, 1859–1862,* University of Michigan Press, 1959, page 190.

The stress on the "real" is no fluke but central to a whole range of native thought & poetics. And the sense of the problematic/elusive nature of that reality comes across in related works; e.g., the Pawnee:

> can this be real?
> can this be real?
> this life I am living?

or the death song questioning the singer's own guardian power:

> Big Bear:
> you deceive me.

A view-of-the-world, in short, open enough to put questions above answers as the mark of a truly human life.

J.R.'s working of sacred curing songs from the Society of the Mystic Animals (also called: Society of Shamans), taking into account all elements of the original (including the non-verbal) but translating the melody in particular into equivalent visual patterns that hold the page. The twelve opening songs are sung by the *hajaswas* or leader of the event; the others are "individual" songs following the *hajaswas'* directions to "open the bag of songs & sing whichever you want." The pumpkin rattle passes counter-clockwise around the circle, each one taking it in turn & singing a Society song of his choice. Songs can be grouped in sets by coincidence of melody & similarities in content, but on a given occasion they may happen in any order. In these versions, R.J.J. provided the basic translations (sometimes the idiom as well), & J.R. worked them into paginal structures. By this process it is our hope that the originals (wherein resides the power) remain with the Senecas, where they in fact belong.

The Seneca name for the ceremony is I'dos (pron. ee-dos); the common term for it in English is "Shaking the Pumpkin."

Addenda. (1) "Seneca poetry, when it uses words at all, works in sets of short songs, minimal realizations colliding with each other in marvelous ways, a very light, very pointed play-of-the-mind, nearly always just a step away from the comic (even as their masks are), the words set out in clear relief against the ground of the ('meaningless') refrain. . . . Given the 'minimal' nature of much of the poetry (one of its *strongest* features, in fact) there's no need for a dense response in English. Instead I can leave myself free to structure the final poem by using the English of my Seneca co-translator as a base: a particular enough form of the language to itself be an extra tool for that 'continuation of journalism by other means' that Walter Lowenfels defined poetry as being in the first place." (J.R., "Total Translation: An Experiment in the Translation of American Indian Poetry," in *Pre-Faces & Other Writings,* pages 76–92). The resemblance of Seneca verbal art to concrete & minimal poetry among us was another (if minor) point these translations were making.

(2) Work on this series was carried out under a grant-in-aid from the Wenner-Gren Foundation for Anthropological Research. Other workings begun under their auspices appear on pages 4 & 294–297, above.

SOURCE: Knud Rasmussen, *The Netsilik Eskimos,* Report of the 5th Thule Expedition, Copenhagen, 1931, *passim.*

In *Magic Words for Hunting Caribou,* Field as final translator fuses poems by Orpingalik (see above, page 144, & commentary, page 377), Inutuk & Nakasuk; in *Seal Hunting,* parts of poems by Orpingalik & Nakasuk. The fantastic opening statement on "magic words," etc., is fused also, from a longer commentary by Nalungiaq, "just an ordinary woman" (she says), who learned it from an old uncle, Unaraluk the shaman, whose helping spirits — his dead father & mother, the sun, a dog & a sea scorpion — enabled him "to know everything about what was on the earth & under the earth, in the sea & in the sky." As elsewhere (see below, page 377) the Eskimo consciousness is notable in its understanding of basic poetic process. "Mighty magic is a mother," writes poet R. Creeley of where it all comes from: thus toward the same comprehension as the Eskimo. Of their actual practice of "magic words" [= poetry], Rasmussen informs us that the usual thing was not to employ ordinary speech but the special language of the shamans (= seers, or proto-poets), in which language (according to Peter Freuchen) "all things and all beings were called by other than their usual names or by circumlocutions. This immediately put a whole new set of images at their disposal. Also, their trade required that they always have numerous magic formulas ready for use when needed. These formulas would lose their power if used by anyone else. Therefore, within the rules of the polysynthetic language, they would make their own word compositions, not understandable to other people. Since the formulas lost their power after too much use, they had to be constantly renewed, & the angakoks [shamans] thus trained themselves in new and unusual word combinations. As a result they could write many poems." (Freuchen, *Book of the Eskimo,* pages 205–206.)

Addenda. (1) CEREMONY BEFORE SEAL-HUNTING, to accompany the "magic words for hunting seal": A handsome lemming skin, flayed off whole like a small bag, is filled with miniature carvings of seals, harpoons & harpoon heads, & then as an offering to Nuliajuk, is sunk in *atuArutit,* the tide-water crack that always runs along a little way out from the shore. (Thus: Rasmussen, *Netsilik,* page 169.)

(2) Nuliajuk the sea goddess — the story of whose origins the words for seal-hunting get down clearly enough — lives in terrifying presence in a house at sea-bottom. Many of the great shaman spirit journeys recorded here & elsewhere are directed toward confronting her & her

surrounding retinue of monsters in times of famine or danger, or to win abundance of seals, who by the story are manifestations of her own being. Another shaman practice is to attempt to draw her to the surface of the land by "making a hook fast to the end of a long seal thong & throwing it out of the entrance passage: the spirits set the hook fast in her, & the shaman hauls her up into the passage. There everybody can hear her speaking. But the entrance from the passage into the living room must be closed with a block of snow, & this block of snow Nuliajuk keeps on trying to break into pieces in order to get into the house & frighten everybody to death. And there is great fear in the house. But the shaman watches the block, & so Nuliajuk never gets into the house. Only when she has promised the shaman to release all the seals into the sea again does he take her off the hook & allow her to go back down into the depths." Elsewhere in the Eskimo world, Nuliajuk is called Sedna.

(3) While the coaxing sound in some of the "magic words" is self-explanatory as a strategy, the reader should also note the Eskimo belief that a seal is possessed of a perishable body but an immortal soul, & that a man may catch a seal many times if he only once wins its soul over.

(4) Of the words themselves & his own relation to them, Rasmussen writes further: "Translating magic words is a most difficult matter, because they often consist of untranslatable compounds of words, or fragments that are supposed to have their strength in their mysteriousness" — *coefficient of weirdness* is Malinowski's good term for it — "or in the manner in which the words are coupled together." Obviously comprehension by others isn't the issue here "as long as the spirits know what it is that one wants" — although the level of articulation would seem to have varied from shaman to shaman. For example, the poet Orpingalik (see page 377, below) "uttered [his magic words] in a whisper, but most distinctly and with emphasis on every word. His speech was slow, often with short pauses between the words. I have endeavored to show the pauses by means of a new line of verse" (*Netsilik,* page 14) — that last a clear insight on Rasmussen's part into poetry's origins in other-than-song.

(5) For more on shamans-as-poets, etc., see *Technicians of the Sacred,* revised edition, pages 485 ff.

Page 45   MOON ECLIPSE EXORCISM

SOURCE: Prose texts in Leo J. Frachtenberg, *Alsea Texts and Myths,* Bureau of American Ethnology, Bulletin 67, 1920, pages 227–229.

The image of the bloody-yellow water is from a parallel sun eclipse exorcism, while the rich man whose death the event prefigures measures his wealth in dentalia shells.

Page 46   POEM TO EASE BIRTH

SOURCE: Eduard Seler, *Gesammelte Abhandlungen,* Volume 2, 1902–1915, page 1045.

The lady-who-sits-on-the-tortoise is Mayuel, goddess of pulque, who came to it from observations of a mouse nibbling on maguey cactus & surely acting like no mouse she'd ever seen, so that she looked up closer at the "strangely clouded sap" collecting on the maguey stem, got an idea & fed it to her husband, it acting like a damn strong aphrodisiac with the result that she had lots of children & became not only goddess of pulque but patroness of childbirth, entitled by that latter designation "to the respect given to warriors who have been heroes in fierce battles." Thus: C. A. Burland's account of the myth but also of the myth-become-propaganda of the first great military state in the history of North America.

Page 47   CROW VERSIONS

SOURCE: Robert H. Lowie, *Crow Texts,* University of California Press, 1960.

As with other tribal poetry, these Crow songs & prayers came in visions or at other moments of great urgency. Prayers, like the fourth poem here, were addressed mainly though not exclusively to the sun, & sacrifices of the supplicant's own flesh, etc., were offered to him as a kind of over-all deity superseded only on special occasions by personal gods or special sacred objects. (Said One-blue-bead: "The only thing I prayed to specially was my feather. I might pray to the sun any time.") Old Man Coyote, who figures in the sixth poem, "was at times confounded with the sun, though sometimes he himself figures as praying to him." The same might of course be said for most of the other dreamtime beings, especially in a culture, say, where ideology & poetry are responsive to what Cassirer speaks of elsewhere as a "law of metamorphosis" in thought & word. (For which, see pages 389, 396, below, as well as the more specific comment on the fifth poem here.)

Crow Text 1. In a narrative of the Medicine Arrow Bundle, one Hillside tells how his brother's son, Cut-ear, went to a mountain-top, chopped off a finger, & fasted in search of a vision. The Seven Stars appeared to him as seven persons, & sang songs to him. This was the song of the third star.

Crow Text 2. In his vision, White-arm tells us, "I slept near Horn's place. During my sleep I saw a person riding a brown horse toward the top of a mountain & singing. He came toward me. I noticed all the feathers & other ornaments tied to his horse. A hawk was painted on his horse's neck. I took a wing of this bird & used it for my necklace." The person then sang this song to him. White-arm adds: "I joined the Church & now the one who gave me the song is teasing me at night, but I won't listen to him." (Lowie, *Religion of the Crow Indians,* page 338.)

Crow Text 3. Addressed to a whirlwind. The words are like those spoken to a ghost, an implied comparison that conveys "a grave insult."

Crow Text 4. The sweat-lodge was conceived as, above all, an offering to the sun. Writes Lowie: "Sweat-lodges were originally ritualistic, & even those who had the relevant privileges would, according to my informant, sweat only when prompted by a dream. On the other hand, tradition tells of a man who constantly erected sweat-lodges & was accordingly named Sweats-regularly. In the construction of the sweat-lodge, the Crow used willows numbering from twelve to a hundred. Plenty-hawks' (full) prayer specifies lodges of 18, 14, 20, & 100 willows respectively." Merwin's version only gives the section of the longer poem dealing with the 100-willow lodge.

For more on sweat-lodges, etc. see *Sweat-House Ritual #1,* page 229 above, & commentary, page 392, below; also the sweat-lodge section of *66 Poems for a Blackfoot Bundle,* page 173, above.

Crow Text 5. In a narrative by Yellow-brow, a young warrior named Double-face, enduring the typical *ennui* of a Crazy Dog member pledged to self-destructive madness, wanders feverishly around camp the day before battle with the Cheyenne. He says to his older brother: "There are three things I am now eager to do: I want to sing a sacred song; I want to sing a Big Dog song; I want to cry." Then he paints his horse & himself, fits on medicines, & goes into the camp-circle, crying & making others cry, wailing a prayer, part of which Merwin works into the fifth of these Crow versions.

Events of the Crazy Dog Society (but literally Crazy-Dog-wishing-to-die) appear elsewhere in this anthology (for which, see page 160).

Actions were extreme & futile but heroic too: a very literal playing-out of older Plains Indian despair over death & old-age — a kind of behavior not that foreign to our own lives lived at extremes, etc. "Why have you done that?" Spotted-rabbit's mother asked. "You are one of the best-situated young men . . . you are one of the most fortunate men who ever lived . . . & were always happy." But, writes Lowie, Spotted-rabbit was bored with life because he could not get over his father's death. Or again, when Spotted-rabbit receives a gift of plums, he says, "I began to be a Crazy Dog early in the spring & did not think I should live so long; yet here I am today eating plums." Comments Lowie, of such as Double-face & Spotted-rabbit: "We have here reached the peak of the Crow spirit." (*Texts,* 331–334.)

N.B. The reader interested in how men make poetry — i.e. how they use language to take the measure of reality — might also check Lowie's description of the process in Double-face's prayer & elsewhere, by which the man so moved improvises names for a power he feels in the world, not stuck with fixed gods only but making any object he can name a manifestation of that power. Thus, in the section of Double-face's poem that Merwin translates, Double-face is in the act of hypothesizing a location for the power that moves him & which appears elsewhere in the Crow texts in whatever catches the poet's eye & mind:

> Hallo, Little Sweat-lodge, 'We are making it for you,' I said: now I have made it.
> You, mountains of renown, Big Rivers & Small Rivers, smoke it.
> You, Beings Up Above, smoke it.
> Beings in the Ground, smoke it.
> Earth, smoke it.
> Willows, smoke it.
> Hallo, Fat: wherever I go I want to come on something fat.
> Hey, Charcoal, I want to blacken my face with some charcoal.
> Winds, I want you Winds to smoke, I want the Winds to blow toward me.
>
> (*Crow Indians,* page 115)

Not reification, then, & the contemporary sickness of an ecological life-death, but a life-investing process & ongoing deification! And if that ain't the red-hot/white-hot sense-of-the-world that Radin spoke of [for which, see page 361, below], then the present editor is damned if it meant anything at all in the first place.

Crow Text 6. From one of more than six versions of the Crow "Earth Divers" (origin accounts) collected by Lowie. Of the considerable variations in the narrative, he writes: "Obviously there is no one standard version: each narrator works into his cosmogony what seem to him suitable incidents." An example of tribal "freedom," etc., as commented upon by Lowie, Radin, Diamond, & many others.

For more on Coyote the reader can check the commentaries on page 366, below. Among the Crows, as in other Indian religions, he appears as the Supreme Trickster but also as the first maker of the earth & all living things. "He was a great trickster & our ruler," says another narrator. "And since he was a great trickster, we are that way also." But he adds: "All the ways of the Indians he made for us. He put us to sleep, he made us dream, whatever he wanted us to do we did. He put the stars into this world in the beginning; they were dangerous." (*Religion of the Crow,* page 320) Thus Old Man Coyote is the imperfect (= dangerous) creator of an imperfect (= dangerous) universe — a view which, being more empirical & rational in the first place, presents fewer problems to rationalize than the Christian view, say, of a perfect god & universe, etc.

Page 52   *From* THE CHANTS

SOURCE: Álvaro Estrada, *María Sabina: Her Life and Chants,* Ross-Erikson Publishers, Santa Barbara, 1981, pages 112–114. Recorded July 21–22, 1956, by R. Gordon Wasson in Huautla de Jiménez, Oaxaca (*Mushroom Ceremony of the Mazatec Indians of Mexico,* Folkways Records, FR 8975).

A major Wise One (= shaman) among the Mazatecs of Oaxaca, Mexico, María Sabina receives her poems/songs through use of the psilocybe mushroom at all-night curing sessions (veladas): a practice going back to pre-Conquest Mexico & witnessed by the Spanish chronicler who wrote: "They pay a sorcerer who eats them [the mushrooms] & tells what they have taught him. He does so by means of a rhythmic chant in full voice." The sacred mushrooms are considered the source of Language itself — are, in Henry Munn's good phrase, "the mushrooms of language." Thus, writes Munn as witness, "if you ask a shaman where his imagery comes from, he is likely to reply: I didn't say it, the mushrooms did. No mushroom speaks, only man speaks, but he who eats these mushrooms, if he is a man of language, becomes endowed with an inspired capacity to speak. The shamans who eat them . . . are the oral poets of the people, the doctors of the word, the seers and oracles, the ones possessed by the voice. 'It is not I who speak,' said Heraclitus, 'it is the logos.'" Of this language & her own relation to it, María Sabina says: "I cure with Language, the Language of the *saint children*. When they advise me to sacrifice chickens, they are placed on the parts where it hurts. The rest is Language."

The selection presented here departs from the more extended, even "grandiloquent" language of most of the Chants, relying instead on techniques of fragmentation & the use of nonsemantic sound (meaningless syllables, humming, clapping, whistling, etc.). The session itself goes on for a whole night, with many of the images, "self"-namings, etc., established early & repeated throughout in full or fragmented form.

Cayetano García, in whose home the session took place, acts also as the principal respondent. "The tone of voice in which this passage [begins]," writes Henry Munn, "is definitely playful, and at one point the man laughs with pleasure at her song. He thanks her for the beauty of her words."

Page 56   ARCHAIC SONG OF DR. TOM THE SHAMAN

SOURCE: Collected by James A. Teit, in Morris Swadesh & Helen H. Roberts, *Songs of the Nootka Indians of Western Vancouver Island*, Transactions of the American Philosophical Society, Volume 45, Part 3, 1955, pages 230–231.

The words used by the singer (a Thompson River Indian named Nêluk) are in Chinook jargon & "in imitation of those used by Dr. Tom." In a typical doctoring performance, songs were "sung only by the doctor or his wife or helpers, and the words were mumbled so that usually only the doctor understood what they were. He would breathe on the patient as he sang." The power of the words, then, is clearly more than a matter of their immediate — or even eventual — comprehension.

Addenda. The commentary on Dr. Tom identifies him as "an old Indian from the coast who traveled in the Interior. . .and doctored the sick. He had formerly traveled with a white man's circus (for two or three years) and knew a lot of the sleight-of-hand tricks used by white performers as well as other tricks known to the Coast Indians. These tricks he used to good effect in conjunction with his doctoring. He was driven out of the interior by the missionaries & the police for obtaining money under false pretenses, and was in jail for a while. A favorite trick of his was to show things he claimed he had taken out of the bodies of the sick." About "tricks," though, the reader should note Knud Rasmussen's story of a young Copper Eskimo named Taiphuina who told how she "had once been a shaman disciple but had given it up, as 'she could not lie well enough,'" to which the shamans present responded with much good-

natured laughter, knowing (Rasmussen writes) that "the relationship be-
tween the natural and the supernatural is in itself so problematic that it
is of no consequence if there is some 'cheating' in the ritual during an
invocation."

N.B. For a major attack on this concept of poetry & art (namely, that
of the trickster-poet), the reader may again check the 10th book of Plato's
Republic; he may also ponder how Plato's apparent rationality & love-of-
the-truth have contributed to getting us where we are today & may devise
his own game-theory as a start at extrication.

Page 57   MAGIC WORDS *from* RUN TOWARD THE NIGHTLAND

SOURCE: Jack Frederick Kilpatrick & Anna Gritts Kilpatrick, *Run toward the
Nightland: Magic of the Oklahoma Cherokees,* Southern Methodist University Press,
Dallas, 1967, *passim.*

Translated from manuscripts written in Sequoyah's Cherokee sylla-
bary, usually in medicine books owned by shamans, wizards, etc., but
by interested laymen also. The power, though, remains in voice &
thought, the part of the ritual that "consists of what one says (or merely
thinks) or sings," of which the written poem is only a reminder. The
words, if fixed to a finer degree than in oral tradition, are open to mod-
ifications in performance: e.g., "the repetition of a key word the sacred
four times, the interjection of the supremely sacrosanct numeral seven;
the insertion of the pronoun *ayv* ('I'), & a hiatus in which the reciter thinks
intently upon the purpose of the ritual." (*Nightland,* page 7) A master may
also improvise a text if the spirit so moves him, but obviously subject to
those limits that will make the spell work. The second element of
Cherokee magic ritual, i.e. the accompanying "physical procedures"
(= events), while often recorded, are clearly subordinate to the words —
though a better way of looking at the process (as with other mixed-media
situations) may be as a total pattern of events, in which the word-events
are themselves physical procedures but with a greater "power" attributed
to them as the only elements necessary to each performance.

Some of the language-events also show the level of "abstraction" pos-
sible in the poetry-of-magic, as in any poetry that groups words toward
the creation &/or implementation of a possible or existing music. For
example, the Cherokee use of color is both symbolic & expressive (as all
living language tends to be), with fixed associations for color words on
the one hand, & on the other a heightened ability to produce & induce
"thought-paintings" (the Kilpatricks' term for it), not on the basis of what-

the-eye-sees but in "abstract" combinations that may then have image-making functions of their own. (For which, see also the immediately following commentary, on *The Killer*.) The use of "seven!" as an interjection is another example of words acting apart from their usual meaning: here as a pure power-word that strengthens the whole mix.

Addenda. Even more important in Cherokee is the use of numbers in determining the structure of the spells. Thus the translators write: ". . . Anyone who can read Cherokee can readily see that religious, medical and magical texts are built upon patterns that take full advantage of the powers resident in the minor sacred numeral four or major sacred numeral seven. This accession to numerological fiat usually results in a given text's being structured into four or seven lines, into four or seven groups of lines, or into major divisions subdivided into units of four or seven." Some such insistence on symmetries & the relevance of abstract detail is, in fact, one of the strongpoints of Indian poetry & performance in general: not as a question of dead metrics, etc. (= literature), but as a key to the living world.

Page 60   THE KILLER

SOURCE: James Mooney, *Sacred Formulas of the Cherokees,* Bureau of American Ethnology, 7th Annual Report, 1891, page 391.

This poem, from the manuscript book of A'yunini (Swimmer), is typical in fact of the Cherokees' use of colors beyond their (mere) symbolic values (for which, see the preceding commentary) to achieve striking effects by juxtaposition, etc. as with the introduction of the conflicting color in the following:

> As the Red Cardinal is beautiful, I am beautiful
> As the Red Dhla:nuwa is beautiful, I am beautiful
> As the Red Redbird is beautiful, I am beautiful
> As the Blue Cardinal is beautiful, I am beautiful

much as in *The Killer* itself for that matter. Says Jack Kilpatrick, who translated the red & blue piece: "Something peculiarly Cherokeean in the unexpected dissonance"; or as Mooney explained it way back then: "As the purpose of the ceremony is to bring about the death of the victim, everything spoken of is symbolically colored black. . . . The declaration . . . 'It is blue,' indicates that the victim now begins to feel the effects of the incantation, and that as darkness comes on, his spirit will shrink and gradually become less until it dwindles away to nothingness."

358

N. B. The editor has discussed the "obsessive, single-color imagery" of *The Killer* elsewhere (*Technicians of the Sacred,* revised edition, page 496) & has compared it to other tribal poetries & to the practice of modern poets like Lorca & Wakoski, among many others. This is not merely to point to analogues for their own sake, but in the hope that all such "devices" & modes-of-thought may be of interest to the reader in considering the possibility of poetry in his/her own life.

Page 61   WIZARDS

SOURCE: Allan F. Burns, *An Epoch of Miracles: Oral Literature of the Yucatec Maya,* University of Texas Press, Austin, 1983, pages 136–138.

A part of the Mayan tradition of narrative as conversation/discourse (see page 375), the present account is from a body of lore called *secreto'ob,* or secrets. Writes Burns: "These narratives are not thought of as secret in the usual sense of the word: they are not made up of knowledge which is guarded. Instead, the narratives deal with esoteric phenomena of the nonordinary world of the Maya, the world seen in dreams or during visitations by supernatural beings. In everyday parlance, Mayan people often refer to the events of the 'nighttime' world as the converse of those found in the 'daytime' world. The nighttime world is inhabited by beings in the form of children, *aluxo'ob,* who play practical jokes on people who venture out in the dark. The nighttime world is also the realm of deer and other animals which are hunted and the world of poisonous snakes which can kill the unwary."

The *saastun* mentioned in the poem is the small round crystal with which a *hmem* (shaman/Maker) diagnoses illness. (See page 419, below.)

Page 64   A SONG *from* RED ANT WAY

SOURCE: Hoijer, McAllester, Wheelwright, et al., *Texts of the Navajo Creation Chants,* Peabody Museum of Harvard University, pamphlet to accompany record album, ca. 1950. The original singer was Hasteen Klah (1929).

A version of the Red Ant Way myth begins: "The fact is that the Ant People did not originate here, but their origin is traced below this earth to earth twelve, called the Dark One, on the surface of which they were the very first to come alive." And it adds: "There, you see, many of them began to live in human form . . . and to kill one another by every possible means." But all of that is part of the acute sense the first poets showed not only of the animal world at its farthest morphological remove from us (the Navajos, e.g., identify 35 different types of ant by name, some say as many as 70) but of the use to which it could be put to describe the human world as well. Both in fact as part of a continuum. The Ant people (basically dangerous or "evil" but like all things never completely so) were, especially when molested (e.g., pissed upon or otherwise disrupted in their anthills), the direct cause of a variety of diseases. For these & other sicknesses related to them by an intricate network of symbol & myth, the Red Ant Way chant-event system was a cure.

Like other Navajo ceremonials, Red Ant Way contains hundreds of songs in its various versions, along with other ritual-events such as sand painting, body painting, prayerstick planting, pollen events, herb events, etc. The whole chantway system is so complicated in fact that the individual medicine man or chanter (*hatali*, literally a keeper-of-the-songs) can rarely keep-in-mind more than a single ceremony — the nine-day Night Chant, for example — sometimes only part of one. As with other "mixed media" art of this complexity (& the Navajo includes dozens of multi-layered ceremonials like Ant Way & Night Chant) translation for-the-words-alone may hit certain highlights but never the magnitude of the composite work.

Addenda. An attempt at a more comprehensive (i.e. "total") translation of Navajo poem-songs appears above, on pages 294–297; & the same method (of translating both semantic & non-semantic vocalizations) could apply to the whole range of Navajo song as sound-poetry. But the editor doesn't mean by that to play down the effectiveness of translation that focuses on the words alone, being aware of the special sense-of-things that that kind of isolating technique makes possible. The work of new translation, etc., would proceed by *whatever* processes could serve to bring the range & depth of it across.

A further discussion of chant-way as intermedia, etc., appears in *Technicians of the Sacred,* revised edition, pages 502–504.

Page 65   THE DEADLY DANCE

SOURCE: Angel María Garibay K., *Llave del Náhuatl,* Editorial Porrua, Mexico, 1961. Spanish text: pages 229–230; Nahuatl text: pages 145–146.

Page 69   A MYTH OF THE HUMAN UNIVERSE

SOURCE: Charles Olson, *Human Universe & Other Essays,* Grove Press, 1967, pages 13–15.

Olson was in Yucatan December 1950 to July 1951, & other versions of the sun/moon myth appear in *Mayan Letters,* etc. as a poet's real turn-on to an older (poet's) way of ordering things. His own comment at end of this telling (*O, they were hot for the world they lived in, these Maya, hot to get it down the way it was — the way it is, my fellow citizens*) holds true too for new attempts in our own culture "to keep the attention poised," etc., & points to the growing interest in matters of tribal poetics & that search-for-the-primitive Stanley Diamond sees at the center of our post-Romantic development. The reader may also notice how the "hotness" in Olson's description parallels Paul Radin's cry of recognition at presentation of a Pima narrative: *This is a reality at white heat,* & he may consider both against the diminution of said intensity factor among the rulers-of-our-own-lives today & may ponder if the triumph of the American republic didn't in fact accomplish the rub-out of the tribal poets Plato had proposed for all republics, *the way it was — the way it is, my fellow citizens!*

Page 71   *From* THE POPOL VUH: BEGINNINGS

SOURCE: Opening paragraphs from Delia Goetz & Sylvanus G. Morley, *Popol Vuh: The Sacred Book of the Ancient Quiché Maya,* from the Spanish translation by Adrián Recinos, University of Oklahoma Press, 1950, pages 81–82; verse translation from Mayan by Munro S. Edmonson, see below.

Poems-of-origin were part of the sacred oral tradition of all those tribes inhabiting the North American continent before the European conquests. All spoke of the creation or emergence of animals & gods, & of the evolving geography that men learned in their movements through the land. Of these monumental poems, the Quiché Mayan *Popol Vuh* (literally "book of the community") is the oldest written survival. Preserved by Indians in Santo Tomás Chichicastenango & in the 18th century given to Father Francisco Ximénez who transcribed & put it into Spanish, it vanished again & was rediscovered in the 1850s by Carl Scherzer & Abbé Charles Etienne Brasseur de Bourbourg. It existed in picture-writing before the Conquest, & the version used by Father Ximénez (& since lost) may have been the work, circa 1550, of one Diego Reynoso. The book "contains the cosmogonical concepts & ancient traditions of [the Quiché nation], the history of their origin, & the chronicles of their kings down to the year 1550."

For more on the Popol Vuh, see the following commentary, & for a note on Mayan ideas of creation through discourse/conversation (among the gods), see below, page 375.

SOURCE: Munro S. Edmonson, *The Book of Counsel: The Popol Vuh of the Quiché Maya of Guatemala,* Middle American Research Institute, Publication 35, Tulane University, 1971.

"Not the story of a hero," writes Edmonson "[but] of a people." The name, Popol Vuh, means "book of the community" (or "commonhouse" or "council"), & its theme (like other epic works with which it should share prominence — certainly in this hemisphere we would not only live in as intruders) is the history of all of "us" traced back to the beginnings: in this case "the goodness of Quiché: the people, the place, and the religious mysteries which were all called by that name. It is a tragic theme, but its treatment is not tragic: it is Mayan. The rise and fall of Quiché glory is placed in the cosmic cycling of all creation, and when it is ended, like the cycles of Mayan time, it stops. . . . The next cycle will be something else, perhaps the epoch suggested by the closing line of the work, something called 'Holy Cross.'" Or maybe past that too, to a point where we can again see where they were & can join them toward unknown ends in common — for which, see the "proposal" given below, or consider the purposes of this book in general.

Edmonson's translation gets away from the prose of all earlier ones (including the written Quiché), to assert an original "entirely composed in parallelistic (i.e. semantic) couplets," much of it governed by a process he calls "keying. . . in which two successive lines may be quite diverse but must share key words which are closely linked in meaning. Many of these are traditional pairs: sun-moon, day-light, deer-bird, black-white, (but) sometimes the coupling is opaque in English, however clear it may be in Quiché, as in white-laugh," etc. Such associations — as part of the developed poetry of a language — are discussed below (page 401) in relation to a series of Navajo "correspondences."

The excerpt from the Popol Vuh printed here is from early in the work & depicts the beginnings of the career of Alligator (= Cipaena), one of the sons of pride (= 7 Parrot = Vuqub Kaqix), before his destruction by Hunter & Jaguar Deer (= Hun Ah Pu & X Balan Ke), etc.

Addenda. AN ACADEMIC PROPOSAL. For a period of 25 years, say, or as long as it takes a new generation to discover where it lives, take the great Greek epics out of the undergraduate curricula, & replace them with the great American epics. Study the Popol Vuh where you now study Homer, & study Homer where you now study the Popol Vuh — as exotic anthropology, etc. If you have a place in your mind for the *Greek Anthology* (God knows you may not), let it be filled by Astrov's *Winged*

Serpent or the present editor's *Technicians of the Sacred* or this very volume you are reading. Teach courses in religion that begin: "This is the account of how all was in suspense, all calm, in silence; all motionless, still, & the expanse of the sky was empty" — & use this as a norm with which to compare all other religous books, whether Greek or Hebrew. Encourage poets to translate the native American classics (a new version for each new generation), but first teach them how to sing. Let young Indian poets (who still can sing or tell-a-story) teach young White poets to do so. Establish chairs in American literature & theology, etc. to be filled by men trained in the oral transmission. Remember, too, that the old singers & narrators are still alive (or that their sons & grandsons are), & that to despise them or leave them in poverty is an outrage against the spirit-of-the-land. Call this outrage the sin-against-Homer.

Teach courses with a rattle & a drum.

Page 78 THE ORIGIN OF THE SKAGIT INDIANS
        ACCORDING TO LUCY WILLIAMS

Collected & set down by Cary in the narrator's English. About which he writes: "I became aware of this creation myth in 1952 when I was collecting general myths of the Skagit people. Many of the older people denied knowledge of it, or claimed forgetfulness, and I am inclined to believe both because Lucy said very few people knew the myth and very few people cared about it. Even here there appear to be gaps. Lucy didn't remember Swadick or his place of creation and Stoodke has no account. I suspect they belong to neighboring tribes since the Okanagans are an east neighbor. It took Lucy about thirty minutes to tell this story. There were long pauses. The delivery was very slow. But it is restated entirely as it was told to me. I have chosen this form in an effort to maintain her idiom." A recognition, too, that where speech is the vehicle of language, there is no prose, but the speaker's language as it strives toward articulation is forever in the process of becoming a poem. The lack of the old details, etc. — while we would want to have them too — in no sense denies that process, but may in fact intensify it by the nature of the search. Said the Hasidic shaman of my own tribal past: "The fire we can no longer light, the prayer we no longer know, nor do we know the place where it happened in the woods. All we can do is tell the story." And that too, adds the story-teller, proved sufficient.

SOURCE: Erland Nordenskiöld, *Picture-Writings & Other Documents of the Cuna Indians,* Volume 2, 1928, pages 30–35.

Like other Cunas, Slater picked up his knowledge of English (his name too) from sailors he worked with in Panama. He gives the actual source of his narrative as a chief at Aligandi named Iguanigdipipi, & in the absence of better texts, the present editor is offering Slater's written English version as is — & would likely do so anyway, for the high delight it presents of a man mining a language to which he's hardly native. Also that the power's there with very little waste: a power of conception typical (as far as I can tell) of one aspect of Cuna poetry & thought: its ability to arrange all available imageries, etc., toward the geography of a landscape not immediately to hand. This primary surrealism — clear enough here — turns up throughout the various Cuna spirit-journeys now recorded; e.g. the following in *The Journey through the Next World* of Nele Pailibe of Ustúpu (same source as Slater, pages 37–47). Here

— the voyager (= dead man, or shaman as his representative) first goes by canoe on "the mother of all rivers," then on a fast & exceedingly beautiful vessel to a forest where the trees, sand, stones & fruits are all of gold.

— He arrives some time later at the principal water reservoir in the world, with whose manager God communicates by "a sort of telegraph," to warn him of eclipses of the sun, floods, earthquakes, hurricanes, etc.

— At the mid-point between heaven & earth, from which the earth itself looks no bigger than a quarter of a coconut & heaven appears as great palaces off in the distance, he is surrounded by large numbers of eagles, "very sumptuous, of massive gold."

— He later sees a wall made of gold, on which life-sized statues of gold are moving like humans.

— At a house of interrogation, a woman named Ólotilisóbi comes with a bell & summons a group of workers, who arrive by elevator & shut the dead man in a gold chest, first smearing his body with fragrant perfumes. Ólotilisóbi seats herself on the chest; when she gets up, the top of the chest is opened, & the dead man emerges in clothes of gold, & with gold shoes & hat. Even his body is pure gold.

— Ólotilisóbi says to him: "Walk out through that door! Do you see the flag fluttering far away over there? A flag of pure gold." From the top storey he now takes an elevator to the ground floor & goes to the place where the flag was fluttering. This is also a four-storey house, & he goes to its top floor, where he's well received. There are many people there. After a while they show him a large mirror, in which he sees the inside of a human body.

—— Later a railroad train takes him to a river where a woman guards a tree, the branches of which are hung with golden necklaces of all kinds & sizes. He sees another tree whose branches & leaves change into golden mirrors.

—— The dead man crosses a river of cocoa, then a river of brewed coffee, then a river of pineapple juice, etc.

—— On his return journey he takes a train, which brings him to a road, along the sides of which are figures resembling babies. They have a perfectly natural look, & all of them are holding flowers in their little hands.

Then at the top of a very large building which they reach by elevator, the dead man's helping spirit gives another Cuna account of the creation of the world. The earth began as a hen's egg, he tells him, then shows him eggs of all sorts of colors. Any color may be further divided into eight categories, as blue, say, exists in eight shades, some lighter, some darker. The eggs now change into women, & the spirit fetches a very sumptuous chest, in which are cups filled with human sperm & eggs. When he touches these, they turn into children & from the chest come sounds as if from wailing babies. "Thus," he says, "Our Lord created the earth & the human race. The chest represents the womb of woman. The cup is the mould within which the embryo is formed. In the same way as God created man he also created the earth."

Then he concludes: "At no time does the soul reach God: man will never behold him."

Addenda. The poetic process (of vision & language, myth-making, etc.) stays alive in the narratives, both in pulling basic Indian threads through the thin Christian fabric & in introducing elements that are personal to the seer himself as poet (e.g. God creating clothes & ornaments for woman in Slater's creation, etc.). There are also secondary interpretations of many of the images, as Slater's explanation elsewhere that the various colored souls = "menstruation in its various aspects," that the table is "woman's bosom" or her labia spread flat from intercourse, that the white soul on the table is God's sperm, etc. But that much may be the elaboration of theologians & not poets, even if the line between is thin.

Page 83　The Invention of White People

Source: Leslie Marmon Silko, *Ceremony,* The Viking Press, 1977, The New American Library, 1978, pages 139–145.

> I suppose at the core of my writing is the attempt to identify what it is to be a half-breed or mixed blooded person; what it is to grow up neither white nor fully traditional Indian. It is for this reason that I hesitate to say that I am representative of Indian poets or Indian people, or even Laguna people. I am only one human being, one Laguna woman.

Raised at Laguna Pueblo in New Mexico, Silko continues a view of history & myth told from her own (particular & cultural/familial) perspective. Thus, she writes: "White ethnologists have reported that the oral tradition among Native American groups has died out, because whites have always looked for museum pieces and artifacts when dealing with Native American communities. . . . I grew up at Laguna listening, and I hear the ancient stories, I hear them very clearly in the stories we are telling right now. Most important, I feel the power which the stories still have, to bring us together, especially when there is loss and grief." And again:

> You don't have anything
> if you don't have the stories.

Page 89　Coon cons Coyote, Coyote eats Coon, Coyote fights Shit-Men, etc.

Source: Melville Jacobs, *Northwestern Sahaptin Texts,* Columbia University Contributions to Anthropology, Volume 19, 1934.

Coyote appears in the familiar role of primordial shit-thrower, cock-erupter, etc., to satisfy the need for all that in the full pantheon of essential beings. No merely horny version of a Disney character, he is (like other tricksters in tribal America: Rabbit, Raven, Spider, Bluejay, Mink, Flint, Glooscap, Saynday, etc.) the product of a profound & comic imagination playing upon the realities of man & nature. Thus, as Jung writes of the Winnebagos' Trickster in that now-famous essay: he is "absolutely undifferentiated human consciousness. . . a psyche that has hardly left the animal level . . . [but] god, man & animal at once . . . both sub- and super-human . . . an expression [therefore] of the polaristic structure of the psyche, which like any other energic system is dependent on the tension of opposites." Like any genuine poetry system too.

The good-of-him, which should be more apparent after the "counterculture" than before, is at least three-fold:

(1) to find a place for what — as animals, children, etc. — we were & are: to be aware of, even to enjoy, the very thing that scares us with threats of madness, loss of self, etc.

(2) to ridicule our ordinary behaviors by breaking (vicariously at least) their hold on us: to punch holes in established authority (= the way things are) so as not to be its forever silent victims;

(3) where Trickster is creator too, to explain the dangers inherent in reality itself — of a world, that is, that must have such gods at its inception: or as an old Ten'a Indian said to John Chapman, "The Creator made all things good, but the Raven (= Trickster) introduced confusion" (for which, etc. see page 355, above).

Page 91   TELLING ABOUT COYOTE

SOURCE: Simon Ortiz, *A Good Journey,* Turtle Island, 1977, pages 15–18.

A poet of Acoma Pueblo (New Mexico), Ortiz provides a significant continuity between old & new modes, with a strong sense of the possibilities & losses involved therein. (The present extension of coyote-consciousness, e.g., confirms the presence of Coyote as American trickster-saint: a symbol both of exile/wandering & of a dream-of-home.) To the questions, "Why do you write? Who do you write for?" Ortiz replies: "Because Indians always tell a story. The only way to continue is to tell a story and that's what Coyote says. The only way to continue is to tell a story and there is no other way. Your children will not survive unless you tell something about them — how they were born, how they came to this certain place, how they continued." And to the further question, "Who do you write for besides yourself?": "For my children, for my wife, for my mother and my father and my grandparents and then reverse order so that I may have a good journey on my way back home."

For more on Coyote, Trickster, etc., see the preceding commentary & pages 355 & 390–391.

Page 95   THE BOY & THE DEER

SOURCE: Dennis Tedlock, *Finding the Center: Narrative Poetry of the Zuni Indians,* Dial Press, 1972; University of Nebraska Press, 1978.

Tedlock's version of *The Boy & the Deer,* along with his other translations, is a primary example of what the present editor has been calling "total translation," i.e. the attempt to render *all* sounds & repetitions which the translator can be made to perceive in the performed original. By doing this with Andrew Peynetsa's oral narratives, Tedlock has also expanded the area of what "we" can recognize as poetry — I mean as any treatment of language in which all particulars (of movement, phrasing, idiom, etc.) count & have to be accounted for in bringing the work across. He has potentially increased the body of oral *poetry* a thousandfold through the clear recognition that prose doesn't in fact exist "outside the written page." For which & other comments, his own view-of-the-matter follows.

"[TRANSLATING SOUND & SILENCE IN A SPOKEN LITERATURE]: The spoken narratives of the Zuni Indians (like those of other tribal peoples) are events, not just verbal descriptions of events. They sound like poems and plays, but because they are spoken rather than sung or chanted they have always been treated in translation as if they were equivalent to written prose. If one 'listens' only for *meaning* (in the ordinary sense), it is easy to fall into this trap; but if one listens to the *sounds* (with more than the narrow phonetic ear of the linguist) and to the intervening *silences,* it becomes clear that what has been widely called 'oral prose' is in reality dramatic poetry. Indeed, there is ample reason to believe that 'prose' has no existence at all outside the written page.

"What makes written prose most unfit for representing spoken narrative is that it rolls on for whole paragraphs at a time without hesitating or taking a breath: there is no silence in it. To solve this problem I have adopted line changes, which in contemporary poetry usually correspond to pauses in performance. The noticeable silences in Zuni narrative range all the way from about four-tenths second to three seconds, so I have divided them into two types: ordinary pauses, averaging a little less than a second in length and represented by simple line breaks; and long pauses, two to three seconds long and represented by double spaces between lines. A prose presentation would not be much of a guide to these silences: some of them fall between clauses or sentences, but others do not, and some of the clause and sentence boundaries are not accompanied by silence.

"In passing from Zuni to English it is possible to at least approximate the original contrasts in line length. There is no point in preserving the exact syllable counts in translation [these vary anyway from performance to performance — ed.], but radical changes in the original lengths would distort the pace of the narrative. Line length — or, to put it the other way around, the frequency of pauses — is the major cause of variations in the apparent rate at which human speech is delivered: passages with short lines (many pauses) seem slow, while those with long lines (few pauses) seem fast."

[Other sounds attended to — loudness, intonation, vowel lengthening, etc. — are noted in the "Aids to Reading Aloud" on page 116. Tedlock goes on to say about this translation & the boundaries of translation in general]: "Accidents or 'errors,' when recognized, are eliminated in conventional translations, but they are a natural part of performance: keeping them in translation can help preserve the sound-event quality of the original narrative. In the following passage, the line consisting solely of 'you' was a false start on the part of the narrator:

> 'Your belly grew large
> you
> you were about to deliver, you had pains in your belly, you were
>   about to give birth to me, you had pains in your belly
> you gathered your clothes
> and you went down to the bank to wash.'

The repetition of 'you had pains in your belly' might also be considered an error. The narrator is quoting an agitated person and simply gets carried away, making the quotation more realistic in the process.

"In most spoken narrative traditions the audience gives the performer a standardized response. In the Zuni case the response is *eeso,* with the effect of 'ah yes' or 'yes indeed,' given after each of the two introductory lines and otherwise scattered here and there among the pauses in the body of the story. The presence of a tape-recorder inhibits this response, and so it occurs only five times (each marked *audience*) in the present narrative; under more normal circumstances it might have occurred something like twenty times."

The reader should also note that other words in the original — the opening & closing formulas, proper names without meaning, etc. — are brought across (translated, so to speak) without being changed: an optional strategy even in a "total" translation. Kachinas are (as elsewhere among the Pueblos) the ancestral gods impersonated in masked dances; their village "lies beneath the surface of a lake and comes to life only at night." The translated term, "daylight person," refers to all living human beings, while "all other beings, including animals, some plants, various natural phenomena, and deceased humans (kachinas), are called 'raw people,' because they do not depend on cooked food. The boy is partly daylight, since his mother is daylight, and partly raw, since his father is the Sun and since, as Andrew Peynetsa points out, 'he was the half-son of the deer mother, because she gave him her milk.'" On death he becomes completely "raw," thus "enters upon the roads of his elders," going back to the deer forever. This may partly explain why the narrator himself interprets the boy's death as a suicide.

For more on "total translation," particularly in the area of song & sound-poetry, see J.R.'s working on pages 294–297, above, & the commentary thereto on page 411, below.

Page 119 WOLF SONGS & OTHERS OF THE TLINGIT

SOURCE: John R. Swanton, *Tlingit Myths and Texts*, Bureau of American Ethnology, Bulletin 39, 1909, *passim.*

Koller's workings probably deliver much more than Swanton — describing the poems as "highly metaphorical" & hard to understand — thought possible to get across. But good poets have the advantage of not believing in metaphor, therefore not being conned by its presumed presence. What emerges, anyway, is a cumulative picture of Tlingit life & attitudes (given above without a break for singers' names, etc.) that the present editor finds almost unbearable in its clarity & directness.

If it's not otherwise apparent to the reader, note should also be made that many of the animal references (Wolf, Eagle, Crow, etc.) are to clans in the original, though Koller has chosen to emphasize their natural & totemic significances. "Crow" in the Tlingit is more like "raven." Notes on individual songs & poets follow.

Song No. 1 (I keep dreaming . . .) Composed by Qaqatcguk after his dream on the island.

Song No. 2 (Shaman Song) A spirit song composed by a shaman called Luswat.

Song No. 3 (Throw him into . . .) A spirit song composed by Kasenduaxtc.

Song Nos. 5–8 (Cradle Songs) Sung over a child & used sometimes at feasts. When a man died his brother married the widow — as with the old Hebrew tribes.

Song No. 9 (Funeral Song) Composed by Hayiaku, also called Small-Lake-underneath. "It is used when a feast is about to be given for a dead man, & they have their blankets tied up to their waists & carry canes."

Song No. 10 (That's a rich man . . .) Used by all families of the Wolf phratry, who sing it all together just as they are coming to a feast.

Song No. 11 (We've all been invited . . .) Composed in Tsimshian & used at a great feast. Songs in other languages — like the following one too — were in fact common.

Song No. 12 (How is it all...) Composed by a Haida who was popularly called Haida Charlie. A dance song at feasts.

Song No. 13 (I wonder what eagle...) Composed by Gaxe (Crying-Wolf).

Song No. 14 (I think about you...) Composed by Yuwaku & "addressed to the rest of his group."

Song No. 15 (I know how people...) Composed by Andeyek (name means: For-a-town-spirit) to denounce strangers to town who paid no attention to his people.

Song No. 16 (You surprise me...) Composed by Nigot.

Song No. 17 (I'm gonna die...) Composed by Tsakak.

Song No. 18 (Song on the Way to Jail) Composed by Kakayek about his brother's wife. She does the speaking in anticipation of being sent away by the Whites for drunkenness (her actual rejoinder in fact is two songs down). Kakayek's own name probably meant something like wolves-howling-in-the-distance.

Song No. 19 (Song for the Richest Woman) Composed by Guxnawu (Dead-Slave) about a woman named Kahantiki (Poor-Orphan).

Song No. 20 (I don't know why...) Composed by Toxaoci in reply to No. 18.

Song No. 21 (It's only whiskey...) Composed by a shaman named Kagank.

Song No. 22 (My wife went away...) Composed by Katda (Around-A-Flat-Basket), whose wife her people took back.

Song No. 23 (If you'd died...) "This is sung when peace is being made after a great war." It can be sung for any clan by inserting the clan's name.

Song No. 24 (Before he died...) Part of a song composed by a man named Łquena, when he was the only one of his people saved & his enemies wanted to make peace with him. He danced as a deer, singing his song, & at the end of it, cut the man standing next to him in two.

Song No. 25 (It would be very pleasant...) Composed by Yełdugu (Raven-skin) when his sweetheart abandoned him.

Song No. 26 (He followed...) A mourning song.

SOURCE: Schwerner's translations from *Poèmes Eskimo* by Paul Emile Victor, Pierre Seghers, Paris, 1958.

The range of Eskimo poetry has easy extensions into the everyday & personal: areas (they used to say) too particular for the likes of primitive hunters & gatherers. But Rasmussen showed long ago how Eskimo songs, etc. got down precisely "the thoughts and moods of people journeying or hunting in solitude . . . hummed at home in the snow hut or tent in the evenings . . . but in company with the drum they are also the central point in the *qagsgé*," i.e. a big house built for the public song festivals, where large groups met after feasting in private homes, to hold song contests, etc.

The reader may also be interested in Orpingalik's song (page 144, above, & the commentaries thereto) for a major Eskimo work in this mode. As a contrasting type, the Eskimo *Magic Words* (pages 41–44, above) are also available.

Page 128 KIOWA "49" SONGS

SOURCE: Alan R. Velie, *American Indian Literature: An Anthology,* University of Oklahoma Press, 1979, pages 176–179.

A popular form of contemporary Indian lyric, "49" songs show up throughout the States "at powwows and other social gatherings, usually late in the evening after other types of dances and songs are completed." The origin of the name has been variously explained — in Velie's version, as derived from a burlesque show of the 1920s that toured Kiowa country with a California gold rush theme & the repeated refrain, "See the girls of '49, see the '49 girls." Applied to Kiowa women who were singing semi-traditional "war-journey songs" with transformed lyrics, the name (so they say) stuck & passed into the pan-Indian culture.

"In singing '49' songs" — writes Velie — "the singers chant a nonverbal refrain to an accompanying drum beat. After an extended period of chanting, they sing the short lyric once, either in Kiowa or in English." The words in the present versions are the original English — a good example of how a feeling for the "luminous detail" & for the ironies of language & behavior can be brought into an altered context.

Page 129　Two Divorce Songs

Translated by Cary from his own gatherings in the Kispiox-Hazelton country of British Columbia, summer 1968.

Page 130　Tsimshian mourning song

Source: Garfield, Wingert & Barbeau, *The Tsimshian: Their Arts & Music,* Publications of the American Ethnological Society, Volume 18, 1951, pages 155–156.

The type of song called a *lin* (= lament), it was sung immediately after the death of a relative & again a year later. The present version belonged to the family of the singer, a man named Weerhæ, English name: Robert Pearl.

Page 131　insult before gift-giving

Source: ditto, page 123.

A potlatch (= giveaway) song of the Eagle clan to accompany gifts of food to the guests at feasts. The singer in this instance was one Tralahæt, also called Frank Bolton; the interpreter was Pahl (Charles Barton). Recorded in 1927.

(1) While the idea was to "roast the guest before making gifts to him" (thus: Charles Barton), the poem isn't an example of N.W. Coast meanness, etc., so much as an indication of the use of language (poetry) to experience & bring-to-surface threats to group stability: why real poets (who even today remember their roots in the primitive) often appear anti-social or (merely) negative to those who no longer understand poetic process & modes-of-thought. But poetry either explores the area of the socially & spiritually destructive or becomes (as it often has) an instrument for its own emasculation.

(2) "Some of the words," writes Barbeau, "are Gitksan & others Niskæ — side by side," a use of foreign languages fairly common in tribal practice & another reminder that "power" & not immediate or total comprehension was the primary poetic value. Expressions like "Now the words!" or "Sing louder!" were usually interjected by the singer himself; "they were meant to call the attention of the listeners to the theme of the song."

SOURCE: Frances Densmore, *Music of the Tule Indians of Panama,* Smithsonian Miscellaneous Collections, Volume 77, Number 11, 1926, page 31.

(1) "The boy and the older girl are 'doctors' (possessors of mysterious powers). . . . The Tule had seen spyglasses but did not own one." Other Tule (Cuna) journeys were, however, carried on into earth, air & sea, as in the trip of Nele Pailibe (see page 364) or that along Muu's way (pages 256, 401). The spyglass, then, is confirmation of powers attested to in other songs; thus:

> Go to sleep & dream of many animals — mountain lions & ocean lions
> You will talk to them & understand what they say
> & when you awake you will be a shaman like me.

(Densmore, Tule, page 18)

(2) Densmore's recordings were made during a Washington visit by eight Tule Indians in 1924. The typical Tule song (she tells us) is in the form of a "simple, continuous narrative" with hardly any repetitions, etc. — often acting as a kind of scenario for the actions it accompanies. The way the words are sung "suggests melodic speech" (rather than chants) "in which the rhythm is determined by the accents and lengths of the words." It's also common to improvise, i.e. "the substance of the words and the general character of each song is 'learned,' but . . . each performance of the song is an improvisation. . . . The Tule said they did not intend to 'sing a song always the same.'"

Page 134 TWO CHEYENNE POEMS

SOURCE: Lance Henson, *In a Dark Mist,* Cross-Cultural Communications, 1982, pages 16–19.

A member of the Dog Soldier Society & the Native American Church, Henson works both Cheyenne & English toward a continuity of tribal traditions & language. Final aim of the Cheyenne poems (he says) is their incorporation into ritual performance.

AUTHOR'S NOTES. "Little Fingernail kept a ledger inscribed with buffalo blood depicting Cheyenne scenes. He was killed at Buffaloswallow after the Fort Robinson outbreak.

"Charles White Antelope is a Native American Church elder in Chapter Number One, Calumet, Oklahoma."

Page 136 CONVERSATIONS IN MAYAN

SOURCE: Allan F. Burns, *An Epoch of Miracles: Oral Literature of the Yucatec Maya,* University of Texas Press, Austin, 1983, pages 35–37.

The Mayan word *tzichal* ("conversation") covers a range of language events from "small talk" to "stories" per se to the "secrets" & "ancient conversations" of the myth-world. The point in common is that a principal narrator/speaker works through dialogue with a respondent ("the person who knows how to answer the speech") in an always two-sided performance act. "In Yucatec Mayan," writes Burns, "it is not possible to say 'tell me a story.' Instead, the only way to bring a story into verbal expression is to ask someone to 'converse' a story with you. It is especially difficult for those of us who are used to listening to monologues in our mass media to recognize the importance of conversation and discourse in Yucatec Mayan oral literature. In the opening lines of the Quiché Mayan book of counsel, the *Popol Vuh* [page 71, above], the gods Tepeu and Gucumatz create the world by holding a conversation: 'Tepeu and Gucumatz talked together. They talked then, discussing and deliberating; they agreed, they united their words and their thoughts.' In contrast, in the Bible of Western European heritage, the Word is singular and it creates the world through a monologue, not a dialogue."

In the present instance, the conversation/dialogue emerges naturally from language lessons between Alonzo Gonzales Mó as narrator & Burns as the still silent but necessary respondent. Here Mó dictates the sequences, which Burns writes down in Mayan as "a kind of silent 'responding' to his speech." As outline of a language & a life, they resemble other conversations-of-the-actual (= poems) by contemporaries of his & ours.

Page 138 NAVAJO ANIMAL SONGS

SOURCE: David P. McAllester, *Enemy Way Music,* Papers of the Peabody Museum of American Archaeology & Ethnology, Harvard University, Volume 41, Number 3, page 80.

A group of moccasin game songs, as given by Son of Bead Chant Singer. When he recorded "wildcat," McAllester writes, "he was so amused he had difficulty finishing the song, and his daughter laughed so loud she had to sit down on the ground. The first line of the song was enough to set the audience laughing in anticipation of what was to come."

Writes Reichard of moccasin game songs in general: "Matthews, in an early work, 'Navajo Gambling Songs,' refers to the large number of songs concerned with the moccasin game. One old man said there were four thousand, and another that there was no creature that walked, flew or crawled in all the world known to the Navajo that had not at least one song in the game and that many had more. The reason is almost certainly that the game originated as a contest for day and night in which all living things participated." (Reichard, *Navajo Religion,* page 287) The reader should remember too (especially if he still tends to equate sacred & sober, etc.) that laughter is itself an old form of religious language, if a dangerous one. Says McAllester about the thin line walked here: "It is interesting that the moccasin game songs which contain laughable remarks about various animals and birds are sung only after the first killing frost when it is safe. There is a minimum of danger from retaliatory lightning, snake bite or damage to crops after this time of year."

Page 140 THREE CREE NAMINGS

SOURCE: Howard A. Norman, *The Wishing Bone Cycle: Narrative Poems from the Swampy Cree Indians,* Ross-Erikson Publishing, Santa Barbara, 1982, pages 57–58, 50–51, 86–87.

"Affiliations with animals are the most common sources of the old ways of naming in Swampy Cree tradition (i.e., those not designated under the auspices of a church). Names may be acquired several ways. A boy called 'Loud Lynx,' for example, may have inherited the name from a grandfather who said it still had useful powers. Or his parents may have requested an elder or 'medicine-seer' to interpret his next dream or vision into a name. [Those unhappy with their original names for various reasons may also request new names of their own invention.] . . .

"The personal name-origins translated here were told by Samuel Makidemewabe, a Swampy Cree elder. He lived several places in north-central Manitoba Province. One of his jobs in the community was to chronicle, in stories, how people earned their names, mainly during childhood. . . . Makidemewabe wasn't present for all the incidences from which these names derived. He was right there for some of them. With the others, basic information was brought to him. These stories, then, illume every storyteller's option to embellish as long as the necesssary core of historical fact is clearly preserved. . . . Makidemewabe said, 'To say the name is to begin the story,' which leads us into these name-origins." (Howard A. Norman, pages 46, 48–49)

For more on naming, etc., see pages 158, 243, & the accompanying commentaries.

Page 144 ORPINGALIK'S SONG: IN A TIME OF SICKNESS

SOURCE: Knud Rasmussen, *The Netsilik Eskimos,* Report of the 5th Thule Expedition, Copenhagen, 1931, pages 321–323, 324–327.

Orpingalik (the name means man-with-willow-twig) was a shaman, poet & hunter, "notably intelligent & having a fertile wit" (writes Rasmussen), who could move, like other big poets, between personal modes (as here) & "magic words" of the kind given elsewhere in these pages (for which, see pages 41-44, above). Obviously into it up to his elbows, he called this song "my breath" because (he said) "it is just as necessary to me to sing as it is to breathe." That breath, which is all the more visible where he came from (in the language of the Netsilik shamans, e.g., a living person is "someone smoke surrounds"), becomes the physical projection of the process of thought, etc. that goes on inside a man. Thus, Orpingalik describes an order of composition something like "projective verse" as follows:

> Songs are thoughts, sung out with the breath when people are moved by great forces and ordinary speech no longer suffices. Man is moved just like the ice floe sailing here and there in the current. His thoughts are driven by a flowing force when he feels joy, when he feels fear, when he feels sorrow. Thoughts can wash over him like a flood, making his breath come in gasps and his heart throb. Something like an abatement in the weather will keep him thawed up. And then it will happen that we, who always think we are small, will feel still smaller. And we will fear to use words. But it will happen that the words we need will come of themselves. When the words we want to use shoot up of themselves — we get a new song. (*Netsilik,* page 321)

As for the extent of his own involvement therein, he says elsewhere:

> How many songs I have I cannot tell you. I keep no count of such things. There are so many occasions in one's life when a joy or a sorrow is felt in such a way that the desire comes to sing; and so I only know that I have many songs. All my being is song, and I sing as I draw breath.

The particular circumstances behind "Sickness" were very much as the poem describes them. For other Eskimo poems, etc., about people & animals, see above, pages 124–127.

Page 147 A BOOK OF EVENTS (I)

This book of events is presented as a sequel to one in *Technicians of the Sacred*. As there, the editor has taken a series of rituals & other programmed activities & has, as far as possible, suppressed all reference to accompanying mythic or "symbolic" explanations. This has led to two important results: (1) the form of the activities is, for the first time, given the prominence it deserves; & (2) the resulting works bear a close resemblance to those mythless activities of our own time called events, happenings, de-coll/age, kinetic theater, etc. It may be further noted that most of these "events" — like the (modern) intermedia art they resemble — are parts of total situations involving poetry, music, dance, painting, myth, dream, etc., as are many of the songs & visions presented elsewhere in this anthology. But a crucial point of tribal poetry-&-art is precisely that it calls for total performance & participation: a maximization of human activities to allow the world to remake itself at that level of intensity (= *reality at white heat*) that Radin spoke of.

Having revealed this much, the editor again doesn't wish to obscure by a series of explanatory footnotes the forms that have been laid bare. While absence of such notes may result in some distortion, that surely isn't more than what results from the usual presentation of the words-of-the-event (= poem) apart from the rest. But the work of poets is poetry in whatever medium it takes place!

Addenda. (1) Other presentations of poetry beyond speech- & song-utterances will be found in *A Book of Extensions (I)*, pages 239–275, above, & in *A Book of Extensions (II): Soundings,* pages 277–297, above. The editor feels this approach to be vital to an adequate comprehension of the ways in which the "word" (= *logos*) manifested itself among the American tribes in a complex of moves in which word, event & image were generated by a single impulse toward "vision" or whatever term of ours would fit the bill today.

(2) The contemporary word "happening" — as cover-all for these kinds of events — itself has counterparts in, e.g., the Navajo word for their own (intermedia) ceremonials, which (Kluckhohn & Wyman tell us) translates literally as "something-is-going-on"; or in the widespread use by the Iroquois & others of the English word "doings."

(3) Since writing the above, the editor has become aware of new occurrences in contemporary happenings & theater that have gone beyond the mythless presentation of events to first attempts at a redefinition of the content-of-reality itself: in other words, to a renewed willingness to define content before the event rather than after it. This shift from an inductive to a deductive art has often involved some sense of Indian or tribal heritage as model.

Page 149 DREAM EVENT I & DREAM EVENT II

Anthony Wallace's "Dreams & Wishes of the Soul" (available, say, in *Magic, Witchcraft & Curing,* ed. J. Middleton, Natural History Press) is the going account of Iroquois dream practice back to the 17th century *Jesuit Relations.* Said Father Fremin: "The Iroquois have, properly speaking, only a single divinity — the Dream." But dream was central to the creative & intellectual experience of most Indian groups — as source of vision & song, & key to that "dream-time" to which the Australian aborigines ascribed all outcroppings of the sacred, etc.

Page 150 A MASKED EVENT FOR COMEDIAN & AUDIENCE

SOURCE: Bernhard J. Stern, *The Lummi Indians of Northwest Washington,* Columbia University Contributions to Anthropology, Volume 17, 1934, pages 57–59.

Page 150 BUTTERFLY SONG EVENT

SOURCE: Leslie Spier, *Yuman Tribes of the Gila River,* University of Chicago Publications in Anthropology, Ethnological Series, 1933, page 231.

Compare not only the construction of mobiles, windworks, etc. in contemporary art, but transposition of voice & other body sounds to visual media.

Page 151 AUTUMN EVENTS

SOURCE: Franz Boas, *The Central Eskimo,* Bureau of American Ethnology, 6th Annual Report, 1888, pages 200–201.

Page 152 TAMALE EVENT

SOURCE: Bernardino de Sahagún, *Florentine Codex,* tr. Arthur J. O. Anderson & Charles E. Dibble, University of Utah, Part 2, page 163. The present version is unaltered from the Nahuatl translation.

Compare the event itself with the poems from it on pages 319–321. Animal events of this sort are notably widespread — & probably no more baroque among the Aztecs, say, than with the Lummi of Northwest Washington, for which see "Animal Spirit Event" on page 160, above.

Page 153 MUD EVENTS

SOURCE: Gladys Reichard, *Social Life of the Navajo Indians,* Columbia University Contributions to Anthropology, Volume 7, 1928, pages 132–133.

For other acts of earth- & body-rootedness the reader may compare contemporary performance works that involve daubings, etc. (as Allan Kaprow's *Soap;* instructions for the 2nd evening

>   bodies dirtied with jam
>   bodies buried in mounds
>   at the sea edge
>   bodies cleaned by the tide)

— but remember too the generations of experience that gave these Navajo events their context.

Page 154 DAKOTA DANCE EVENTS

SOURCE: Lewis Henry Morgan, *The Indian Journals 1859–1862,* University of Michigan Press, 1959, page 146.

Highly condensed scenarios as given to Morgan, circa 1860. The ordeal of "Moon Event" more commonly turns up in Plains Indian sundances. "Half-Man Event" has numerous contemporary analogues in body art & painting, polar images, etc.

Page 155 Gift Event

Source: as originally printed in J.R.'s *Technicians of the Sacred,* based on native accounts in "The Amiable Side of Kwakiutl Life: The Potlatch & the Play Potlatch," by Helen Codere, *American Anthropologist,* Volume 56, Number 2, April, 1956.

Compare Alison Knowles' *Giveaway Construction* (1963):

Find something you like in the street & give it away. Or find a variety of things, make something of them & give it away . . .

among many contemporary performance works, etc., that involve gift-giving. Part of the redistribution pattern for valued objects, or way of creating new value, but no more sinister (as potlatch or as art) here than there.

Page 156 Language Event I

Source: Knud Rasmussen, *The Netsilik Eskimos,* Report of the 5th Thule Expedition, Copenhagen, 1931, pages 307–314. For more on shaman language, etc. see the commentaries (pages 350–351, above) on "magic words."

Page 157 Language Event II

Source: Gladys A. Reichard, *Navajo Religion: A Study of Symbolism,* Bollingen Series, XVIII, Pantheon, 1950, 1963, page 270.

Among other Navajo forms of "altered language": this one, not surprisingly, for use in the Rain Ceremony. But the reader might take it from there, & see what results would follow the application of the single rule to a wider series of situations.

Page 157 Picture Event, for Doctor and Patient

Source: Washington Matthews, *The Night Chant, a Navajo Ceremony,* Memoirs of the American Museum of Natural History, 1902, page 129.

Compare this to contemporary self-destroying art, say, or to the notion that a work-of-art's survivability may *not* be the real measure of why we bother in the first place. (See also pages 263, 404.)

Page 158 NAMING EVENTS

SOURCE: Ruth Underhill, *Social Organization of the Papago Indians,* Columbia University Contributions to Anthropology, Volume 30, 1939, pages 174–178.

For naming as a fundamental source of poetry, see *Technicians of the Sacred,* revised edition, pages 448–451, & Gertrude Stein's reminder therein that "that is poetry really loving the name of anything & that is not prose."

Page 159 PEBBLE EVENT

SOURCE: Alice C. Fletcher & Francis LaFlesche, *The Omaha Tribe,* Bureau of American Ethnology, 27th Annual Report, 1905–1906, pages 565–566.

This is the major ritual-event of the Pebble Society, for which *Sweat-House Ritual No. 1* (page 229, above) is a preparation. For more on the accompanying sacred narrative, etc., see commentary, page 392, below. Another example of simultaneous recitation appears above, on pages 282–286.

Page 160 CRAZY DOG EVENTS

SOURCE: Robert H. Lowie, *The Crow Indians,* Holt, Rinehart & Winston, 1935, 1956, pages 330–331.

The events resemble Dada activities, say, & also the political gestures of the provos & crazies, etc. of the late 1960s. But the phenomenon (contraries, warrior clowns) was by contrast a *deep-seated* aspect of Plains Indian life, not unlike traditions of the Japanese & others. Ran the Crazy Dog prayer: "I do not want to live long; were I to live long, my sorrows would be overabundant. I do not want it!"
For more on this, see pages 353–354, above.

Page 160 ANIMAL SPIRIT EVENT

SOURCE: Stern, *Lummi,* as above, pages 63–64.

An immediate comparison is to the Aztec event ("tamales," etc.) above, but the experience of another animal's nature (or even that of an

inanimate *thing*) was one of the major achievements of Amerindian poets
& visionaries. Not a masquerade either, for when Lowie, say, writes in
a passage that my eye just now lights on, of a Crow man who "could not
eat a cherry without going into an ecstatic condition & acting like a bear,"
there is a level of experience & an utterly sane blowing-of-the-mind, so
to speak, that transforms events into vision & from which the words will
then emerge as song or narrative, etc.

Page 161 Vision Events I, II & III

Source: (I) & (II) from Peter Freuchen, *Book of the Eskimos,* Fawcett World
Library, 1961, pages 158, 159; (III) a *highly condensed* version of the Plains
Indian "vision quest" as initiation into manhood, etc.

Page 165 The Horse Dance

Source: *Black Elk Speaks: Being the Life Story of a Holy Man of the Oglala Sioux,* as
told through John G. Neihardt, William Morrow & Co., 1932, University of
Nebraska Press, 1961, pages 166–180.

Hehaka Sapa, or Black Elk. Born "in the Moon of the Popping Trees
[December] on the Little Powder River in the Winter when the Four
Crows Were Killed [1863]." Died August 1950 on the Pine Ridge Reser-
vation, Manderson, South Dakota. Given a "great vision" in his
childhood (comparable in its complexity to that of biblical Ezekiel), he
was a "holy man" or "priest" (*wichasha wakon*) of the Oglala Sioux &, like
his second cousin Crazy Horse, a great "visionary seer." But unable to
live out his visions for the rescue of his people, he did finally deliver to
strangers a record of those sightings & of the rituals entrusted to him by
the former "keepers of the sacred pipe."

The Horse Dance, as presented here, is as extraordinary a work (of
mind & spirit) as the Great Vision from which it was derived. And it
blows skyhigh the notion of tribal ritual (Indian or other) as fixed & in-
flexible: repetition rather than creation. What we have in fact is a
description of ritual theater *in the making*: a work keyed to the particulars
of the vision it's enacting. That vision — with its attendant imagery &
language — remains incomplete, a torment to the visionary himself, until
it's given a public form, objectified by the shamans/makers, & witnessed
by the community at large. The relation between private vision & public
art has never been more clearly stated, & that may be a triumph in its
way as significant as the "defeat" projected elsewhere in his book.

Page 173 SIXTY-SIX POEMS FOR A BLACKFOOT BUNDLE

SOURCE: Clark Wissler, *Ceremonial Bundles of the Blackfoot Indians,* Anthropo-
logical Papers of the American Museum of Natural History, Volume 7, Part 2,
1912, pages 215 et seq.

Imperfect scenario based on Wissler's incomplete description, but a
lot of poetry anyway & gives you some idea of what else was going on.
The bundles themselves were "wrapped-up aggregations of sacred ob-
jects" (thus: R. Lowie): medicines whose powers were put to a number
of curative & other religious ends. The principal item in the present bun-
dle was the *natoas,* a ceremonial bonnet made of turnip leaves, etc. but
also the other objects handled in the ritual-event or mentioned in the
accompanying myth-of-origin. Much obviously remains untold here,
but the sheer action of the piece may be sufficient news to us outsiders.

Page 184 A DISPUTE BETWEEN WOMEN

SOURCE: Tom Lowenstein, *Eskimo Poems from Canada and Greenland,* Allison &
Busby, London, 1973, pages 85–89. Based on Danish translation in Knud
Rasmussen, *Myter og Sagn fra Groenland* ("Myths and Legends from Greenland"),
Gyldendal, 1921.

Fundamental (in Rasmussen's words) to "the public justice of the
Eskimos," song contests point to the energies of poetry as something
more than "pretty words," etc. The reader can compare these to the
work of African abuse poets or to the flytings, etc. of pagan Europe,
& can sense in them as well the origins of drama per se as the
enactment-of-a-conflict.

Addenda. DIRECTIONS FOR A SONG CONTEST. "If two men or two women
fall out (even to the extent of becoming mortal enemies) the quarrel can
be resolved in a song contest. The enemies stand in the middle of the
floor, surrounded by spectators. The challenger must speak first, and
he dances and beats the drum as he sings. The one who succeeds best
in ridiculing his opponent is jubilantly declared victorious."

ALTERNATIVE PROCEDURES. "The Canadian Eskimos combined boxing
with their songs, while in East Greenland blows with the head were dealt
with such violence, that a man's eyes would often swell and quite close
up. A return bout came another evening: during the whole of a song the
'recipient' had to stand smiling and take both mockery and beating

without showing they affected him at all. When eventually everything had been fought out, old grudges were usually forgotten, and the combatants became such good friends that they swapped wives and exchanged gifts as tokens of reconciliation." (After Knud Rasmussen, in Lowenstein, *op. cit.*, pages 107–108)

Page 188 Rabinal-Achí: Act IV

Source: Translated from the Quiché & French edition of Brasseur de Bourbourg, Paris, 1862, & the Spanish edition of L. Cardoza y Aragón (from an unpublished French version by Georges Reynaud, 1928): *Anales de la Sociedad de Geografia e Historia,* Volume 6, Numbers 1–4, Guatemala, 1929–1930. Translation © 1971, 1972, and 1985 by Nathaniel Tarn.

One of the great Maya classics from highland Guatemala — along with the *Popol Vuh* (see above, pages 71 & 73) & the *Annals of the Cakchikels* — the *Rabinal* is a dance-drama, virtually the only Maya one in existence. Except for the absence of religious ritual, which may have been deliberately excised, this version seems by most accounts to be authentically pre-Hispanic.

(Writes Tarn): "The *Rabinal* was found in the town of that name in the Verapaz region of Guatemala by the pioneer Americanist, the Abbé Brasseur de Bourbourg. After hearing from some servants about the legendary Knight of Rabinal, Brasseur cured the wife of one Bartolo Ziz who, in gratitude, visited the Abbé and declared himself ready to reveal the text of the drama he had performed thirty or forty years before on his father's and grandfather's orders. The dictation took twelve days. After this, Brasseur worked to obtain a performance, frightening the Indians into it by quoting lines from the drama at them and pretending to know everything there was to be known of their customs better than they did themselves. On January 25th, 1856, with financial aid from the Abbé and with his blessing in Church, the *Rabinal-Achí* was performed in Rabinal. . . .

"The play itself concerns the capture by the Knight of Rabinal of a neighboring Knight of the Quiché, his bringing before Rabinal's father and his ultimate sacrifice by Rabinal's soldiers after consuming his captor's food and drinks and dancing with his captor's wife. Georges Raynaud has suggested that, but for truncating of the text, the sacrifice would have included the presentation of the heart to the gods and the cardinal directions.

"I have tried for a straight, text-faithful but colloquial translation, setting the text out to exploit the parallelisms and stylistic redundancies. There has been no attempt, or little, to get rid of the repetition by one speaker of what his interlocutor has just said. The salutations alone are an invention of mine based on a mixture of Quiché and English phonetics: I think they give something of that solemn, almost harassing, repetitiousness characteristic of the *Rabinal* as I read it."

While translations exist in French, Spanish & German, Tarn's is the first significant go at it in English — & the first, certainly, as verse.

GLOSSARY (of Maya words not translated in the text). *Ahau:* Chief. *Achí:* man, in the sense of Latin *vir* opposed to *homo* (= Maya *vinak*). *Galel Achí:* Eminent *Achí. Balam:* Sorcerer; also: Jaguar. *Cala:* a hailing term, as also *yeha. Cavek-Quiché:* one of the tribes of the *Quiché* people. *Cot:* Eagle. *Hobtoh:* Five-Rains, alluding to birthday of the Chief. *Ixtatzunin:* meaning uncertain. *Ixtaz:* frog. *Oyeu:* Brave, Valiant. *Rahaual:* High Chief, Governor, Prince. *Tun:* two-tongued wooden drum, like Nahuatl: *teponàztli. Toltec:* a Mexican (plateau) culture which had great influence in Highland Guatemala.

Page 211   THE LITTLE RANDOM CREATURES

SOURCE: Prose text in William Jones, *Fox Texts,* Publications of the American Ethnological Society, Volume I, 1907, page 79.

The present working is from a narrative Jones translated as "The Little-Creatures-of-Caprice Ensnare the Sun," which creatures themselves turned up (he noted) in various other stories not recorded in *Fox Texts.* Of interest too to the reader who wants to keep track of the diversity of modes in Amerindian poetry, etc., is Jones' stress on the great preference shown by Fox narrators for brevity & a kind of "rapid narrative" — an almost opposite technique from other North American story-tellers (for which, e.g. see Tedlock's total translation of a Zuni narrative, etc., page 95, above). Thus, Jones' description of a Fox narrative performance: "When the weather begins to chill and the nights become raw, the fire of the lodge is then the center of a circle of men and women, some sitting and others lounging, with the feet always toward the fire. By and by someone spins a tale; the next person tells another, and so round the circle. . . . They soon get under way and hurry on with little or seldom any by-play, and come up at the end with a suddenness that is often startling. The result is a tale generally so elliptical that it would not be altogether clear to an outsider who was not familiar with its setting." If such condensation is a general characteristic of "poetry" (it isn't always, but let it go, by Pound's definition, at that), the Fox narratives would clearly so qualify. But then the reader should remember that in an oral culture (where the movement of the voice carries all the language & where justified margins just don't exist) there's no such thing as prose in the first place.

Addenda. NARRATIVE EVENT (Fox)

Sometimes a man goes into a fast to tell stories. He paints his whole face black. This is at night, and when he begins to tell stories it is to be for all that night.

Often he does not eat in the morning, nor for the whole day. His eating is at midnight. He shells off two rows of white corn from a cob of eight rows. The corn he makes into *tagwahani* and cooks in a small kettle. The amount that he eats at this time is very small.

All this is that he may have good health and that he may have long life.

— From William Jones, Ethnography of the Fox Indians, *page 109*

Page 212   FIVE FLOWER WORLD VARIATIONS

SOURCE: Jerome Rothenberg, *15 Flower World Variations: A Sequence of Songs from the Yaqui Deer Dance,* Membrane Press, Milwaukee, 1984. Based on literal translations in Carleton Wilder's *The Yaqui Deer Dance* (1963).

> The small nouns
> Crying faith
> In this in which the wild deer
> Startle, and stare out.
> *— George Oppen*

"Flower world," "enchanted world" & "wilderness world" are among the English terms used to describe the other-than-human domain surrounding the settled Yaqui villages: "a region of untamed things into which man's influence does not extend" (E. Spicer). In mythic times that world *(huya aniya)* may have been *everything,* later reduced (so Edward Spicer tells us) "to a specialized part of a larger whole, rather than the whole itself. . . . Not replaced, as the Jesuits would have wished, . . . it became the other world, the wild world surrounding the towns." (*The Yaquis,* page 65.) Within the frame of a native & independent Catholicism, it persists in the present, into which it brings the mythic figures of sacred Deer Dancer & Pascola clowns. The songs accompanying the very taut, very classical Deer Dance are, in their totality, an extraordinary example of traditional poesis: the cumulative construction by word & image of that Flower World from which the dancer comes.

Such uses of flower & deer symbology, etc., are widespread throughout Mexico — their sources deep into the native past. (See, for example, pages 305, 309, & the accompanying commentaries.)

Page 215 THE EAGLE ABOVE US

SOURCE: Konrad Theodor Preuss, *Die Religion der Coraindianer,* Volume I, 1912, page 43.

Sung by one Santiago Altamirano for the eagle whose eye is the sun. Hollo has translated about half the original text.

Page 217 A SONG OF THE RED & GREEN BUFFALO

SOURCE: William Whitman, *The Oto,* Columbia University Contributions to Anthropology, Volume 28, 1937, page 109.

The song was taught to him as a boy. He had been "painted up with mud & dressed in a little buffalo hide with the tail round [his] middle," & so taken on a long walk to the Buffalo Medicine lodge for his induction. Along the way the older men taught him by speaking & singing. Would later become a good doctor & famous hunter — also a leader of the Peyote religion among the Oto.

BUFFALO DANCE EVENT, *for men & women.* (1) Dress up like buffalos. Let some of the dancers wear buffalo caps; let others wear buffalo robes or tails; & let some be plastered with mud & clay. Have some of the dancers blow whistles of cane, & certain women shake rattles of buffalo hooves. (2) Have everyone paint up. Let the kinds of painting come from visions. Use red paint freely but also use dirt from the earth. When someone has been painted have him sing a paint song of his own. Let him sing a set of buffalo songs, & let others join him when he calls on them. Feast on meat. Then have each member sing a separate quitting song together. Then quit.

BUFFALO NARRATIVE

A journey through the seasons
            came in summer
      to a field of buffalos
      saw

old buffalos were covered head & back
with goldenrods
      & some   with sunflowers
           wrapped around their horns
in winter
it was gone
        he changed
        along with it
    had been a boy
    that spring
    that same day maybe
    or that evening
was an old man now
a doctor

& it began to snow

     — Origin myth of the Buffalo Medicine Lodge, after Whitman
      (pages 107–108)

Page 218 *From* THE WISHING BONE CYCLE

SOURCE: Howard A. Norman, *The Wishing Bone Cycle: Narrative Poems from the Swampy Cree Indians,* Ross-Erikson Publishing, Santa Barbara, 1982, pages 29–30, 38–39.

(1) Trickster stories go far back in Cree culture (as elsewhere), but the figure here is the invention, specifically, of Jacob Nibenegenesabe, "who lived for some ninety-four years northeast of Lake Winnipeg, Canada." Nibenegenesabe was also a teller (= *achimoo*) of older trickster narratives, the continuity between old & new never being in question. But the move in the Wishing Bone series is toward a rapidity of plot development & changes, plus a switch into first-person narration as a form of enactment. In the frame for these stories, the trickster figure "has found the wishbone of a snow goose who has wandered into the Swampy Cree region and been killed by a lynx. This person now has a wand of metamorphosis allowing him to wish anything into existence; himself into any situation." Norman's method of translation, in turn, involves "first listening to the narratives over & over in the source language, then re-creating them in the same context, story, etc., if notable, ultimately to get a translation word for word."

The poems, as delivered here, represent a major example (both contemporary *and* tribal) of the "law of metamorphosis in thought & word" spoken of by Cassirer (below, page 396), the Surrealists, & others. Thus Ezra Pound, circa 1918: "Our only measure of truth is. . . our perception of truth. The undeniable tradition of metamorphosis teaches us that things do not remain always the same. They become other things by swift and unanalysable process. It was only when men began to mistrust the myths and tell nasty lies for a moral purpose that these matters became hopelessly confused."

(2) Writes Norman, further: "The Swampy Cree have a conceptual term which I've heard used to describe the thinking of a porcupine as he backs into a rock crevice: *usá puyew usu wapiw* ('he goes backward, looks forward'). The porcupine consciously goes backward in order to speculate safely on the future, allowing him to look out at his enemy or just the new day. To the Cree, it's an instructive act of self-preservation. Nibenegenesabe's opening formula for the wishing bone poems (and other tales) consisted of an invitation to listen, followed by the phrase: 'I go backward, look forward, as the porcupine does.'" (1976) The act of telling, then, is one in which traditional ways (as process) do not imprison but free the mind to new beginnings & speculations. This is the basis in fact of the "oral" as a liberating possibility: an interplay that preserves the mind's capacity for transformation — as important in an ecological sense as that other preservation (of earth & living forms, etc.) that we now recognize not as nostalgia but a necessary tool for our common survival.

(3) For more on tricksters, etc., see above, page 366, & elsewhere in this volume.

Page 221 THE GREAT FARTER

SOURCE: Prose text in Knud Rasmussen, *The Netsilik Eskimos,* Report of the 5th Thule Expedition, Copenhagen, 1931, page 448.

More scatology turns up, say, in the Coyote story on page 89, & it's almost needless to say that the recovery of all of that today opens the possibility of digging a highly developed, highly surreal aspect of the tribal imagination that earlier generations would have dismissed as mere barbarism or would have translated into dead Latin. Which dismissal, in its various aspects, has left its mark too on those Indians who are doubtful of where the power lies or has its public limits.

Page 223 ONE FOR COYOTE

Translated by Cary from material he collected around 1951. He writes of it: "When Harry told it to me he chuckled and poked me slyly. His wife, Jessie, big woman, shook her head unhappily. Harry moved quickly to an ending in which Coyote threw bumblebees at the woman and ran away laughing. It's taken a long time for the story to grow to what I feel is Coyote, as the transformer according to Radin and the trickster cycle he set down. Anyway I do feel it true according to every sensitive groping backwards. The 'primitives' had their jokes and the creator carried the burden. I won't do it, but I think there's a definite similarity between Loki & Raven-Coyote etc."

More on Coyote turns up in the present "service," but the narratives on pages 89 & 91, say, are particularly relevant to the present working.

Page 224 HOW HER TEETH WERE PULLED

SOURCE: Isabel Kelly, "Northern Paiute Tales," *Journal of American Folklore,* Volume 51, 1938. Ramsey's working "synthesizes several versions of the story."

Elsewhere the toothed-cunt may turn up as one with thorns, even (among the Pomos, say) as one filled with live rattlesnakes — like that very medusa-head-as-pubic-hair-tangle of Sigmund Freud's nightmares. Among the tribes, too, it isn't merely expressive of fear but of the "power" (always ambivalent & dangerous) a man must take the teeth from, they thought, to make it amenable to his life.

For other versions of that female aspect, its place among the powers, etc., see above, pages 231–232, & commentary.

Page 225 THREE SONGS OF MAD COYOTE

SOURCE: From Herbert J. Spinden, "Essay on American Indian Poetry," in his *Songs of the Tewa,* 1933, page 21. Reissued by the Sunstone Press, Santa Fe, New Mexico, 1976.

Spinden identifies the first as a "dream song of Silu-we-haikt (Eyes-around-the-Neck), first revealed in the annual Guardian Spirit Dance, where each dreamer costumed himself according to the nature of his vision." For more on Nez Percé visions of Coyote, myths about his eyeballs, etc., see page 89, above, & commentary. Coyote material from elsewhere also appears in the present gathering.

Page 226　A Story of the Eaters

SOURCE: W. S. Merwin, *Selected Translations 1968–1978,* Atheneum, New York, pages 84–85. Based on translation by Katherine B. Branstetter.

"The Eaters are members of a group of demons (*pukuh*) who are found in an important genre of cautionary tales in the oral literature of the Tenejapa Tzeltal Maya of Highland Chiapas, Mexico. Eaters are unusual among demons because they are not known by their appearance. They serve as messengers of God (in some versions they serve deities of the traditional Mayan religion), stealing souls away to 'Veracruz' in the low country. The bodies of their victims then sicken and die if prayers are not properly carried out." (Katherine B. Branstetter, personal correspondence.)

The singular verbs with the plural noun are features of the Tzeltal original carried over into Merwin's version.

Page 228　Things That Were Truly Remarkable

SOURCE: N. Scott Momaday, *The Way to Rainy Mountain,* The University of New Mexico Press, 1969, pages 97-100.

"Mammedaty was my grandfather, whom I never knew . . . [He] was the son of Guipagho the Younger and of Keahdinekeah, one of the wives of Pohd-lohk. His grandfather Guipagho the Elder was a famous chief, for whom the town of Lone Wolf, Oklahoma, is named, and like his father, Mammedaty lived in the reflected glory of a large reputation. All in all, he bore up under the burden, they say, with courage and good will. His mother, Keahdinekeah, was the daughter of Kau-au-ointy, a woman of strong, foreign character. There was a considerable vitality in him, therefore, and a self-respect that verged upon arrogance. He was born in 1880." (N.S.M., *The Names,* page 26)

Page 229　Sweat-House Ritual No. 1

SOURCE: Alice C. Fletcher & Francis LaFlesche, *The Omaha Tribe,* Bureau of American Ethnology, 27th Annual Report, 1905–1906, pages 571–573.

The sweat-lodge in question was used as a preparatory rite by the Pebble Society (lit. "they who have the translucent pebble"), & the words of the ritual belonged to Waki'dezhinga, a former Society leader, who used them "as he entered the sweat lodge to make ready for his duties toward the sick." Membership in the society followed a dream or vision of water or of its representative, the pebble, or a dream or vision of the "water monster." Devices indicating such dream animals, etc. were painted on the bodies of participants. (For a scenario of other events in the ceremonial, see above, page 159.)

The old man of the poem is the "primal rock" of the Omaha dream-time: an aged being sitting in the midst of water that's impossible to traverse, spoken of as having "persisted through all time since the gathering of the primal seven, to have sat at the center where the paths converge, & endured the shock of the four winds, those mighty forces which bring life & can destroy it," etc. The sacred narrative of the Pebble Society — at least in Waki'dezhinga's telling of it — places the dream-time history as follows:

> At the beginning all things were in the mind of Wakonda. All creatures, including man, were spirits. They moved about in space between earth and the stars. They were seeking a place where they could come into a bodily existence. They ascended to the sun, but the sun was not fitted for their abode. They moved on to the moon and found that it also was not good for their home. Then they descended to earth. They saw it was covered with water. They floated through the air to the north, the east, the south, and the west, and found no dry land. They were sorely grieved. Suddenly from the midst of the water uprose a great rock. It burst into flames and the waters floated into the air in clouds. Dry land appeared; the grasses and the trees grew. The hosts of spirits descended and became flesh and blood. They fed on the seeds of the grasses and the fruits of the trees, and the land vibrated with their expressions of joy and gratitude to Wakonda, the maker of all things. (*Omaha*, pages 570–571.)

In the actual ritual (see description, below), the stones in the sweat-house represented the old man & were so addressed, while the steam was equated with the primal water, etc. The "children" of the poem are the patients about to be ministered to, & the winds are "the messengers of the life-giving force, winds of the four directions, into whose midst the child is sent, to reach the four hills of life." What we have here, in short, is a religion & poetry at a point of high & complex development.

Addenda. (1) SWEAT-HOUSE EVENT (Omaha)

A framework of slender poles is bent so as to make a small dome-shaped frame; this is covered tight with skins. Stones are heated over a fire, then placed in the center of the tent. The bathers enter, carrying a vessel of water with them. The coverings of the sweat-house are then made fast, & the participants sprinkle water on the heated stones & sit in the steam while singing songs & chanting the words of the sweat-house ritual. After a sufficient sweat has been experienced, they emerge from the sweat-house & plunge into cold water, after which they rub themselves dry with artemisia or grass. (*Omaha,* page 585.)

(2) The movement of the poem, in its cumulative juxtaposition of divine attributes, etc. is typical of that tribal poetry which attempts to realize a form & shape for powers that have been experienced in dream & vision before or during the event. While the poem's contents may finally be fixed, as here, there are other instances where it involves an ongoing activity, e.g. in the Crow sweat-house poem (pages 47–48, commentary, page 353) & Lowie's description of the process by which the supplicant (= poet) articulates his sense-of-reality, etc. through language.

(3) A cross-reference of a very different kind is to the avatar of Quetzalcoatl as old-man in the Aztec myth of his transfiguration:

> . . . And it is said, he was monstrous.
> His face was like a huge, battered stone, a great fallen rock; it [was] not made like that of men. And his beard was very long — exceedingly long. He was heavily bearded.

Thus, Sahagún's informant in the 16th-century *Florentine Codex,* to say nothing of the Ancient-of-Days & those primal rocks of our own tribal poetries, etc.

Page 231   A POEM TO THE MOTHER OF THE GODS

SOURCE: Sahagún's 16th-century gatherings, as rendered into Spanish in Angel María Garibay K., *Poesía Indígena,* Ediciones de la Universidad Nacional Autónoma, Mexico, 1952, pages 11–12.

For the power of the imagination (Indian, Aztec, etc.) to give a face to its gods, the reader should check again the art of the ancient codices (for which see e.g. page 242, above) & such overwhelming statues as *la Gran Coatlicue,* that "Lady-of-the-Serpent-Skirt" & mother of the gods, "whose head is twin serpents, whose necklace human hands & hearts, whose feet & hands are claws, whose skirt is made of writhing snakes," etc. but depicted elsewhere as a mother carrying a baby in her arms. Garibay's note to this poem gives the name of the mother goddess as

Teteo innan, but he points also to her many other names & aspects. Her worship was *sumamente antiguo* in Anáhuac.

The *holy thigh* of the goddess (another version has the thigh skin painted on her face) probably goes back to a sacrifice for the goddess Toci in which the victim was flayed & her thigh worn as a conical cap by a young priest acting as her son, Cinteotl. *Tamoanchan* is, literally, house-where-they-come-down or where-they're-born: the Aztec place-of-emergence. The *Nine Plains* (probably "high arid regions") are part of the imagery of subsequent Aztec migrations into Mexico, on one of which she was said to have manifested herself as *obsidian butterfly* (Itzpapalotl) on rounded (melon) cactus. *Xiuhnel* & *Mimich,* who witnessed her avatar as deer, were likely gods of that place & seem to have played a key role in the wanderings. The deer itself was sacrificial victim before they turned to humans (thus: Garibay), but a later form of human sacrifice involved daubing of victims with white plaster & feathers. The poem itself may represent a fusion of goddesses—easy enough in mythic thought.

Addenda. (1) While such information as here given has its uses, the reader should not be discouraged from focusing his own mind on the actual image-of-the-god, to follow that wherever it may lead him; or, as Mr. Joseph Peynetsa of Zuni said to our friend Dennis Tedlock: *When they tell those stories do you just write them down, or do you see them with your mind as well?* The poem, then, as a process of bringing-the-image-forward.

(2) "And the costume of Teteu innan was as follows: there was liquid rubber on her lips and a circle of rubber on each cheek. She had cotton flowers. She had a ball with palm strips. She had a shell-covered skirt, called a star-skirt. She had the star-skirt. Eagle feathers were strewn over her skirt — it was strewn with eagle feathers; it had white eagle feathers, pointed eagle feathers. Her shield had a golden disc in the center. She carried the medicinal herb, *totoicxitl.* She used a broom; she carried a broom." (Sahagún, *Florentine Codex,* Book Two: "The Gods," 8th Chapter.)

Page 233 BEFORE THEY MADE THINGS BE ALIVE THEY SPOKE

SOURCE: Constance Goddard DuBois, *Religion of the Luiseño Indians,* University of California Publications in American Archaeology & Ethnology, Volume 8, Number 3, 1908, page 139.

An excerpt from what DuBois labeled "Luiseño Creation — 4th Version," it was narrated by Lucario Cuevish, "an old man blind from his youth." DuBois herself pointed to the "tendency to variation in the (telling of) myths," which we can now recognize as part of the frequent *de facto* freedom of the tribal/oral poet, whose sacred "texts" are in a constant process of self-correction & transformation. The mode of the narrative (lost in the carry-over) involves the extensive use of gesture language & a "groaning style" in (especially) the dialogue; i.e. that utterances are often drawn out &/or punctuated with a groan-like sound, han-n-n-n-n — though it's not clear from her own notations that that would be the case with the lines excerpted here. At any rate the present editor has restricted himself to compressing (on basis of the apparent Luiseño text & notes for a literal reading) what seemed to be heavy paraphrases & expansions in DuBois' translation.

About the basis for such expansions & the implications of just such passages as this one, she writes: "Much of this mythology is abstraction, belonging to the domain of metaphysics." With which the present editor would likely agree, being reminded too of abstract/concrete workings from the other India; lines, say, like these from the Brihadaranyaka Upanishad:

> In the beginning there was nothing to be seen here . . . but it was all concealed by death — by hunger, for death is hunger. Then Death was first & thought to have a body. Death moved about & worshipped & his worship produced water.

> And what was there was froth of water, it was hardened & became the earth. Death rested on the earth & being rested he grew warm, & Agni flared up full of light

who was the sacred fire, etc. — as in the Luiseño, the union of the earth & Death (but after a detailed exploration of each other's bodies) first generates the sacred objects: nets & baskets, red paint, thorny plants, salt grass, & woman's menses. All of which would indicate, perhaps, where some of that was headed at the point of its disruption.

Page 234 SIOUX METAMORPHOSES

SOURCE: Frances Densmore, *Teton Sioux Music,* Bureau of American Ethnology, Bulletin 61, 1918, *passim.*

(1) " . . . Life is not divided into classes and subclasses. It is felt as an unbroken continuous whole which does not admit of any clean-cut and trenchant distinctions. The limits between the different spheres are not insurmountable barriers; they are fluent and fluctuating. . . . By a sud-

den metamorphosis everything may be turned into everything. If there is any characteristic and outstanding feature of the mythical world, any law by which it is governed — it is this law of metamorphosis . . . the deep conviction of a fundamental and indelible *solidarity of life* that bridges over the multiplicity and variety of its single forms. . . . The consanguinity of all forms of life seems to be a general presupposition of mythical thought." (From E. Cassirer, *Essay on Man.*)

(2) On the PLANET, EARTH, September, 1969

The unanimous Declaration of Interdependence

When in the course of evolution it becomes necessary for one species to denounce the notion of independence from all the rest, and to resume among the powers of the earth, the interdependent station to which the natural laws of the cosmos have placed them, a decent respect for the opinions of all mankind requires that they should declare the conditions which impel them to assert their interdependence.

We hold these truths to be self-evident, that all species have evolved with equal and unalienable rights, that among these are Life, Liberty and the pursuit of Happiness. — That to ensure these rights, nature has instituted certain principles for the sustenance of all species, deriving these principles from the capabilities of the planet's life-support system. — That whenever any behavior by members of one species becomes destructive of these principles, it is the function of other members of that species to alter or abolish such behavior and to re-establish the theme of interdependence with all life in such a form and in accordance with those natural principles, that will effect their safety and happiness. Prudence, indeed, will dictate that cultural values long established should not be altered for light and transient causes, that mankind is more disposed to suffer from asserting a vain notion of independence than to right themselves by abolishing that culture to which they are now accustomed. — But when a long train of abuses and usurpation of these principles of interdependence, evinces a subtle design to reduce them, through absolute despoilation of the planet's fertility, to a state of ill will, bad health, and great anxiety, it is their right, it is their duty, to throw off such notions of independence from other species and from the life support system, and to provide new guards for the re-establishment of the security and maintenance of these principles. Such has been the quiet and patient sufferage of all species, and such is now the necessity which constrains the species Homo Sapiens to reassert the principles of interdependence. — The history of the present notion of independence is a history of repeated injuries and usurpations all having in direct effect the establishment of an absolute tyranny over life. —

To prove this let facts be submitted to a candid world. — 1. People have refused to recognize the roles of other species and the importance of natural principles for growth of the food they require. — 2. People have refused to recognize that they are interacting with other species in an evolutionary process. — 3. People have fouled the waters that all life partakes of. — 4. People have transformed the face of the earth to enhance their notion of independence from it and in so doing have interrupted many natural processes that they are dependent upon. — 5. People have contaminated the common household with substances that are foreign to the life processes which are causing many organisms great difficulties. — 6. People have massacred and extincted fellow species for their feathers and furs, for their skins and tusks. — 7. People have persecuted most persistently those known as coyote, lion, wolf, and fox because of their dramatic role in the expression of interdependence. — 8. People are proliferating in such irresponsible manner as to threaten the survival of all species. — 9. People have warred upon one another which has brought great sorrow to themselves and vast destruction to the homes and the food supplies of many living things. — 10. People have denied others the right to live to completion their interdependencies to the full extent of their capabilities.

We therefore, among the mortal representatives of the eternal process of life and evolutionary principles, in mutual humbleness, explicitly stated, appealing to the ecological consciousness of the world for the rectitude of our intentions, do solemnly publish and declare that all species are interdependent; that they are all free to realize these relationships to the full extent of their capabilities; that each species is subservient to the requirements of the natural processes that sustain all life. — And for the support of this declaration with a firm reliance on all other members of our species who understand their consciousness as a capability to assist all of us and our brothers to interact in order to realize a life process that manifests its maximum potential of diversity, vitality and planetary fertility to ensure the continuity of life on earth.

(Signed)   ECOLOGY ACTION

(3) For everything that lives is holy. — W. Blake.

Page 239 A BOOK OF EXTENSIONS (I)

The two "books of extensions" present an exploration of other-than-speech or -words (the non-verbal, conceptual, pictorial, graphic, etc.) as the medium of poetry or as part of a continuum with poetry itself. Such merging of arts & shifting of boundaries ("our" arts & boundaries,

I mean) are not beside the point, but directly at the heart of the great tribal poetries of North America — to see which at their fullest, it's no longer possible to stick with the limited categories of western poetics. In the first Book of Extensions, the work explored includes: (1) the extension of language into non-verbal media, but especially through pictures & writing where these aren't merely a shorthand for speech & an aid to memory but develop further as distinct (if rarely isolated) activities; (2) poetic process as observed in the movements of language itself or the ways in which particular cultures construct or associate words & concepts; & (3) games that program words & utterances toward particular realizations as play, etc. (for which, see also the "language events," pages 156–157, among other items in this book).

Page 241 THE TABLET OF THE 96 HIEROGLYPHS

SOURCE: Enrique Juan Palacios, "Inscripción recientemente descubierta en Palenque," *Maya Research,* Volume 3, Number 1, New Orleans, 1936, facing page 3.

(Wrote poet Charles Olson, back in 1951 or so): "Christ, these hieroglyphs. Here is the most abstract & formal deal of all the things this people dealt out — & yet, to my mind, it is precisely as intimate as verse is. Is, in fact, verse. Is their verse. And comes into existence, obeys the same laws that the coming into existence, the persisting of verse, does." (*Mayan Letters.*)

Page 242 FROM A BOOK OF THE MAYA

SOURCE: From the pre-Conquest Dresden Codex, as given in Eduard Seler, *Gesammelte Abhandlungen zur Amerikanischen Sprach- und Altertumskunde,* Berlin, 1908, Volume 3, page 683.

"According to the early sources" (thus: Michael Coe) "the Maya books contained histories, prophecies, songs, 'sciences,' and genealogies. . . .: thousands of books in which the full extent of their learning and literature was recorded." The three which survived the onslaught of the Spanish civilizers "are written on long strips of bark paper, folded like screens and covered with gesso. . . . [Of these three] the most beautiful and earliest . . . [is] the Dresden codex."

SOURCE: Leona Cope, *Calendars of the Indians North of Mexico,* University of California Publications in American Archaeology and Ethnology, Volume 16, Number 4, 1919. A selection, from which the present group is taken, appeared in Richard Grossinger's *Io,* the "ethnoastronomy issue" of summer 1969.

The present editor suggests (1) that giving a name to something is a fundamental act of poetry, & (2) that a language in which names convey real information may be superior because of that to one whose proper nouns, etc. have been stripped of all significance. But the reader might consider the possibility of using the Indian ones as models toward construction of his own calendar of names by which he & his children could govern their lives.

For another aspect of naming, see the "naming events" on page 158, above, & the commentaries thereto; also the Swampy Cree namings on pages 140, 376.

Page 246 LEAN WOLF'S COMPLAINT

SOURCE: Garrick Mallery, "Sign Language Among the North American Indians," *Bureau of American Ethnology,* 1st Annual Report, 1880, pages 526–528.

"The whites have had the power given them by the Great Spirit to read & write, & convey information in this way. He gave us the power to talk with our hands & arms, to send information with the mirror, blanket & pony far away, & when we meet with Indians who have a different language from ours, we can talk to them in signs." Thus: Iron Hawk, a Sioux Chief, as quoted back in 1885 in William P. Clark's *Indian Sign Language.*

Page 249 ZUNI DERIVATIONS

More searchings for the poetic processes inherent in the language itself — or how it goes about its work. A question then arises of the degree to which language or its elaborations may have been the invention of "poets," i.e. of people hot in their seizing of reality through language, their willingness to play therewith, etc. But instances of specific tribal inventions, e.g. of shaman language (pages 156, 350, above), water language (page 157, above), etc. — not only Indian but worldwide — point to this as a distinct possibility in the self-transformation (= evolution) of the human.

Page 254 N<small>AVAJO</small> C<small>ORRESPONDENCES</small>

S<small>OURCE</small>: Gladys Reichard, *Navajo Religion*, Bollingen Series, XVIII, Pantheon, 1950, pages 518–521. Selected from sixty-five such groupings & arranged in sets by J.R.

Reichard speaks of such correspondences ("associations" her word for them) as "key to the Navajo system of symbolism" & maintains that they "are by no means 'free,' but are held together in a stipulated pattern which only the details that compose it can explain" — details, however, which she finds impossible to get at, therefore no "explanation" presently possible, etc. While the present editor accepts all that as "true enough," it seems to him that there's also a level at which the combination of images (poised between languages & cultures) has a way of opening *our* eyes to possibilities of relationships it would be hard to reach by following our own set habits-of-thought. And while it's interesting to learn in relation, say, to the fifth group in the third set, that the "ax which destroyed anyone who took hold of it, other than the owner, was possessed by Frog, Gambler & Old Age," it seems obvious that the matter didn't end there but might itself be changing under the influence of transmission through succeeding generations or as touched by the vision of a single seer (= "poet") — which is something that is always going on.

Page 256 M<small>UU'S</small> W<small>AY</small> *or* P<small>ICTURES FROM THE</small> U<small>TERINE</small> W<small>ORLD</small>

S<small>OURCE</small>: Nils Holmer & S. Henry Wassén, *The Complete Mu-Igala in Picture Writing: A Native Record of a Cuna Indian Medicine Song*, Etnologiska Studier, Number 21, 1953, Göteborg (Sweden), pages 71–75, 144–146.

The transposition of song to picture writing was the work of Guillermo Hayans, who was mostly using the "less evolved type" of Cuna writing "according to which sentences or situations are represented rather than single words or parts of words." Where single words are shown, "this is done according to phonetic rather than to semantic principles" — punning, for example, as bird (*nuu*) in the pictures = teeth (*nuka*) in the text, worms (*nusu*) in the pictures = penis (*nusupane*) in the text, etc. But the man who makes the pictures is not only a transcriber but an active intelligence.

The song (657 lines in this version from Nele de Kantule, the shaman who was Hayans' teacher) is used to cure whatever complications of childbirth follow capture of the pregnant woman's soul by Muu, the power who "forms the fetus in the womb of the mother & gives it its characteristics, or talents, *kurgin*." In this case the archetypal shaman journey

401

(to free the soul, etc.) is understood as a uterine voyage, in which the road to the goddess Muu is also the vagina of the sick woman, her home the woman's uterus, etc. To get there the shaman & his helpers (carved dolls, in fact, that he's turned into "shamans") enter a world, writes Lévi-Strauss, of fantastic animals & monsters, etc. "darkened & completely covered with blood . . . (through which they find their way) by the white sheen of their clothing and magical hats," to come on her at last in her dark whirlpool (of the "woman's turbid menstruation" & place-of-the-fetus). A reconciliation is then accomplished, but even so the way out of Muu's world must be blocked, the vagina "sealed" after birth, etc. — thus the nets, entanglements & striking-with-sticks of the passages given here.

All of which the reader may want to set against other images of the subterranean goddess, lady-of-birth who eats back her young, etc. — for which see the Aztec Teteo innan (pages 231–232, above) or Eskimo Nuliajuk (page 350) or even, say, the great toothed mother (page 224). The danger of precisely these necessary (= natural) forces is fundamental to the outlook of much tribal poetry &/or religion, which may be at home with the Earth all right, but aware too of the void on the other side of the rise.

Addenda. Lévi-Strauss' description of the technical accomplishment of the *Mu-Igala* is worth a look at as further testimony to the powers latent in poetry & language, "effectiveness of symbols" that aren't read as such, etc. Thus he contrasts the detailed frame-by-frame description of movement in the early sections of the poem ("as if . . . filmed in slow-motion") with the use in the uterine voyage itself of "an appropriate obsessing technique" to bring across the "lived experience" of the body in its sickness, i.e. "a rapid oscillation between mythical and physiological themes, as if to abolish in the mind of the sick woman the distinction between them." In doing which, the songs "relate in detail a complicated itinerary that is a true mythical anatomy, corresponding less to the real structure of the genital organs than to a kind of emotional geography . . . [giving a] picture of the uterine world peopled with fantastic monsters and dangerous animals" like a "hell à la Hieronymus Bosch." The shaman who does this "provides the sick woman with a *language,* by means of which unexpressed, and otherwise inexpressible, psychic states can be immediately expressed . . . [toward] the reorganization, in a favorable direction, of the process to which the sick woman is subjected. . . . Thus" (he concludes) "we note the significance of Rimbaud's intuition that 'metaphor' can change the world." (For more of which, see his essay, "The Effectiveness of Symbols," in *Structural Anthropology,* pages 181–201.)

SOURCE: Weston La Barre, *The Peyote Cult,* The Shoe String Press, 1959, page 75.

From the time of John Wilson (also called Nishkuntu, or Moon-Head), an early revealer of peyote in the 1890s, the poetic & religious imagination of many leading peyotists has gone into the devising of highly symbolic altars, or "moons," which can themselves be read as (concrete) poems. As with poems, the readings of the altars vary from maker to maker, while elements like the crescent-shaped upper portion remain basically fixed. In the present Enoch Hoag moon (in use among the Caddo), the elements make up a face: "a star and a heart at the hair-parting or forehead, . . . ash mounds simulating eyes, an inverted heart at the crossing of the altar-lines as a nose, four concentric lozenges for an oracular mouth, and another heart east of this resembling a cleft chin; the moon itself is the figure's hair." Among the Osage, they "call the three hearts of the altar the 'Heart of Goodness,' the 'Heart of the World,' and the 'Heart of Jesus'; others interpret the 'world' as the 'sun.' The ashes are the graves of Christ and Wilson for some, the dividing of the Red Sea for others. Some say the whole firepit is the grave of Christ, and the ash mounds his lungs, as the figure under the fire is his heart." The altar may also be marked with the leader's initials or "footprints" — as W's or M's for Wilson or Moon-Head. With a cross at center, the whole altar may be said, in the words of Wilson's vision, to map "the 'Road' which led from the grave of Christ to the Moon in the sky, which Christ had taken in his ascent."

Addenda. For a thoroughly aboriginal imagery-of-peyote, etc., see the Huichol poems on pages 305–308 & the accompanying commentaries. Of the practice of the Native American Church, as in the present selection, Ruth Underhill writes: "The Peyote religion teaches an ethical doctrine much like those of the monotheistic religions. However, it eschews specific Christian theology, its exponents often stating that while Christ came to the whites, Peyote came to the Indians. . . ." [Or, says a Comanche to J. S. Slotkin, himself a member: "The white man talks *about* Jesus; we talk *to* Jesus," etc.] "[Their meetings] are held in a tepee strewn with white sage in the Plains manner and with a half-moon shaped earthen altar as in some Kiowa ceremonies. During the evening, a drum and rattle are passed around clockwise, one man singing a song, supposedly of his own composition, while a man on one side of him drums and one on the other side rattles. Meanwhile heads of the cactus, usually dried, are passed around, each person expecting to eat eight during the evening. After midnight, when the round has been made once, there are testimonials from individuals who have been helped to follow the 'straight road,' giving up liquor and other faults. At dawn comes a token meal of old Indian foods, then prayers asking God's help for Indians, whites and all the world."

Page 263   THE PICTURE WITH THE WATER FRINGE MOUTHS

SOURCE: Washington Matthews, *The Night Chant, A Navajo Ceremony,* Memoirs of the American Museum of Natural History, 1902, pages 181–182.

Yei — masked gods or Holy Ones of the nine-day Night Chant, from which its common Navajo name, *Yeibichai.*
Bitahatini — literally, the Visionary/the Prophet: shamanic founder of the Night Chant.

Sandpaintings, or drypaintings (the pigments are rarely sands as such), were part of the complex Navajo chantway system (above, page 360), along with songs, masked dances, & a range of smaller & larger event-pieces that worked toward a balance of negative & positive elements in the patient & the world. In the narrative behind the Night Chant, the Visionary is the shaman-chanter who first enters the frame of the painting to absorb its powers & to leave his own negative traces behind. The sandpainting, then, functions as a map, the image of a segment of The People's sacred geography into which successive generations have entered. The relation to song is evident in the section of the myth related here.

N.B. After the elaborate construction & ritual employment of each sandpainting, the image, which has been nearly obliterated by the patient's presence in it, is gathered up & disposed of in a prescribed (= holy) manner. (See above, pages 157, 381.)

Page 265   THE STORY OF GLOOSCAP

SOURCE: Garrick Mallery, *Picture-Writing of the American Indians,* Bureau of American Ethnology, 10th Annual Report, 1888–1889, page 474.

Page 266   OJIBWA LOVE POEM

SOURCE: Same as the preceding, page 363.

Page 267 STRING GAMES

SOURCE: Franz Boas, *Bella Bella Texts,* Columbia University Contributions to Anthropology, Volume 5, 1928, pages 151–155.

String games with verbal read-outs like these (as songs, chants, narratives, etc.) were fairly widespread — thus the possibility that the game may have been played under circumstances conducive to the sacralizing (= "poetic") process. Which wouldn't be at all surprising. But with read-out or not, it can be seen as a (damn near) universal game-of-changes not far from the activity of magicians & poets.

Page 269 POEMS FOR THE GAME OF SILENCE

SOURCES: Frances Densmore, *Chippewa Music-II,* Bureau of American Ethnology, Bulletin 53, 1913, page 303; & Densmore, *Mandan and Hidatsa Music,* B.A.E., Bulletin 80, 1923, page 171.

The "game of silence" consisted of keeping still as long as possible in the face of songs whose non-sequential & far-out expressions were meant to cause laughter. Here directed at children, the mind's activity reflects the same energy present in more serious tribal poems: for the pleasure of the game, say, or as a simple exercise for developing & keeping all those faculties alive.

For a sacred version of the above, check out the "masked event for comedian & audience" on page 150 of the present work.

Page 270 SONGS & SONG PICTURES

SOURCE: Frances Densmore, *Chippewa Music,* Bureau of American Ethnology, Bulletin 45, 1910, *passim.*

Recorded circa 1907, the "song pictures" (as she called them) are ideographs recorded on birch bark, representing individual songs & extended series of songs that can be read-out from them. According to Densmore the pictures use certain "established" (but apparently very open) symbols common to Midē drawing (see below) & rearranged & elaborated for each particular occasion. But W. J. Hoffman's earlier readings show departures from the mere representation of the songs' contents to the presentation of new information not supplied by the words.

The songs so depicted are almost all from the *Midēwiwin* (Society of the Midē or "shamans"), the basic organizational form of the tribal religion. The artists—Odenigun (numbers 82–87), Debwawendunk (number 17), Becigwizans (numbers 66–69), & Nawajibigokwe (all the rest)—had all been initiated through the various grades or degrees of the society, toward a gradual opening-up of sense perception, powers to heal, etc. Again & again Densmore tells us that even in the recording of songs for her information, singers & artists treated the events, i.e. the singing & drawing, as an experience of some intensity, an occasion for prayer, tobacco offering & (sometimes) meditative withdrawal. There are 107 song pictures in *Chippewa Music;* I follow Densmore's own numbering therein.

Song Picture 17. For initiation into the sixth degree of the Society. Before singing, Debwawendunk ("an old man...and a most devout adherent of the Midē") smoked in silence, then made a speech as follows: "I am not doing this for the sake of curiosity, but I have smoked a pipe to the Midē manido from whom these songs came, and I ask them not to be offended with me for singing these songs which belong to them."

Song Pictures 27, 29, 30, 34. All relate to the water spirit (manido)— his dwelling, his actions & his manifestation as male beaver. To induce visitations from such "in the form of water animals, mermaids & mermen...it is not unusual for a member of the Midēwiwin to sit beside the water for hours at a time, singing Midē songs and beating the Midē drum or shaking a rattle."

Song Pictures 54, 56, 58, 64. All sung after a man has been initiated & given a medicine bag corresponding to the degree he's taken. (54): Again a water spirit, this time in form of a *migis* = white shell used in initiation, shot into candidates & then removed; its purpose was "cleansing." [See *Pebble Event,* page 159, above, & accompanying commentary.] (56): The double line at left divides the series in half on the birchbark strip; participants dance during the second part.

Song Pictures 66, 68, 69. Sung during the dance which follows the initiation ceremony, when members sing songs for their special medicines. "It is said that a man whose hunting medicine is particularly strong may rise and dance and sing his hunting-charm songs" joined by others who know them. Sung otherwise at the start of a hunt. (68): refers to a Midē bag made of marten skin with "power to drive together animals from all parts of the earth."

Song Picture 71. Not used ceremonially.

Song Pictures 82, 83, 85, 86, 87. All deal with "rare medicines" & can be sung only by those who purchase the right to sing them. (82): Composed by a starving man, who then tried it out himself in hunting bear. (83): Sung in a "round dance" around the grave of a person whose death had been avenged by a war. At the end, poles with scalps were stuck into the ground at the head of the grave, "to stay there until the poles should decay and fall." (85): Two women had "crab-skin" medicine bags that let them hold on to everything good — like crab-claws, etc. (86): Song of a man who put medicine on his feet & body, so could walk on fire without being burned, hold hot stones in his hands, etc. (87): Of a man starved out by people from another camp; a Midē sends a woman to steal a small bone, puts medicine on it & sings this song until the people in that camp can get no game. "But the man whom he was helping could get all the game he wanted."

Page 277   A BOOK OF EXTENSIONS (II): SOUNDINGS

An exploration in this section of poetries where the sound heard at surface is stripped of apparent meaning or imbued with meaning & function beyond the words as such, or where words are absent or are distorted from their normal forms. Otherwise the conventions of song & poem are followed, toward the creation of a sound-poetry that has been brought to a high development in the Indian Americas, but has been aimed at in divergent ways by other poets in the contemporary culture.

If meaning-as-explanation or for the sake of convincing an audience, etc. is absent here (or beside the point of the whole process), it's hardly that the poems are "meaningless." Rather that they develop an immediately functional language — a special language, of magic, etc., in which the power of sound & breath & ritual is used to move an object toward ends determined by the poet-magus. Such special languages, extraordinary in their nature & effect, unite the user (through what Malinowski calls "the coefficient of weirdness") with the beings & things he's trying to influence or connect-with for a sharing of power, participation in a life beyond his own, beyond the human, etc. Or, from a somewhat different point of view, what's happened here can be seen as a system of native American mantra — for those for whom that kind of comparison would bring it closer.

What follows, then, is a selection of ways in which the older American poetry has moved beyond words toward a redefinition of language itself or to the discovery of those deeper sources from which language comes.

An earlier discussion of tribal & contemporary sound-poetry (on a worldwide level) appears on pages 442–447 of *Technicians of the Sacred* (revised edition). Further commentaries — on special languages, etc. — are scattered through the present work.

Page 279 SOUND-POEM NO. 1
Page 280 SOUND-POEM NO. 2

SOURCES: Number 1 from Washington Matthews, *The Night Chant, a Navajo Ceremony*, Memoirs of the American Museum of Natural History, 1902, page 152; Number 2 transcribed from an original composition by Richard Johnny John & set on the page by J.R., July 1968.

The first of these functions in the old sacred (tribal) context, with some possibility of words interjected in the 13th & 15th lines (translated: the rain comes down / the corn comes up) but with considerable distortion. The second is a contemporary woman's dance ("social") song, but with distinct echoes (Johnny John tells me) of older, fixed sounds taken from their original places & collaged into the new works. An ongoing tradition of wordless songs (= sound-poems) throughout native America — & still hasn't played itself out.

Page 281 A POEM FROM THE SWEATBATH POEMS

SOURCE: Truman Michelson, *Contributions to Fox Ethnology*, Bureau of American Ethnology, Bulletin 85, 1927, page 77.

Page 282 *From* CEREMONY OF SENDING: A SIMULTANEITY FOR TWENTY CHORUSES

SOURCE: Francis LaFlesche, *The Osage Tribe: Rite of the Chiefs*, Bureau of American Ethnology, 36th Annual Report, 1921.

Presented here in simulation of the actual method-of-performance are "two of the twenty prayers recited simultaneously by the twenty-three clans present during the initiation of a new chief." Of these twenty-three, twenty (namely, the Elder Water People, White Water People, Star People, Deer People, Bow People, Hidden People, Golden Eagle People, Black Bear People, Mountain Lion People, Elk People, Crawfish People, Wind People, Sun People, Sun-carrier People, Night People, Red

Eagle People, Last Sky People, Buffalo-back People, Men of Mystery, & Bull Buffalo People) recite their particular prayers, while three clans (Turtle, Cattail, & Buffalo-face) remain totally silent.

Writes Barbara Tedlock, after LaFlesche: "The candidate and all the totems mentioned are located in the center of the House of Mystery with the clan members, arranged in the three main divisions Sky, Earth and Water, surrounding them. After the candidate distributes all his fees — buffalo meat, sweet corn, dried squash, lotus roots, horses, clothing, weapons — to the individuals present, all the clanspeople (with the exception of the three silent clans) begin reciting their prayers. This recitation is not in unison but is simultaneous" [a type of performance not uncommon in Plains Indian ritual-events, as also in those contemporary "happenings," etc., in which (writes John Cage) "everything will eventually be happening at once: nothing behind a screen unless a screen happens to be in front"]; "the prayers vary in length from 17 lines to 179 lines."

She writes, too, of her own translation: "The phrase *said'nth'house* on the left hand margin is a refrain or burden said after each of the longer phrases on its right . . . I've written it as a vocable phrase because of its natural collapsing from *said in this house* during recitation. The Hidden People are in regular type while the Star People are indented and in italics. The double spacing in the second half represents the silence of the Star People who've already finished."

Page 287   TEPEHUA THOUGHT-SONGS

SOURCE: Charles L. Boilès, "Tepehua Thought-Song," *Ethnomusicology*, Volume II, Number 3, 1967, pages 267 et seq.

Songs without words or other vocalizations but with a built-in system of "semantic signaling" that permits all the participants to read-out texts, etc. from melodies played on guitar & violin. Nor is it a case (as with us, say) of silently thinking the words to an instrumental version of a song we know, but that the musical phrases themselves are codes for concepts that can be further modified or expanded in combination. The songs presented here are from a collection of forty-five recorded in Pisaflores, Veracruz, in 1966. The accompanying read-outs were provided by Pedro Hernandez, a Tepehua priest, & were translated by José Marquez, one of the village elders. Also, writes Boilès, these are long versions, whose "wealth of detail" goes beyond the "basic message content" of the song, to "explain the subliminal context in which the song is heard & understood." But the thought process & resulting composition have been directly generated by the music.

The ceremony itself is called Halakiłtunti (literally, the moving-of-things, or priest's manipulation of sacred objects at an altar) & can be turned to purposes of curing, invigorating, "restoring harmony to daily life," etc. But beyond that, too, communion is established with Thought itself; namely, with the "seven sacred thoughts of god" represented by the Marijuana goddess, lakatuhún hatupasdíqał (Spanish: Santa Rosa). This takes place in the second part of the ceremony, when the participants have all taken on otherworldly roles: priest has become a spirit priest; tables, altars & all other objects have turned to gold; priestess has become the Great Midwife ("our-grandmother-of-the-vapor-bath"); two men & two women have become the four guardians of the great table which is the world, etc. Through the thought-songs, then, & by chewing marijuana leaves, the participants come to know the thoughts of the goddess Thought. She "enters" finally & order is restored to the world, ending when "the four guardians seize the corners of the table and begin to dance, moving the table around, causing the earth to resume its proper movement."

In all of this the songs are so central that (as Boilès points out) the "songs associated with the marijuana spirit can induce euphoria even without actual use of the drug. Any time that the songs are played, it is believed that the physical and spiritual worlds are drawn together and that candles and incense must be burned and a libation poured for the spirits."

Page 290 *From* THE HAKO: A PAWNEE CEREMONY

SOURCE: Alice C. Fletcher, *The Hako: A Pawnee Ceremony,* Bureau of American Ethnology, 22nd Annual Report, 1904.

Hako was the name given by Alice Fletcher to a Pawnee version of a ceremony once widespread among Plains Indians. On one level it functioned as a rite of adoption between groups & "a prayer for children, in order that the tribe may increase and grow strong." Fundamentally "hako" means *sound.* Literally "a breathing mouth of wood" (i.e., the drum), it also includes the pulsation of voice generated in the throat & by the beating of a hand against the lips. Finally hako is everything in the ceremony, for everything, the leader tells us, *speaks:* "The eagle, Kawas, speaks; the corn speaks; so we say Hako — the voice of all these things."

In the version given here, Tahirussawichi (himself a *ku'rahus,* or ceremonial leader) gives a syllable-by-syllable breakdown of the words, giving them ritual as well as lexical meanings. Thus *h'* is a breath & the breathing forth of life itself. What's revealed is a system of meditation — a change of state through concentration on the words & sounds. The process of transcription & of syllable-by-syllable & symbol-by-symbol exegesis then brings Tahirussawichi to a sort of meditation on the meditation itself.

Page 294 THE 12TH HORSE SONG OF FRANK MITCHELL
Page 296 THE 13TH HORSE SONG OF FRANK MITCHELL

SOURCE: Jerome Rothenberg, *The 17 Horse Songs of Frank Mitchell: Nos. X–XIII,* Tetrad Press, London, 1970.

[A NOTE ON TRANSLATION AS "TOTAL TRANSLATION"]: This is my almost final working (the "final" one would *not* be written down) of the twelfth & thirteenth of 17 "horse songs" in the blessingway of Frank Mitchell (1881–1967) of Chinle, Arizona. Their power, as with most Navajo poetry, is directed toward blessing & curing, but in the course of it they also depict the stages by which Enemy Slayer, on instructions from his mother Changing Woman, goes to the house of his father The Sun, to receive & bring back horses for The People. The Navajos, of course, had no horses before the coming of the Spaniards, but a short time after the actual delivery, the myth had already taken shape, translating history into the Eternal Dreaming. The 12th Song marks the point in the narrative where Enemy Slayer contemplates returning home with his father's horses & other good gifts; the 13th Song is his prevision of their beauty on the earth.

I've been attempting "total" translations of all the horse songs, accounting not only for meaning but for word distortions, meaningless syllables, music, style of performance, etc.; &, since translation is at no time mere reproduction, even the music isn't free from changes. The idea never was to set English words to Navajo music, but to let a whole work emerge newly in the process of considering what kinds of statement were there to begin with. As far as I could I also wanted to avoid "writing" the poem in English, since this seemed irrelevant to a poetry that had reached a high development outside of any written system.

Under the best of circumstances translation-for-meaning is no more than partial translation. Even more so for the densely textured Navajo. Right from the start, then, the opening line of the first horse song, reading something like this:

> *dzo-wowode sileye shi, dza-ŋa desileye shiyi dzaŋadi sileye shiya'e*

is really a distortion of the phrase "dząądi sila shí" repeated three times. A literal translation (i.e. "for meaning") would say something like "over-here they-are-here (&) mine" three times over, which would fail to get the sense of one statement presented as three distinct oral events. To do more than that, a total translation must distort words in a manner analogous to the original; it must match "meaningless" syllables with equivalents in our very different English soundings; it may begin to sing in a mode suitable to the words of the translation; & if the original pro-vides for more than one voice, the translation will also.

The translation of the 12th Horse Song follows some such program. David McAllester provided me with tapes of Frank Mitchell singing & with texts that included transcriptions of the words-as-sung, indications of how they would be sounded in normal Navajo speech, literal & general translations, footnotes, & ready answers to such questions as I still had. I translated first for meaning & phrasing in English, adding small words to my text where the original had meaningless syllables; then distorted, first the small words so that they approximated to "mere" sound, then within the meaningful segment of each line toward more or less the dens-ity of the original; e.g. "& by going from the house the shining home but some are & are gone to my house" >"& by going from the house the shahyNshining hoganome but some are & are gone to my howinow *baheegwing.*" Most of the distortions were carried out on the tape recorder, & as part of the process I went from speaking toward singing, moving rapidly from Mitchell's version to soundings of my own. Since the open-ing of each song (typical of Navajo) is a string, small or large, of mean-ingless syllables, I let my equivalents for these introductory sounds serve as "key" to which I could refer in determining my moves within the poem. Similar sounds & distortions had naturally to be carried over from song to song.

The final step in the process was a departure from the Mitchell tape, but in line with McAllester's description of how the songs would be sung ceremonially. The typical Navajo performance pattern calls for each per-son present to follow the singer to whatever degree he can. Thus group singing is highly individualized (only the ceremonial singer is likely to know it all) & leads to an actual indeterminacy of performance. Those who can't follow the words at all may make up their own vocal sounds — anything, in fact, for the sake of participation.

To simulate this in recording, I used a four-track system, on which I laid down the following:

TRACK ONE. A clean recording of the lead voice.

TRACK TWO. A voice responsive to the first but showing less word distortion & occasional free departures from the text.

TRACK THREE. A voice similar to that on the second track but provided with significantly less information — i.e. recorded without written text while listening to a playback of the first two voices at a barely audible level.

TRACK FOUR. A voice limited to pure-sound improvisations on the meaningless elements in the text, recorded under circumstances like those for the third voice.

When I had recorded the four tracks, I had them balanced & mixed onto a single tape. [A later, significantly different version of the multitrack horse songs was published as *6 Horse Songs for 4 Voices* (New Wilderness Audiographics, 1978).]

In all this what matters to me most as a poet is that the process has been a very natural one of extending the poetry into new areas of sound. Nor do I think of it as poetry plus something else, but as *all* poetry, *all* poet's work, just as the Navajo is all poetry, where poetry & music haven't suffered separation. In that sense Frank Mitchell's gift has taken me a small way toward a new "total poetry," as well as an experiment in total translation. And that, after all, is where many of us had been heading in the first place.

N.B. For more on "total translation," particularly in the area of spoken narrative, see the commentary to Dennis Tedlock's working of the Zuni *Boy & Deer* (pages 95–116, above). J.R.'s versions of *Shaking the Pumpkin* (pages 13–37, above) are attempts at "translating" words, sounds & (to some extent) "melody" onto a visual field.

Page 301 THE NET OF MOON

SOURCE: Prose text in Alexander Lesser, *The Pawnee Ghost Dance Hand Game,* Columbia University Contributions to Anthropology, Volume 16, 1933, page 96.

Told by Mark Evarts in a narrative full of good visions. The man who cried was Louis Behaile.

With the coming of the Ghost Dance in the 1890s, the Pawnees revived many old activities, e.g. the hand-game being played here, which was (a) sacralized & (b) delivered in various new forms through individual visions — much in the manner of song-transmission through dream, etc. Writes Lesser: "Once the games were begun, whether it was by [Tom] Morgan or by [Joseph] Carrion, by direct inspiration or through borrowing from the Arapaho, the idea of learning Ghost Dance hand games in visions spread like wildfire and the games sprang up like mushrooms. . . . For a game to persist after it was once created, the owner had to be well thought of by his people . . . and had to believe in the supernatural sanction of the game. Many games were probably demonstrated briefly and then forgotten.

". . . The game visions were supposed to give full directions to the visionary as to the details of the game. This included the essentials of the ritual aspects (such as offerings and ceremonial arrangements), the character of the hand game set, the way to play the game." (Lesser, pages 155–156.) Unlike sacred games elsewhere, no actual gambling was involved.

Addenda. (1) THE HAND GAME VISION OF JOSEPH CARRION. . . . *Saw a large circle of people above. In a vision on the fourth day . . . saw things whirling round in the sun, crows flying round the sun & flying over him & an eagle feather in the whirling sun. Then he saw a black sun streaked with white coming toward him & fell over. When he stood up he saw a buffalo bull stick his head out of the sun, & just before sundown Jesus standing in the western sun with one hand extended toward him.* (Lesser, 233) INTERPRETATION: as a gift of the hand game. The circle of people were the players, & Christ held the set of sticks in his extended hand. As he held them extended downwards toward Carrion, so in the intervals of Ghost Dance hand games the beneficiary must hold them aloft toward the heavenly bestower, etc.

(2) The vision of the moon comes to the man who was ready to be caught by it. Everyone was having visions in those days, as Evarts tells it: the air was heavy with them, the process one of a continuing re-creation & renewal through dream — as with so much tribal activity in the absence of a final text. Anything — a song, a stone, a gamblers' game, an odd way of walking — could be made sacred thereby & renewed, which was also the essential "freedom" within the great Plains culture, that man was not only bound to the tribal unit by cultural forms, etc., but could develop his special take on them through the poetics of his own mind.

(3) For more on the Ghost Dance, see the poems on page 341 & the commentaries thereto.

Page 302 ESSIE PARRISH IN NEW YORK

SOURCE: George Quasha, "Somapoetics 73: Essie Parrish in New York," *Alcheringa,* old series, Volume I, Number 1, 1975, pages 27–29.

Essie Parrish, a Kashia Pomo healer from California, spoke at the New School for Social Research on March 14, 1972. The poem is a reconstruction of her narrative of a dream-vision, based on notes Quasha took as she spoke. He remarks that "the greater portion of the lines are as I wrote them in the notebook. I'm just a humble scribe." And again:

> I know a bit about how it must have felt to be jotting down Mayan or whatever over the centuries: you sit there concerned only to get it down. Before it returns to the silence ungrasped. So the text seems to me *interesting* — as an oral performance, but not in the usual sense. Essie was speaking to anthropologists — or, rather, white people with "professional" interests. She speaks almost as she would to children, and yet she's in awe — still — before her own story. She gets back into the journey itself, and some qualities of the vision are carried over into the pacing of her account. Changes in tone of voice, syntax, "time" or verb tense, and diction are unpredictable, and yet they seem to mark the inner contours of the sweep of her mind. I have not emphasized any kinds of shifts over others: . . . the time is simply continuous and the shifts occur where they do, however awkward they may seem. My only "formal" concern was to distort her tone and overall temporal curve as little as possible.

Page 305   FOR THE GOD OF PEYOTE

SOURCE: Spanish versions by Marino Benzi in *Correspondencias,* Number 1, Mexico, May–June 1966.

Aboriginal images & transformations within the Huichols' localized (tribal) religion. Blue Stag is Tahumatz Kauyumari, culture hero of the Huichols, messenger between the gods & man. Stag-Peyote-Maize form the Huichols' mystic trinity: the three are one. Roses, wind, etc. are symbols of the same. Blue Stag's home & place-of-origin (Wirikota) is in the East & acts as focus for the Huichols' 250-mile "peyote hunt" & pilgrimage.

Continuity of sun-&-flower images from ancient Mexico, for which see the following set; but also pages 212, 387, above. The peyote practices described on page 403 are, by contrast, from the widespread but *inter*tribal Native American Church·in the United States.

Page 309 THE FLOWERING WAR

SOURCE: Angel María Garibay K.'s Spanish versions in his *Poesía Indígena,* Ediciones de la Universidad Nacional Autónoma, Mexico, 1952. Poems are Aztec but earlier too.

The "flowering-war" image in Mexican poetry becomes one of the basic symbols of Nahuatl spiritualism. As Laurette Séjourné summarizes it in her book *Burning Water*: "To reconcile the matter and spirit of which he is formed, individual man must all his life keep up a painfully conscious struggle; he is a battle-ground in which two enemies confront each other pitilessly. The victory of one or other will decide whether he lives or dies; if matter conquers, his spirit is annihilated with him; if spirit wins, the body 'flowers' and a new light goes to give power to the Sun. . . . This 'flowering war,' continually renewed in every conscious creature, is symbolized by two divergent currents, one of water, one of fire — which at last unite." The actual military orders of Eagles & Tigers (Jaguars) would then be taken as prototypes of those enlisted in that struggle: on some "real" battleground (in the latter & grotesque Aztec view of it) or in man as "meeting ground of opposing principles, which die in isolation when they are removed from it."

For more on this, see *Technicians of the Sacred,* revised edition, pages 501–502. The imagery & ritual of flowers continues into contemporary Mexico, e.g. in the Huichol peyote songs, pages 305–308, & in those from the Yaqui Deer Dance, pages 212–214.

Page 316 WHAT HAPPENED TO A YOUNG MAN IN A PLACE WHERE HE TURNED TO WATER

SOURCE: Pliny Earle Goddard, *White Mountain Apache Texts,* Anthropological Papers of the American Museum of Natural History, Volume 24, Part 4, 1920, pages 128–131.

Hollo's condensation & working from prose-&-song texts given by Goddard. Not only did the boy come back to hunt deer but brought back water-songs (like the second section here, etc.) for a new water ceremony:

He asked for a sweathouse to be built. When it was ready the boys went in and were singing inside. The young man who had been turned into water started to sing water-songs. Inside he wove lightning together again. There had been no water-songs

and now they existed. That's how medicine men for water came
to be.

(Goddard, page 131)

The story, writes Goddard, "was told by Frank Crockett's father who
practiced the ceremony." It was for the recovery of those made ill by the
floods due to thunderstorms.

Page 319 POEM TO BE RECITED EVERY 8 YEARS WHILE EATING UNLEAVENED
TAMALES

SOURCE: Eduard Seler, *Gesammelte Abhandlungen zur Amerikanischen Sprach- und
Altertumskunde,* Berlin, 1904, Volume 2, pages 1059–1061.

"Thus was respite given the maize every eight years. For it was said
that we brought much torment to it — that we ate it, we put chili on it,
we mixed salt with it, we mixed saltpeter with it; it was mixed with lime.
As we troubled our food to death, thus we revived it. Thus, it is said, the
maize was given new youth when this was done." (Sahagún, *Florentine
Codex,* Part 2, page 164).

Of the parties named in the poem, Tlaçolteotl was patroness of all that
ecological renewal — "goddess Desire" certainly but also our-Lady-of-
the-Bunghole, in which earth-fertilizing guise her name (as Seler tells
it) was Tlaelquani = Lady *Dreckfresser* — & was equated with that same
Teteo innan (see above, page 394) who mothered maize-god Cinteotl
& must later have had an eye out for him as Kid Fertility (= Piltzintecutli
= Xochipilli, flower god) though he was on his own by then & busy shag-
ging Xochiquetzal = Flower Bird, etc. A story & cast-of-characters,
then, that touches all bases on the fecundity front & goes to show you
how the Nahuatl poets, etc., saw earth's life transfigured into beings
"without check with original energy" (Whitman) — before the advent of
prose redactions & the secularization of dreams.

For a scenario of part of the eighth-year ceremony, see page 152,
above.

Page 322 HEAVEN & HELL

SOURCE: Prose text in Knud Rasmussen, *The Netsilik Eskimos,* Report of the 5th
Thule Expedition, Copenhagen, 1931, pages 315–317.

Page 324 *From* THE BOOK OF CHILAM BALAM

SOURCE: Ralph L. Roys, *The Book of Chilam Balam of Chumayel,* University of Oklahoma Press, 1933, 1967, pages 125–131.

Chilam Balam (but literally the Prophet Balam or Prophet Jaguar) was the "last & greatest" of the Mayan prophets, in the line of Ah Kauil Chel, Napuctun, Natzin Yabun Chan, & Nahau Pech. He "lived at Mani during the reign of Mochan Xiu" & made the great prophecy that "in the Katun 13 Ahau following, bearded men would come from the east and introduce a new religion" — by which he meant the Mexican god-king Quetzalcoatl (Mayan: Kukulkan) & his white-robed priests. But the actual appearance (in his own lifetime) of the Christian conquerors did in fact "so enhance his reputation as a seer that in later times he was considered the authority for many other prophecies" both before & after him, & his name was put to various books (of prophecies, chronicles, rituals, almanacs, catechisms, etc.) written in the Mayan language but in European script. Besides the present version from the town of Chumayel, the two major books of Chilam Balam are those from Tizimun & Mani; but no collection now extant was compiled earlier than the last part of the 17th century & most are from the 18th.

The mix of Christian & Mayan things in the present chapter is typical of the work as a whole: a natural enough process for the mind operating under pressure of conflicting imageries. Apparently, in this catechism, "the details of the crucifixion of Christ... recalled to the Maya mind some of the ceremonies connected with human sacrifice, in which the victim was probably considered the representative of the god. Like the crown of thorns, a paper crown was placed on his head, & the spear which pierced Christ's side appears to have reminded the Maya writer of the arrow with which the priest struck blood from the thigh of the sacrificial victim. It is also possible that the legend of the stone arrow-points, which entered the mythical rocks at the four corners of the world, was associated in the mind of the writer with the rocks which were rent at the time of the crucifixion." Anyway, from the ninth or tenth line, say, the imagery is almost pure Maya, in a process of generating sacred riddles, etc., that's poet's play & verbal vision at its wildest.

Page 328 HER ELEGY

SOURCE: Prose account in Ruth Underhill, *Papago Indian Religion,* Columbia University Contributions to Anthropology, No. 33, 1946, page 266.

The divining crystals, common to shamanism not only in North America but in other tribal cultures as well, were the Papago shaman's "most precious possessions." They shed light "'like your car lamps' on the seat of disease. . . . According to legend these flakes of quartz" — usually four in number — "are the solidified saliva of I'itoi" — child of Earth & Sky, & creator of life along with Coyote & Buzzard — "who spat on the head of the first shaman so that saliva entered the man's heart." In general the crystals didn't come from outside but grew within the shaman's body, "lots of them" (said the informant to Ruth Underhill) "like honey in a honeycomb." But the possibility existed too of their withdrawal (as in the present poem) or loss. Thus the same narrator told of her brother who was a shaman "but had a bad wife who came to sleep with him while she was menstruating. That killed his crystals so that they rotted away, and another shaman who looked into his heart, saw it like an empty honeycomb." (Underhill, page 271) Said yet another shaman, when asked to show his crystals: "I keep them in my heart. I never show them."

The delivery or creation of a song or special words as part of the shaman vision should be noted too, & is obviously a key to that link between shamans & poets commented on elsewhere (for which, see in the first place the commentaries on shamanism in J.R.'s *Technicians of the Sacred,* revised edition, pages 485–491, as a quick review of all of that & an attempt to connect the experience to tribal & contemporary views of basic poetic process).

Addenda. Though Papago girls like this one sometimes had the unbidden initiatory visions typical of shamanism, "most women were discouraged from practicing shamanism until after childbearing age, and the prowess they could attain after such a late start never gave them important standing." Adds Underhill: "As in White society, women doctors usually confined themselves to obstetrics & children's diseases." (Page 267)

Page 329 THEY WENT TO THE MOON MOTHER

SOURCE: Barbara Tedlock, "The Beautiful and the Dangerous: Zuni Ritual and Cosmology as an Aesthetic System," in *Conjunctions* 6, New York, 1984, page 260.

Tedlock cites the poem-song — dated summer of 1972 — as an example of the Zuni concept of *tso'ya:* a "multisensory aesthetic of the beautiful." "A beautiful song text," she writes, "consists of simultaneously literal and allegorical levels of meaning. . . . A Zuni performer-composer explained to us that this song is simultaneously about two stars (Mars as morning star and Aldebaran as Lying Star) and two American astronauts each wearing two stars on his helmet, who may or may not have been lying about their ride to the Moon Mother on the White Man's dragonfly: a rocketship. They report back to the people on earth via their sacred rainmaking bundle, Houston Control, that the moon will bless them with silt, alluvial deposits of the kind thought by scientists to be on the moon and present in the Southwest after every heavy rain. The reiterated 'stretching, stretching, stretching' refers to corn plants reaching out for the rain, people reaching old age, and the rocketship reaching the moon. This song, a Zuni favorite that summer, was repeated more than twenty times by request of the Mudhead clowns who are the ultimate judges and critics of all masked performances."

Page 330 FOUR POEMS

SOURCE: Ray Young Bear, *Winter of the Salamander,* Harper & Row, 1980, pages 49–50.

An example of contemporary work (Indian & otherwise) in which the poem, like many of its traditional counterparts, is not so much a *document* of vision as its *instrument*: "that which causes to see" (G. Oppen). That process begins, he tells us, in his native Mesquaki & moves, by an act of translation as *poesis,* into English.

Page 332 DANCE OF THE RAIN GODS

SOURCE: Konrad Theodor Preuss, *Die Religion der Coraindianer,* Volume I, 1912, pages 48–49.

Page 337 A KALAPUYA PROPHECY

SOURCE: Free working after materials in Melvile Jacobs, *Santiam Kalapuya Ethnologic Texts,* University of Washington Publications in Anthropology, Volume II, 1945.

Page 337 THE REMOVAL

SOURCE: Frances Densmore, *Seminole Music,* Bureau of American Ethnology, Bulletin 161, 1956, page 201.

The forced removal of large numbers of Seminoles from Florida to Arkansas & Oklahoma followed the Seminole War of the 1830s, but the resistance continued well into the present century. (The name Seminole itself is from a Creek word meaning "separatist" or "runaway.") The singer of the present version was Susie Tiger (Seminole name: O'mala'gi), who was born at the time of the Removal. Recorded circa 1932, southwest of Lake Okeechobee in the Florida Everglades.

Page 338 HUNGER

SOURCE: Prose text in Knud Rasmussen, *The Netsilik Eskimos,* Report of the 5th Thule Expedition, Copenhagen, 1931, pages 138–139. Part of a longer account by Samik.

Page 339 THE CRIER

SOURCE: Dell Hymes, *"In vain I tried to tell you": Essays in Native American Ethnopoetics,* University of Pennsylvania Press, 1981, pages 203–205.

Performed in English & Wishram by Philip Kahclamet (d. 1958), "who spoke it the night of 25 July 1956 in a booth in the Rainbow Cafe, just across the Deschutes River from the eastern edge of the Warm Springs Reservation, Oregon." As a representation of the traditional crier/orator, the performance begins in English & concludes with a reclaiming of the native language, to set a message of Indian (Nadidánwit) uniqueness against white (= Christian) claims to universal truth, etc. The last two sentences (in Wishram) translate: "Jesus Christ is a Jew. That Pentecostal, Catholic, Presbyterian, Methodist, and that Shaker (church), don't concern yourselves with them. Don't believe in them." Writes Hymes in summation:

> Christianity is particularized in terms of its eponymous founder, Christ, as a Jew, not of or for the Indians (not even in some sense properly a Christian?), and in terms of specific Christian groups (five of them, including the Indian-founded Shaker Church). The particularization in terms of Christ, as Jew, seems to imply that Christianity is to be understood, not as a world religion, a religion for the world, but as a matter of particular groups — ethnic (the Jews), institutional (the churches), and whites collectively. The Indians are a group on the same footing. Since this is our country, not theirs; since their religion is of and for them, not us; the line of division is clear. The Great Spirit for us, SHuSúgli [Christ] for them. (*"In Vain,"* page 206.)

SOURCE: James Mooney, *The Ghost-Dance Religion and the Sioux Outbreak of 1890*, Bureau of American Ethnology, 14th Annual Report, 1896. The condensation follows Margot Astrov's moves in *American Indian Prose and Poetry*.

The late-19th-century messianic movement called the Ghost Dance was not simply a pathetic reaction to white rule or a confused attempt to suck up Christian wisdom. The ritual use of ecstasy & the dance is clearly more Indian than Christian, & the movement's central belief that the present world would go the way of all previous worlds through destruction & re-emergence had been (for all the Christian turns it was now given) widespread throughout North America & at the heart, say, of the highly developed religious systems of the Mexican plateau.

The "messiah" of the religion was Wovoka, also called Jack Wilson, who circa 1889 was taken up to heaven by God & there given the message of redemption, invulnerability, return of the dead, etc. In trance or dream, dancers would receive the words & music of songs, which they would ecstatically project: "no limit to the number of these songs" (writes Mooney) "as every trance at every dance produces a new one. . . . Thus a single dance may easily result in twenty or thirty new songs." This intense existence at the level of poetry was an abiding characteristic of those nations of poets (= vision questers) who were defeated or driven onto reserves by armies of European businessmen & farmers. But, wrote Gary Snyder at a time of later struggles: "The American Indian is a vengeful ghost lurking in the back of the troubled American mind. Which is why we lash out with such ferocity and passion, so muddied a heart, at the black-haired young peasants and soldiers who are the 'Viet Cong.' That ghost will claim the next generation as its own. When this has happened, citizens of the USA will at last begin to be Americans, truly at home on the continent, in love with their land. The chorus of a Cheyenne Indian Ghost Dance song — 'hiniswa'vita'ki'ni' — 'We shall live again.'"

And even so, the pronoun of the song — the "we" — still seems elusive: the Indians refuse to be mere "ghosts," while the realities of language & of culture, built over centuries, remain the hardest to hold onto or to claim as something new.

POST-FACE

I am not doing this for the sake of curiosity, but I have smoked a pipe to the powers from whom these songs came, & I ask them not to be offended with me for singing these songs which belong to them.

(1907) / 1971

JEROME ROTHENBERG is the author of over forty other books of poetry and translation, of whom Kenneth Rexroth wrote: "[He] is one of the truly contemporary American poets who has returned U.S. poetry to the mainstream of international modern literature.... No one writing today has dug deeper into the roots of poetry." Described as a "master anthologist" by Richard Kostelanetz, his assemblages, besides *Shaking the Pumpkin,* include such works as *Technicians of the Sacred* and, with Diane Rothenberg, *Symposium of the Whole: A Range of Discourse Toward an Ethnopoetics.* He has taught for many years at the University of California, San Diego, and recently held the Aerol Arnold Chair in Literature at the University of Southern California and was the first Visiting Writer-in-Residence at the New York State Writers Institute in Albany. His *Pre-Faces* (1982) received the Before Columbus Foundation American Book Award.

ALSO BY JEROME ROTHENBERG

POEMS

White Sun Black Sun (1960)
The Seven Hells of the Jigoku Zoshi (1962)
Sightings I–IX (1964)
Between: Poems 1960–1963 (1967)
Poems 1964–1967 (1968)
Poems for the Game of Silence (1971)
Poland/1931 (1974)
A Seneca Journal (1978)
Vienna Blood (1980)
That Dada Strain (1983)

TRANSLATIONS

New Young German Poets (1959)
Hochhuth's *The Deputy,* playing version (1965)
Enzensberger's *Poems for People Who Don't Read Poems,* with Michael Hamburger (1968)
The Book of Hours & Constellations, or Gomringer by Rothenberg (1968)
The Seventeen Horse Songs of Frank Mitchell X–XIII (1970)
15 Flower World Variations (1984)

ANTHOLOGIES

Technicians of the Sacred (1968, 1985)
Shaking the Pumpkin (1972)
America a Prophecy, with George Quasha (1973)
Revolution of the Word (1974)
A Big Jewish Book, with Harris Lenowitz & Charles Doria (1977)
Symposium of the Whole, with Diane Rothenberg (1983)

PROSE

Pre-Faces & Other Writings (1981)